TWO CHURCHES ONLY
THERE IS NO MIDDLE GROUND

STEVEN SEGO

Library of Congress Control Number: 2023942240
                    Paperback: 978-1-961119-16-1
                    eBook: 978-1-961119-17-8

CONTENTS

INTRODUCTION

I am writing this book to talk about how great God is and about His mercies toward His children. He has told us in black and white who He is, what He is going to accomplish by creating this earth, and why He is allowing us to live on it. However, we are not always paying attention or obedient but rather going about thinking of ourselves and trying to fulfill our own selfish desires.

In writing this book, it is my intent and desire to give the reader a greater understanding of just how good God is toward all the children of men and to help put the puzzle pieces together in understanding our relationship to Him and just how really simple the gospel of Jesus Christ is. I am writing this mostly for the benefit of my children, wanting them to understand the hows, whens, whys, whos, and wheres and other pertinent questions concerning the mysteries of God. I am dedicating this work to all my children, whom I love very much.

God has blessed me with much knowledge about Him, which has come to me through great faith and trials and many hard knocks, to the extent that what I am saying I know is true. I am relying on the Bible as the main source of my search and then back it up with other books, experiences, opinions, and insights that have helped me in the past to understand. Because of these things, I am able to draw educated conclusions and opinions.

I was born in Alamosa, Colorado, on April 16, 1958. I was the thirteenth out of fourteen brothers and sisters. After the first seven, my parents—Raymond Rexford Sego and Neva Wilson Sego—never bothered giving the rest of us middle names. My parents divorced after my little brother, Michael, was born. My mother married again and had two more girls. The first seven children had left home by the time the other seven were in grade school, and half of them were still babies, including myself. My father moved to the Northwest with the latter seven children after my mother gave up custody. We settled in western Montana, where I pretty much grew up in and around the towns of Troy, Libby, and Noxon.

I had a great desire to grow and understand the mysteries of God. My best example and great friend was my elder brother John. He inspired me by his kindness, patience, and understanding. He always tried to be a good brother by spending time with the younger ones, teaching us to fish and hunt. He gave me my first fishing pole. We younger children grew up without a mother, so we really loved having the elder ones around. John fulfilled a mission for the Church of Jesus Christ of Latter-day Saints by going to Peru for two years, where he learned the Spanish language.

My other example was my other brother, Daniel, who fulfilled a mission for two years in New Zealand. Daniel was a great gospel teacher, whom I loved dearly, and I wanted to understand the gospel and be able to teach it like him. I developed the motto "I want to grow," and I set about to do just that.

Before Daniel had left on his mission, my little brother, Michael, was killed in an unfortunate accident, which hurt me deeply, causing me to reflect, meditate, and pray to know what the afterlife is like, and wanting to understand God. My main subjects of thought were where we came from, why we are here, and where we are going when we die. I missed my younger brother badly, even though I tried not to let on too much. This period affected all of us greatly.

I graduated from Noxon High School in Noxon, Montana, in 1976. I was a serious-minded young man with only one goal, and that was to follow in the footsteps of my brothers and also go on a mission for the Church of Jesus Christ of Latter-day Saints. As hard as it was, I avoided the temptations of chasing wild women and drinking, which so many young men and women do at that age. The peer pressure was great, but I managed to make it until the next year, when I went on a mission.

I went on my mission in 1977–1979 to Hong Kong, where I learned Cantonese. I taught the gospel to the Chinese people in their own language. The Chinese people are wonderful. They are very smart, kind, and industrious; and as I was over there, my understanding of the truth of the gospel seemed to expand beyond my wildest dreams. The understanding of God seemed to swell and grow within me until I was obsessed with having a greater understanding of God. I made many friends while in Hong Kong, I learned to love the Chinese people, and I know that God loves them too, just as much as I know He loves me.

When I came home after my mission, I went to visit a pretty girl I had been writing to while I was in Hong Kong. I was planning to marry her when I got back home to the States, but it wasn't meant to be. I had been writing to her most of the time I was in Hong Kong, but for some reason, she stopped writing. This happens to a lot of young men while on their missions. Many times, well-laid plans get dashed. I guess the thing with plans sometimes is that it will be a good idea to tell the other party about your plans. There is so much for young people to learn as they grow up as sometimes, they assume too much and try to guess their way through parts of their lives until it hurts so badly that they don't want to do it that way anymore.

After not getting to marry the girl I had planned to, I dropped out of college and moved to Salt Lake City, Utah. I had a lot of family in Utah, so I was able to feel at home. I got a job and was working, but I still missed the beautiful Northwest. The high mountain lakes and the deer, elk, and bear hunting called to me continually. However, while I was in Utah, I met a girl whom I married on the rebound because of the pressure the church put on young return missionaries to get married. I wish I hadn't now because I really didn't get to know her very well. I knelt at the altar with her to get married, and I had the greatest urge to get up and walk out at that time but didn't because I wanted to spare the feelings of her family as well as my own. Doing so would have spared us both the misery the latter years yielded.

Knowing what I know about God, government, and jurisdictions, to this day, I recollect how—as belonging to the Church of Jesus Christ of Latter-day Saints—while kneeling at the altar in the house of the Lord, I was joined in holy matrimony by someone who allegedly held the priesthood of God, which means having the authority to act in the name of God, yet had to show a marriage license from the devil's kingdom to get it done. So who is greater, God or Satan? The answer, of course, is God. So why then does a man supposedly having authority to act in the name of God, while he is in the house of God, need to ask permission from the devil to perform an ordinance of God? These are some of the questions that continued to play on my mind in the next years.

From this marriage were born five beautiful children, Steven, Amelia, Ryan, Benjamin, and Amber. The woman turned out to be a liberal and a real trial until it came to the point that I had enough and had to move on for the sake of my own sanity. As soon as I made the decision that I couldn't tolerate her liberal ideas anymore, a whole new world opened up to me.

In 1992, I met a beautiful young woman named who lived in Northern Ireland. We started out as pen pals, and sometimes I called as we began to get serious, until one day I asked her what her parents would think if she was to marry a Yankee. I proposed to her at that time. She accepted graciously, and my heart leaped with joy. I went over to Northern Ireland for the wedding, and we were married on February 17, 1992, in a Free Presbyterian Church in Ahoghill, Northern Ireland, which was the best day of my entire life. I married my very best friend that day and have never looked back. She is a good conservative; she loves God, she believes in hard work, and she loves her family. She is a real blessing from God, and she has enriched my life by her example and her faithfulness. I love her deeply, and she became a naturalized American citizen on March 21, 2019.

My wife and I have four beautiful children, who are sharp as tacks. There are three really pretty girls—Stevana, Olivia, and Grace—and one big strapping boy named Jordan. I am so proud of all of them. The girls are so clean and have developed a great love of God. My son is now a firefighter and has served in Afghanistan in the military. He is now married to a really nice young lady. I love all of them dearly. God has blessed me and has made me feel so rich.

My wife is of a great conservative mindset, like myself, and being married to her is like rays of sunshine compared with the night that I have come through from the former marriage. Since then, I have received much knowledge and understanding from the Lord Jesus, about Him, God the Father, and His purposes. This knowledge has come in the forms of light bulbs going on, experiences, and visions, which I want to share with the reader. I hope to put the puzzle pieces together enough to help the reader get a glimpse of eternity.

Growing up as a young boy, I used to listen to my father and brothers talk somewhat about the current events and what was going on in the world. I listened to their opinions, which helped shape some of mine. As a Christian, the Church of Jesus Christ of Latter-day Saints served as a rich resource of knowledge. I learned through the scriptures, the prophecies, and the teachings of Christ of the nature of man and how God is going to deal with people who disobey His commandments. I learned of people who, because of their disobedience, have gone into bondage and, through the mercies of God, have been led out again. It has proved that every time a nation goes into bondage, it is from disobedience to God's commandments; and while in bondage, the people sustain insurmountable misery and suffering before God remembers them. It is like teaching a horse to respect a bit. The horse won't respect it when you pull on the reins the first time, so the best way is to make the horse inflict pain on itself, and then the process makes it easier for it to understand what it doesn't want. Even then, some are so thickheaded that they will learn either harder or not at all. This is how people are.

As I got older, I began to realize that all people must make that choice of who they were going to follow. Will they follow God, or will they follow Satan? In school, I learned history, which I really learned to love and thrive on because it was so interesting. I learned of the Dark Ages and the wars of the different kingdoms striving for domination and control. The most appalling was the Catholic Church and their control over the kingdoms of Europe through the Dark Ages. These kinds of things hit so close to the heart, knowing how that church ruled with such blood and horror and suppressed the thinking of mankind to actually have a period of no light in the world, literally causing the Dark Ages. Then I learned of the world wars and how evil men wanting control were the cause of so many lost lives unnecessarily, and then I grew up in the period of the Vietnam War, causing the same destruction.

These kinds of things caused much concern and reflection on how evil men had such disregard for life. I myself, being a graduate of high school in 1976, was wondering if I would be drafted to fight in Vietnam. God was good to me as I missed the draft by one year. The war ended on April

30, 1975. I was grateful as I had seen a lot of my older friends go to Vietnam. Some didn't come back, and some came back all shot to pieces.

I often wondered about life and why we are here, if we are not important to God. We are told that we are His children, but who is He? Where did we come from? Where are the men and women who dye the battlefield red or die of old age, sickness, and disease, or die as a child. Is there life after this life? What is going on? So I read the Bible and the standard works of the Mormon Church over and over, not wanting to miss anything. I wanted to see the whole picture, and I began receiving knowledge a little here and a little there, listening to insight from other people who talk and want to know many of the same things, but still not seeing the whole picture.

It wasn't until I joined a group of conservatives called the Concerned Citizens for Constitutional Government of Idaho that I began to learn that the Bible, history, and government are all tied together. By learning more about one, I learned more about the other, and knowledge and understanding began to pour in like water. I started to see a communist/socialist a mile away. I saw the lies and deception that had compromised the people's freedoms. I realized that the Left was pushing an agenda of slavery, and I never would have dreamed that I would grow up in an era where there was slavery, especially finding myself on the threshold of this abomination.

I realized that if I didn't want to be a slave, then I needed to get into the fight and make a difference. For this reason, I refused to any longer file any income taxes. The last year I ever filed income tax was 1993 because it is unconstitutional. At this time, I lived at 17825 North Atlas Road, Rathdrum, Idaho 83858. We had bought ten acres, logged it, drilled a well on it, and pulled a mobile home onto it. There, I fought the IRS and the banking system. The land was paid off, free, and clear until I bought a semi-truck, using my property as collateral, and then went trucking.

By this time, I was about thirty-five and still learning about government and the ways and deceitfulness of the things of the world. I learned that the banking system is one very evil institution, if not the evilest. I still had a great desire to learn about the things of God and His mysteries. So I promised my wife and family that just because I would be in a truck on

Sunday didn't mean I would drive on Sunday, and I made a commitment to be stopped on the Lord's Day. Because of this commitment, God had spoken to me in visions and in my sleep.

This was a time when I was actually learning more from people outside the Mormon Church than I was from those within. This felt like a period where it seemed the church was going backward rather than forward, and I didn't know why because I loved the church. There was such an ignorant atmosphere among the members of the Mormon Church that going to their meetings at church was like going there just to fight. It got to the point that my family and I just had to stop going. I had my membership challenged by one of the elders quorum councilors, and I wrote a letter to the church asking to take my family and I off the membership roll.

Since Rathdrum, Idaho, my family has lived at 1250 Shady Lane, Tensed, Idaho, where we bought ten acres and did the same, drilling a well and pulling a double-wide mobile home onto it. There, my family and I lived self-sufficient for five years. We had a couple of good draft horses, both weighing about a ton each. We grew our own food, cut hay, put up firewood, and raised cows, bees, goats, sheep, chickens, rabbits, dogs, and a couple of cats, besides four children. We had milk, honey, grain, and vegetables, as we had a big garden. We were up high in the mountain overlooking a beautiful valley of grain fields and forests. We were close to a state park that teemed with deer, bear, elk, pheasant, turkey, grouse, and all manner of other small wildlife. I called it my pantry. It was a wonderful experience depending on God and getting closer to Him and to my family, because we all depended on one another. Then from Idaho, my family and I moved to Wisconsin, where the winters are cold and which is a land full of dairies, cranberries, lakes, and a different sort of fish from what I am used to.

The experiences that I have had through my lifetime are too many to list, but I cherish everyone and every loved one who has come into my life. I have learned to love life and cherish it, and I am so grateful to my Father in Heaven because I now understand how it works. I know who He is, what His work is, and why. I know that the Church of Jesus Christ of Latter-day Saints is the Lord's church, but I also know that it is in the wilderness. It is evident that my Father in Heaven has been telling us all along about something happening before it happens. He has written the play Himself, narrates it, and then throws us all down here at different times as it pleases Him to see what we will do. I am thankful to God for His patience with me; for the gift of the Holy Ghost; for answering my prayers; for my faith; for His Son, Jesus Christ; and for giving me eyes to see.

I know that my Redeemer lives, for I have seen Him, and I know that I am redeemed from the Fall. All people can have this assurance, but I also know that many won't come to Him because they reject knowledge and won't obey the commandments of God. I pray that anyone who reads this book may be enriched by the things they find herein.

Steven Sego

CHAPTER 1

The Purpose of Life: Where Did We Come From?

To have an understanding and knowledge of God and His mysteries, the first step is attempting to understand His language and symbology. The stage that is set for the play of life and our purpose in our world is written and narrated by God Himself before the Creation even began. There is a beginning symbology and procedure that went into the introduction of God, beginning the creation of another world as He has already created "worlds without end."

Isaiah, in the Old Testament, speaks of and implies worlds created without end. *"But Israel shall be saved in the Lord with an everlasting salvation: ye shall not be ashamed nor confounded* **world without end**" *(Isaiah 45:17, KJV).* Then again in the New Testament, it says, *"Unto him be glory in the church by Christ Jesus throughout all ages,* **world without end**" *(Ephesians 3:21, KJV).* Also, it says, *"Hath in these last days spoken unto us by his Son, whom he hath appointed heir of all things, by whom also he* **made the worlds**" *(Hebrews 1:2, KJV).*

The book of Moses in the *Pearl of Great Price*, translated and written by the Mormon prophet Joseph Smith, speaks about the endless creations of God.

And God spake unto Moses, saying: Behold, I am the Lord God Almighty, and Endless is my name; for I am without beginning of days or end of years; and is this not endless? . . . And he beheld many lands; and **each land was called** *earth, and there were inhabitants on the face thereof. And it came to pass that Moses called upon God saying: Tell me, I pray thee, why these things are so, and by what thou madest them? And behold, the glory of the Lord was upon Moses, so that Moses stood in the presence of God, and talked with him face to face. And the Lord God said unto Moses: For mine own purpose have I made these things. Here is wisdom and it remaineth in me. And by the word of my power, have I created them, which is mine Only Begotten Son, who is full of grace and truth. **And worlds without number have I created**; and I also created them for mine own purpose; and by the Son I created them, which is mine Only Begotten. And the **first man of all men have I called Adam**, **which is many**. But only an account of this earth, and the inhabitants thereof, give I unto you. For behold, **there are many worlds** that have passed away by the word of my power, And there are many that now stand, and innumerable are they unto man; but all things are numbered unto me, for they are mine and I know them. (Moses 1:3, 29–35, Pearl of Great Price)*

Then again, it says, *"And Enoch said unto the Lord: How is it that thou canst weep, seeing thou art holy, and from all eternity to all eternity? And were it possible that man could number the particles of the earth, yea, **millions of earths like this**, it would not be a beginning to the number of thy creations; and thy curtains are stretched out still; and yet thou art there, and thy bosom is there; and also thou art just; thou art merciful and kind forever"* (Moses 7:29–30, Pearl of Great Price).

The gospel of John in the New Testament records the position and deity of Christ and His role in the eternal creation of all things now and in the beginning as one of the gods with whom we have to give an accounting. *"In the beginning was the **Word**, and the **Word** was with God, and the **Word** was God. The same was in the beginning with God. All things were made by him; and without him was not anything made that was made. . . . And the **Word** was made flesh, and dwelt among us, (and we beheld his glory, the glory as of the only begotten of the Father,) full of grace and truth"* (John 1:1–3, 14, KJV). These verses establish the fact that Christ is a member of the Godhead, with power to create and govern anything and everything, including the creation of this earth and everything pertaining to it, not to mention the worlds without end before and after it.

Genesis 1:26–27 (KJV) states, *"And God said, let **us** make man in **our** image, after **our** likeness: and let them have dominion over the fish of the sea, and over* *the fowl of the air, and over the cattle, and over all the earth, and over every creeping thing that creepeth upon the earth. So God created man in his own image, in the image of God created he him; Male and female created he them."*

In the Hebrew language, the term *God,* has a plural meaning. It implies there is more than one God or more than one person having the title of God, with the power of God. The Bible speaks about three with this authority—God the Father, the Son, and the Holy Ghost. We know the Son, who is Jesus Christ, and the Holy Ghost is a silent spirit partner whose purpose is to witness and testify about Jesus Christ and the Father. We can compare this to an algebra equation where Godhead = x + Christ + Holy Ghost.

The Bible is the most complete book we have for truth, and anyone who believes in God and His Son must hold on to it as their most precious source of truth. It tells us from the beginning to the end of time, either outright or implied, of anything we should know about God. Many times, the language is different from our understanding; and at other times, we must search for the truth and be able to see the whole picture. We have to pay special attention to the words and teachings of the apostles in the New Testament and the prophets in the Old Testament. The truth is there, but we need to read it over and over again with the firm desire and commitment to understand it and through prayer and meditation, and then the Spirit of the Holy Ghost will bear witness. When Christ Himself says it, then be sure to sit up and take notice. We learn line upon line, a little bit here and a little bit there, until we have an understanding of the truth. *"Whom shall he teach knowledge? And whom shall he make to understand doctrine? Them that are weaned from the milk, and drawn from the breasts. For precept must be upon precept, precept upon precept; line upon line, line upon line; here a little, and there a little: For with stammering lips and another tongue will he speak to this people" (Isaiah 28:9–11, KJV).*

Some churches teach that God is three persons in one body, while others teach three persons who are separate in body, but one in purpose. My purpose is to prove that there are three distinct beings, especially, that Jesus Christ and the Father are separate and independent, both holding the high office of God, and to explain who the Father is. Some churches teach that God doesn't have a body but is spirit. Both the Father and Christ have several titles and offices, God being one of them. Christ holds offices such as Lord, Jehovah, Wonderful, Counselor, Prince of Peace, the Son, and King of kings. No one can name them all. The Father, besides the title, God, holds the titles of Michael the Archangel, who threw Satan out of Heaven; I Am; the Ancient of Days; Alpha and Omega, the beginning and the end; Elohim; and Adam. The office Christ or the Father is filling at the time carries the significant title for that office. It is like a president of the United States or a judge. They keep every title they have earned forever. They may step down from doing the job, but they maintain the title, and it follows them around, whether for good or for evil.

Just as was written in Genesis 1:26–27, when God said, "Let *us* make man in *our* image," there was more than just one God in the Creation, and everything was created in a place other than this earth before it was placed on the earth, including our first parents, Adam and Eve. *"These are the generations of the heavens and of the earth when they were created, in the day the Lord God made the earth and the heavens, and **every plant of the field before it was in the earth**, and **every herb** of the field before it grew: for the Lord God had not caused it to rain upon the earth, and **there was not a man** to till the ground" (Genesis 2:4–5, KJV).*

God knew each and every one of us personally before we were born into this life, just as He told Jeremiah. *"**Before I formed thee in the belly, I knew thee**; and before thou camest forth out of the womb I sanctified thee, and I ordained thee a prophet unto the nations" (Jeremiah 1:5, KJV).* As stated, God has written the play and script for this world and even narrates it Himself through His prophets, and then throws us in, where He wants us to be, to see what we will do. He has included roles for certain key actors through the ages, even telling us their names. God has told us about the first man and woman, Adam and Eve, and about Satan; and through Daniel, we know of the four great kingdoms, us being in the fourth now, which is the Roman Empire, having a stranglehold on the world. God also has mentioned Jesus Christ thousands of years in advance and His role in redeeming mankind. The Bible tells of Christ's coming, when He would be born, and where, which is the city of David, Bethlehem. The scriptures even pinpoint the day and time and who His parents would be, and it happened, even though Mary had to ride ninety miles, sitting on a donkey to get there. This tells us that God is really, really interested in us and that He is also the producer and director of the play, but He allows us to use our free agency to serve either Him, or Satan.

In writing His play, God uses a lot of symbology and normal props to set the scene, such as by placing the man in the garden, by creating Him from the dust of the earth, and by placing the two trees there for Him to choose from when making His decisions. Another symbology is when Lucifer comes to tempt Eve, Eve tempts Adam, and they both do what Lucifer wants and then end up both getting expelled from the garden into the "world." This narration states "worlds without end." This world we are in is just one of the many worlds He has created.

One very important aspect to remember is that we are literally the offspring of God. *"For in him we live, and move, and have our being; as certain also your own poets have said, For **we are also his offspring**. Forasmuch then as **we are the offspring of God**, we ought not to think that the Godhead is like unto gold, or silver, or stone, graven by art and man's device. And the times of this ignorance God winked at; but now commandeth all men everywhere to repent"* (Acts 17:28–30, KJV). Well then, if we are the literal offspring of God, then God was here to build His world on this earth by physically starting His family. God set the scene for peopling this world by planting Adam and Eve here as our first parents, but where is God if we are literally God's offspring, and who is He?

I have my genealogy traced through my grandmother, whose family originated from England. My sister Sharon has been very diligent in this work and ultimately succeeded in tracing it all the way back to Adam and no further because it just doesn't go any further. Adam, being placed in the garden, is just that, as He was already a living soul, along with His wife, Eve, to begin carrying out His own commandment, to multiply and replenish the earth. Adam was placed in the Garden of Eden. The Garden of Eden is symbolic of the earth. The account describing how Adam was made from the dust of the earth is true, except He was not made from the dust of this earth. *"And the Lord God formed man of the dust of the ground, and breathed into his nostrils the breath of life; and man became a living soul. And the Lord God planted a garden eastward in Eden; and there he put the man whom he had formed"* (Genesis 2:7–8, KJV). Remember that everything is created somewhere else before it is placed in the earth.

There are myths about Mount Olympus, the mountain of the gods. There is a lot of truth to these myths, which are stories carried down from long ago. There are myths about Atlas, who held up the world, and about certain people trying to ascend to Mount Olympus in various ways. One tried to make wings to fly there. The children of Babel tried to build a mighty tower to get there but failed because if they succeeded, they would have made a mockery of God.

Kent Hovind from Lenox, Alabama, is a scientist who for many years fought against the schools filling our children's minds with lies concerning evolution. He set out to teach people that evolution is completely false. He described interesting evidence to suggest that during and after the creation of this earth, the world on which God dwelled hovered just over the earth. Ancients could see that vast planet hovering, which also created such magnetic pull on the waters that the waters stood up toward the mount of the gods, making it look like a mighty and strong man was holding up the world—Atlas. One has to reach the conclusion that even after the flood, this phenomenon still occurred until the people, who were all of one language, began building a tower to get to Heaven, or, in other words, up to the mount of the gods/Mount Olympus. It was at this time that the earth was divided, in the days of Peleg, when the heavens fled away. *"And unto Eber were born two sons: the name of one was Peleg; for **in his days was the earth divided**; and his brother's name was Joktan" (Genesis 10:25, KJV).*

When the mount of the gods left and went away, it released the magnetic pull on the great pillar of water. The water then settled onto the earth, making the water deeper and ended the earth as being one landmass. For instance, the English Channel separating England from France is actually shallow, and used to be above water, and acted as a land bridge. Revelation talks about the heavens as having fled away. *"And I saw a great white throne, and him who sat upon it, from whose face the **earth and the heavens fled away**; and there was found no place for them" (Revelation 20:11, KJV).*

Adam, in reality, came from the mount of the gods/Mount Olympus, being placed, or coming here to begin another world with His posterity on it and subjecting Himself; His wife, Eve; and every one of us under the jurisdiction of Satan. They did this by partaking of the tree of knowledge of good and evil, which was placed in the Garden of Eden. The Garden of Eden symbolizes this whole earth, and the tree of knowledge of good and evil symbolizes the world. Each of the two trees symbolize a system of government or a church. Accepting benefits from the devil, which come in many different forms, will place a person in Satan's jurisdiction. Another chapter will cover this subject. The fruit is symbolic of the benefits, but is not fruit like an apple or pear.

Adam, in His great wisdom, showed each of us that we all must go through this dreary world, learn, and choose between God and Satan. We have been given this lifetime to prepare to meet God/Adam again in Heaven, where He is waiting for each of us to return, if we so choose. We are given the ability to choose for ourselves whom we will serve. *"And out of the ground God formed every beast of the field, and every fowl of the air; and **brought them unto Adam to see what he would call them**: and whatsoever Adam called them every living creature, that was the name thereof. And Adam gave names to all cattle, and to the fowl of the air, and to every beast of the field; but for Adam there was not found a help meet for him"* (Genesis 2:19–20, KJV).

Adam was given the duty to name every animal of every kind of all sizes. How was He able to do that if He was not, in fact, God Himself, having created them through His Son, Jesus Christ? We know that the creations of God are vast and numberless.

The Garden of Eden is symbolic and a representation of the whole earth, where God placed the man whom He formed. *"And the **Lord God planted a garden eastward in Eden**; and **there he put the man** whom he had formed. And out of the ground made the Lord God to grow every tree that is pleasant to the sight, and good for food; **the tree of life also** in the midst of the garden, **and the tree of knowledge of good and evil**"* (Genesis 2:8–9, KJV).

God told Adam and Eve that they could eat of every tree or plant in the garden, but of the tree of knowledge of good and evil, they shall not eat, or they shall surely die in the day that they eat thereof. *"And the Lord God commanded the man, saying, of every tree of the garden thou mayest freely eat: But of the tree of the knowledge of good and evil, thou shalt not eat of it: **for in the day that thou eatest thereof thou shalt** surely **die**"* (Genesis 2:16–17, KJV). We know for certain that Adam and Eve did eat from the tree of knowledge of good and evil. *"And when the woman saw that the tree was good for food, and that it was pleasant to the eyes, and a tree to be desired to make one wise, **she took of the fruit thereof and did eat**, and **gave also unto her husband** with her; and **he did eat**"* (Genesis 3:6, KJV).

By this single act of disobeying God, in order to obey a greater commandment, they brought about man's first death, which is the separation of man from the presence of God. Adam lived 930 years before He died, His physical death, but He died as God said He would, within the day that He partook of the fruit of the tree of knowledge of good and evil. *"But, beloved, be not ignorant of this one thing, that* **one day with the Lord as a thousand years**, *and* **a thousand years as one day**" *(2 Peter:3:8, KJV). "And all the days that* **Adam lived were nine hundred and thirty years**: *and he died"* (Genesis 5:5, KJV).

The Mormons' *Pearl of Great Price*, in the book of Abraham, explains better the time and the planet on which the Gods dwelt. *"But of the tree of knowledge of good and evil, thou shalt not eat of it; for in the time that thou eatest thereof, thou shalt surely die. Now I, Abraham, saw that it was after* **The Lord's time**, **which was after the time of Kolob**; *for as yet the Gods had not appointed unto Adam his reckoning"* (Abraham 5:13). So Adam and Eve were on the earth in the presence of God before they partook of the tree of knowledge of good and evil. They were still on the earth afterward also. The difference was that they were in subjection to the devil and not in the presence of God any longer. This is again symbolic of what we have to do. Even though we are the posterity of Adam and He fell into the jurisdiction of Satan, it doesn't make us responsible for what He did; but because of what He did, it makes us liable for the same choices. We have to decide from day to day whether to choose the fruit of the tree of knowledge of good and evil, represented by Satan, or the fruit of the tree of life, which is a representation of Jesus Christ.

Adam came down off His great throne from being God and lowered Himself to the jurisdiction of Satan to die and have a posterity so that we, His children, might have a chance at life experiences. We were organized in the spirit from "intelligences" before we were placed here on the earth in our bodies as babies. We were intelligences before we were spirits and, as James put it, "lights" drifting in space without any goals, without any purpose or experience, and with no sense of time. *"Every good gift and every perfect gift is from above, and cometh down from the* **Father of lights**, *with whom is no variableness, neither shadow of turning. Of his own will begat he us with the word of truth, that we should be a kind of first fruits of his creatures. Wherefore, my beloved brethren, let every man be swift to hear, slow to speak, slow to wrath"* (James 1:17–19, KJV).

Once again, the Mormons answer this question in the *Pearl of Great Price* in the book of Abraham.

*Howbeit that he made the greater star; as, also if there be two spirits, and one shall be more intelligent than the other, yet these two spirits, notwithstanding one is more intelligent than the other, **have no beginning; they existed before, they shall have no end, they shall exist after**, for they are gnolaum, or **eternal**. . ... Now the Lord had shown unto me, Abraham, the intelligences that were organized before the world was; and among all these there were many of the noble and great ones; And God saw these souls that they were good, and he stood in the midst of them, and he said: These I will make my rulers; for he stood among those that were spirits, and he saw that they were good; and he said unto me: Abraham, thou art one of them; thou wast chosen before thou wast born, And there stood one among them that was like unto God, and he said unto those who were with him: **We will go down**, for there is space there, and **we will make an earth whereon these may dwell**; And we will prove them herewith, to see if they will do all things whatsoever the Lord their God shall command them. (Abraham 3:18, 22–25)*

Because of the love and mercy Adam/God had for us, He came down and started another world just for us so that we may have earthly experiences and test us to see if we will have Him to be our God. He created bodies of flesh and bone for us, just like He has Himself. He has given us the ability to be just like Him in every way. We have all the systems our body needs to move and act independently. We have a circulatory system to carry nutrients throughout the body, we can feed ourselves, we have a skeletal system and a muscular system that we need to move freely. We have a lymph system for circulation, we have sight, and our bodies can clean themselves, heal themselves, and even reproduce and communicate. On top of all this, we are given free will. All these things give reason for all to praise God for eternity. *"And all the angels stood around about the throne, and about the elders and the four beasts, and fell before the throne on their faces, and worshipped God, saying, Amen: Blessing, and thanksgiving, and honour, and power, and might, be unto our God for ever and ever, Amen" (Revelation 7:11–12, KJV).*

To understand the significance of God, we need to take the Bible as a whole, both Old and New Testaments, because they imply and hint about God in all their areas. Many scriptures talk about God in the plural, and many areas individualize the member of the Godhead being discussed. For instance, while Adam was on the earth for 930 years, Christ officiated as God because

He also was God. To put it another way, Christ is the second member of the Godhead and can preside in that office in the absence of the first member of the Godhead. After dying at the end of 930 years, Adam returned to His throne as God, and then Christ came down and did His job, which was to redeem the world from the Fall.

Adam and Christ and the Holy Ghost are a team in bringing to pass the immortality and eternal life of man. While Christ was here on the earth, God/Adam officiated on the throne as God and still does. He is our Father on the earth and is also our Father in Heaven now. He is the one who spoke out of the heavens at the time of Christ's baptism, saying, "This is my beloved Son in whom I am well pleased." *"And straightway coming up out of the water, he saw the heavens opened, and the **Spirit like a dove descending** upon him: And **there came a voice from heaven**, saying, **thou art my beloved Son**, in whom I am well pleased"* (Mark 1:10–11, KJV). This instance shows all three members of the Godhead as three separate persons.

Another instance was on the Mount of Transfiguration. *"While he yet spake, behold, a bright cloud overshadowed them: and **behold a voice out of the cloud**, which said, **this is my beloved Son**, in whom I am well pleased; hear ye him"* (Matthew 17:5, KJV). It is extremely apparent that Jesus Christ held the title of God before and after He was born, being the second member of the Godhead, allowing Him to interchange roles with the Father.

Christ often spoke for and on behalf of the Godhead in many instances, such as dealing with Moses and the children of Israel while they were in the wilderness. *"God spake all these words, saying, I am the **Lord God**, which have brought thee out of the land of Egypt, out of the house of bondage"* (Exodus 20:1–2, KJV). Verse 1 tells us that God spoke to Moses, but verse 2 identifies which one of the Godhead is actually doing the speaking. In this case, it is the Lord, which is Jesus Christ. This is just one of many instances where God is present and where the one doing the speaking identifies Himself as the one to which is actually doing the speaking. When Moses was up on Mount Sinai, receiving the Ten Commandments, God wrote on the tablets with His finger, but the tablets were delivered to Moses by the Lord, and the Holy Ghost was there to witness to Moses, of God and the Lord.

The Garden of Eden, as stated, is symbolic of the whole earth, and Adam and Eve had many sons and daughters. Some were giants and were renowned for their prowess. These were the days talked about as the golden age. It had never yet rained on the earth; in fact, it never rained on the earth clear up until Noah was ready to enter the ark, but God watered the earth by sending a mist every day to water it. It was these days that the people didn't have to work very hard to grow food. They simply harvested what grew.

These were the days that dinosaurs, as we call them now, lived. Kent Hovind, founder of Creation Science Evangelism, being a science teacher for many years and a good Christian and family man, studied and talked about dinosaurs. Another title Mr. Hovind carried was Dr. Dino. He said, "A dinosaur is just a big lizard. The longer a lizard lives, the bigger it gets. If you were a lizard that lived over 900 years, how big could you get?" For that matter, how big could a human get if they lived 900 years? They grew to a pretty big size as many were giants.

Job talks about Behemoth.

*Behold now **Behemoth**, which I made thee; eateth grass as an ox. Lo now, his strength is in his loins, and his force is in the navel of his belly. He moveth his tail like a cedar: the sinew of his stones is wrapped together; His bones are as strong pieces of brass; his bones are like bars of iron. He is the chief of the ways of God: he that made him can make his sword to approach unto him. Surely the mountains bring him forth food, where all the beasts of the field play. He lieth under the shady trees, in the covert of the reed, and fens, the shady trees cover him with their shadows; the willows of the brook compass him about. Behold, he drinketh up a river, and hasteth not: he trusteth that he can draw up Jordan into his mouth He taketh it with his eyes: his nose pierceth through snares. (Job 40:15–24, KJV)*

Kent Hovind talks about this period and describes the conditions that existed as having a perfect atmosphere to restrict the ultraviolet rays of the sun from causing man and beast from aging as quickly, thus allowing them to live much longer. He talks of the water level on the earth before the flood, being much lower than it is now, and about the earth being one landmass. This makes sense as it agrees with *Genesis 1:9–10 (KJV)*. "*And God said, Let the **waters under the heaven be gathered unto one place**, and **let the dry land appear**: and it was so. And God called the dry land Earth; and the gathering together of the waters called the seas: and God saw that it was good.*"

Dr. Hovind explains that during this period, from the Creation to the time of Noah, the world on which God dwelled hovered just over the newly created earth, causing a magnetic pull, thus drawing the waters up toward it in what looked like a great pillar. This perhaps is where the myth began as if mighty Atlas were holding up the world. Kent Hovind also touched on the point, that to keep out the sun's rays, there had to be a ring around the earth, perhaps in the form of ice that would melt, adding more water if and when broken. The world where God dwelled, hovering above the earth, also makes sense in the fact that Nimrod, the mighty hunter, began building or had built the Tower of Babel to get to Heaven. *"And they said, Go to, let us build us a city **and a tower, whose top may reach unto heaven**; and let us make us a name, lest we be scattered abroad upon the face of the whole earth"* (Genesis 11:4, KJV).

We know that the ice ring was broken at the time of the flood to add to the amount of water that covered the whole earth. Even the tops of the highest mountains were covered with massive amounts of water. It is hard to comprehend the depths of the seas at that time, but it was caused to go away somewhere, perhaps back to where it was found. The water came from both within the earth and from over the earth. *"In the six hundredth year of Noah's life, in the second month, the seventeenth day of the month, the same day were all the fountains of the deep broken up, and the windows of heaven were opened"* (Genesis 7:11, KJV).

So surely, there were men who saw the world of the gods, or Mount Olympus, where God dwelled, high above them. Most likely, the myths—which are not myths at all—were carried down by the sons of Noah—Shem, Ham, and Japheth—and their posterity through the ages. Actually, there were many who lived after the flood who would have seen these things, who bore witness to this phenomenon. So the story of Mount Olympus was told by many, but because in our day we can't see what they saw, it has become a big story or myth. Even though the flood went away, the mount of the gods was still there above the earth, up until the days of Peleg. We know this because the posterity of Noah, through Nimrod, in the land of Shinar tried to build a tower to get to Heaven.

God used the confounding of the people's languages at the Tower of Babel to scatter the people on the face of the earth. It was after this, in the days of Peleg, that God caused the heavens to flee away, causing the water levels to rise, thus separating the continents and islands from being one huge landmass.

*And the Lord came down to see the city and the tower, which the children of men builded. And the Lord said, Behold, **the people is all one**, and **they have all one language**; and this they begin to do: and now nothing will be restrained from them, which they have imagined to do. Go to, let us go down, and there confound their language, that they may not understand one another's speech. So **the Lord scattered them abroad from thence upon the face of all the earth**: and they left off to build the city. Therefore is the name of it called Babel; because the Lord did there confound the language of all the earth: and from thence did the **Lord scatter them abroad upon the face of all the earth**. (Genesis 11:5–9, KJV)*

It was in the days of Peleg that the earth was divided from being one huge landmass and when the heavens actually fled away. *"And unto Eber were born two sons: the name of one was **Peleg**; for **in his days was the earth divided**; and his brother's name was Joktan"* (Genesis 10:25, KJV). *"And I saw a great white throne, and him that sat on it, **from whose face the earth and the heaven fled away**; and there was found no place for them"* (Revelation 20:11, KJV). I know these things are true.

CHAPTER 2

Adam and Our Relationship to Him

Chapter 1 establishes the fact that there was more than one God involved in the Creation, that the world where God lived during the Creation hovered just above the earth at the time, and that Adam was the first man on the earth. *"This is the book of the generations of Adam. In the day that God created man, in the likeness of God made he him. Male and female created he them; and blessed them, and* **called their name Adam***, in the day when they were created" (Genesis 5:1–2, KJV).* Adam means "the father of all living," and God gave everyone His own name, like a father here on the earth gives his children his name. *Eve* means "the mother of all living." *"And* **Adam called his wife's name Eve; because she was the mother of all living"** *(Genesis 3:20, KJV).* The Mormons, once again, shed more light on Adam as the Father of all living.

And also with Michael, or **Adam***,* **the father of all***, the prince of all, the ancient of days. (Doctrine and Covenants, section 27:11)*

And it came to pass that Moses called upon God, saying: Tell me, I pray thee, why these things are so, and by what thou madest them? And behold, the glory of the Lord was upon Moses, so that Moses stood in the presence of God, and talked with him face to face. And the Lord God said unto Moses: For mine own purpose have I made these things. Here is wisdom and it remaineth in me. And by the word of my power, have I created them, which is mine Only Begotten Son, who is full of grace and truth. And **worlds without number** *have I created; and I also created them for mine own purpose; and by the Son I created them, which is mine Only Begotten. And the first man of all men have I called* **Adam***,* *which is many. But only an account of this earth, and the inhabitants thereof, give I unto you For behold, there are many worlds that have passed away by the word of my power. And there are many that now stand, and innumerable are they unto man: but all things are numbered unto me, for they are mine and I know them. . ... For behold, this is **my work and my glory—to bring to pass the immortality and eternal life of man**. (Moses 1:30–35, 39, Pearl of Great Price)*

As a young man growing up, I was taught in church that I was a child of God, and I had a hard time for many years understanding just how that could be. I have a sister named Sharon, who had been very diligent in searching out and tracing our family's genealogy. She accomplished that through my grandmother Roger's line all the way back to Adam. Since all people must come from Adam, as He is the first man and Eve is the first woman, you may ask, "How is it that you are able to go that far back?" The key is first getting back to someone in the Bible, and then it is much easier as the genealogy of the ancients is recorded there. My family tree ends at Adam and Eve and cannot go back any further, so how can we be the children of God?

I am sure that Adam was placed here on the earth from the world where the gods dwell as the Bible records. The Church of Jesus Christ of Latter-day Saints (Mormons), in their *Pearl of Great Price* in the book of Abraham, makes reference to the place where the Gods dwell, a planet near unto Kolob. They even have a hymn about this in their songbooks. The mythical name is Mount Olympus. Actually, "Adam" is an office or title of God; and when beginning the continuation of His family, He personally—with His wife, Eve—starts another earthly family, just as we mortals begin our families. Adam and Eve have families without end on worlds without end because that is the work and glory of God, to bring to pass the immortality and eternal life of man. *"God who at sundry times and in divers' manners spake in times past unto the fathers by prophets. Hath in these last days spoken unto us by his Son, whom he hath appointed **heir** of all things, by whom also he **made the worlds**; Who being the brightness of his glory, and the express image of his person, and upholding all things by the word of his power, when he had by himself purged our sins, sat down on the right hand of the Majesty on high"* (Hebrews 1:1–3, KJV). The Mormons once again, through Joseph Smith, have answered this question, which supports the Bible entirely. *"That* *by him, and through him, and of him, the **worlds were created**, and **the inhabitants thereof are begotten sons** and **daughters** unto God"* (Doctrine and Covenants, section 76:24). Thus, we are literal children of God, and the identity of God is staring us right in the face. *"The spirit itself beareth witness with our spirit, that **we are the children of God**"* (Romans 8:16, KJV).

It is evident and certain that Adam is our first Father. We belong to the family of God/Adam. He is our beginning and our end. *"I am **Alpha and Omega**, the **beginning and the end**, the **first and the last**"* (Revelation 22:13, KJV). The Mormon prophet Brigham Young stated in his *Journal of Discourses* that "Adam is the only God with whom we have to do."

So this is how it works: Adam/God, with His Son, Jesus Christ, created every living thing in the spirit before it was placed on the earth (*Genesis 2:4–5, KJV*). Adam/God, with His Son, Jesus Christ, then created this world on which all living things might dwell. His greatest interest and the subject of His glory is the immortality and eternal life of man.

Adam/God not only is the Creator of our spirits but also left His throne in Heaven and came to the earth, assuming the title of Adam to also be our Father in the flesh, same as He has always done, worlds without end. He symbolically partook with Eve of the fruit of the tree of knowledge of good and evil. He, Adam/God, fell so that man might be and might have mortal bodies and gain earthly experiences. The plan also had to include a way to get away from the devil's jurisdiction after a probationary period. That plan included the need for us now, as humans, to die to return to the presence of our Father/Adam. However, the point of us all coming to the earth from the world of spirits was to test us, to see if we would do the will of our Father/ Adam.

So this is where His Son, Jesus Christ, comes in. Our ultimate test was, for Adam/God to send His Son, Jesus Christ, to us, to see if we would follow His Son back to His presence. There are many who haven't, nor are following, or will follow Jesus Christ and do the things that we have seen him do. Therefore, they must be separated from God for eternity.

God/Adam and His Son, Jesus Christ, work as a team, worlds without end, to bring to pass the immortality and eternal life of man. *"For since by **man came death**, by **man came also the resurrection of the dead**. For as in*

*Adam all die, even so **in Christ shall all be made alive**. But every man in his own order: Christ the first fruits; afterward they that are Christ's at his coming. Then cometh the end, when he shall have delivered up the kingdom to God, even the Father; when he shall have put down all rule and all authority and power"* (1 Corinthians 15:21–24, KJV).

Adam then begat sons and daughters and lived a total of 930 years before He died. He died within the day that God said He would because He partook of the tree of knowledge of good and evil. To man, 1,000 years is 1 day to God. After Adam died, He ascended back to His heavenly home to sit on His throne as God. Now He is our Heavenly Father as He has done, worlds without end.

While God/Adam was here on the earth, starting His earthly family, Christ—who also holds the office of God—officiated on the throne of God. Christ was the one who came into the Garden of Eden and talked to Adam before and after He fell. Christ officiated for 930 years until Adam died and ascended to His throne again. Afterward, Christ came down from Heaven to do His job, and that was to die and redeem the family of Adam, at least those who would follow Christ back to the presence of our Father, Adam. It was Adam's voice who spoke out of the heavens at the time of Christ's baptism, saying, "This is my beloved Son, in whom I am well pleased." He spoke the same thing on the Mount of Transfiguration about His Son, with the disciples of Christ present and bearing witness (*Matthew 3:17, Luke 3:22, 1 Peter 1:17, KJV*).

We are the children of God/Adam while He was in the flesh, but Christ is the only child of God/Adam born to Him after He ascended back to His throne in Heaven. This is what makes Christ the only "begotten" of the Father in the flesh. *"For God so loved the world that he gave his only **begotten Son**, that whosoever believeth in him should not perish, but have everlasting life" (John 3:16, KJV).*

*"But when the fullness of the time was come, God sent forth his Son, made of a woman, made under the law" (Galatians 4:4, KJV). "And the angel answered and said unto her, The Holy Ghost shall come upon thee, and the **power of the Highest shall overshadow thee**: therefore, also that holy thing which shall be born of thee shall be called the Son of God" (Luke 1:35, KJV).* Adam is the "Highest" that overshadowed Mary.

Christ talks about His father as if it is common knowledge that we should know who He is. He often mentions "the Father." *"Jesus answered them, Is it not written in the law, I said, **Ye are gods?** If he **called them gods**, unto whom the word came, and the scripture cannot be broken; Say ye of him, whom **the Father** hath sanctified, and sent into the world, Thou blasphemist; because I said, **I am the Son of God**? If I do not the works of **my Father**, believe me not. But if I do, though ye believe not me, believe the works: that ye may know, and believe, that **the Father** is in me, and I in him"* (John 10:34–38, KJV). The Father is Adam, the Father of all living. If He is the Father of all living, then He is just not our Father but also Christ's. That means that if we are to be joint heirs with Christ, then we all must have the same Father.

God shows us how much He loves us by letting us create our own mini-world. We create our own world by getting married and producing our own families. This shows us how much He loves us, by letting us share this ability to have children and experience in this joy. We all love our families more than our own lives. The love we have for our children is humongous. However, this ability to rear children is set in the bounds of marriage and obedience to our Father's commandments. Marriage is the covenant between us and God. If we obey these laws on which blessings are predicated, we then will definitely inherit with our elder brother, Jesus Christ, in the world to come. *"And **if children, then heirs; heirs of God**, and **joint-heirs with Christ**; if so be that we suffer with him, that we may be glorified together"* (Romans 8:17, KJV).

As stated earlier, while Adam was here on this earth beginning another family, us, Christ—who holds the same title or office of God—officiated as God in the absence of Adam. They have interchangeable roles and are two separate beings but one in purpose. God/Adam, of course, officiated while Christ was here as a man on the earth while He fulfilled His mission as Savior of the world. Other titles God has besides Adam are I Am, Alpha and Omega, and Michael the Archangel. *"And there was war in heaven: **Michael** and his angels fought against the dragon; and the dragon fought and his angels, and prevailed not; neither was their place found anymore in heaven. And the great dragon was cast out, that old serpent, called the devil, and Satan, which deceiveth the whole world: he was cast out into the earth, and his angels were cast out with him"* (Revelation 12:7–9, KJV).

Joseph Smith answered this question also:

But behold, verily I say unto you, before the earth shall pass away, **Michael,** **mine archangel,** *shall sound his trump, and then shall all the dead awake, for their graves shall be opened, and they shall come forth-yeah, even all. (Doctrine and Covenants, section 29:26)*

And **Michael,** *the seventh angel, even the* **archangel,** *shall gather together his armies, even the hosts of heaven. And the devil shall gather together his armies; even the hosts of hell, and shall come up to battle against Michael and his armies. And then cometh the battle of the great God; and the devil and his armies shall be cast away into their own place, and they shall not have power over the saints any more at all. For Michael shall fight their battles, and shall overcome him who seeketh the throne of him who sitteth upon the throne, even the lamb. (Doctrine and Covenants, (section 88:112–115)*

And the Lord appeared unto them, and they rose up and blessed **Adam,** *and called him* **Michael,** *the prince,* **the archangel.** *(Doctrine and Covenants, section 107:54)*

We are proudly from the family of Adam. He is our Father in Heaven. He was the one, other than Christ, that Joseph Smith had seen in his vision. Adam is also the Ancient of Days as spoken of in Daniel. *"I beheld till the thrones were cast down, and the* **Ancient of Days** *did sit, whose garment was white as snow, and the hair of his head like the pure wool; his throne was like the fiery flame, and his wheels as burning fire. . . .. I saw in the night visions and beheld one like the* **Son of man came** *with the clouds of heaven, and* **came to the Ancient of Days,** *and they brought him near before him. And there was given him dominion, and glory, and a kingdom, that all people, nations, and languages, should serve him: his dominion is an everlasting dominion, which shall not pass away, and his kingdom that which shall not be destroyed" (Daniel 7:9, 13–14, KJV).*

"Then cometh the end, when he shall have delivered up the kingdom to God, even the Father; when he shall have put down all rule and all authority and power" (1 Corinthians 15:24, KJV). We belong to the family of Adam. It is His right to judge His children, and He will do so and no other. I am very grateful for having this knowledge of God/Adam. Having this knowledge of who God truly is and how He works absolutely **destroys all arguments.** It destroys the theory of evolution because we know of a surety that the Creation actually happened. This knowledge of God destroys the

argument of the atheist because God is very real and genuine, and having this knowledge destroys the belief held by the Catholics and other various Christian denominations, such as the Baptists, who believe that God is one person but with three different heads. In reality, God does have a plural meaning in Hebrew. God is three different persons but one in purpose. Knowing these things also destroys the idea of Allah, the God of Islam. There is only one true, all-powerful, kind, and loving God. It is impossible to look to any other when we are allowed to understand that we are family.

We have been given this life to gain experiences in the flesh and to prepare to meet God. These things happened for us to come here and gain a body and prove if we are willing to obey our Father in Heaven through obeying His commandments. He has organized our intelligences into a spirit body *(Genesis 2:5, KJV)*. He then created a world for us to dwell, came here physically, and began His family here, one of many, with empathy and mercy. He, once a glorified being, fell so that we might have life ourselves. It is so fantastic that God has taken our intelligences, placed them into a spiritual body, then came to the earth, and began for us, from the dust of the earth, physical bodies. He fell so that man might be. He then sent His Son to bring us back to Him, after we have been tested and tried.

Men have been rebelling against God from the beginning, thinking that they could outsmart Him and perhaps gain eternal life without obeying the rules. Many have become devilish in all ways possible and imaginable. They have sought to ascend to Heaven and still maintain their selfish ways through money, deceit, and power over their brethren, etc. Men have tried to do what God has done and create men by cloning and by making robots that will do their evil will. The only problem they have is that they can't place the spirit in man, which is a really big problem. Wicked men from the beginning, trying to outdo God, can only copy what He has done, and then, at best, very poorly, usually distorting and destroying God's creations. The work and glory of God is to bring to pass the immortality and eternal life of man. *"For behold, **this is my work and my glory—to bring to pass the immortality and eternal life of man**" (Moses 1:39, Pearl of Great Price)*.

God has created mankind with a body of flesh and bone to carry our spirits/intelligences around. Our bodies are like independent engines, with all the systems necessary to take care of itself. It has a bone structure to hold the body up. It has a muscular system allowing it to move, a system of circulation, a system to take nutrients throughout the body, a smelling system, a system of sight, of hearing, of breathing so that oxygen can get to the body. It can feed itself; It has a system to clean itself; it can reproduce, and on top of all these systems, God has given us self-will, but has given commandments to govern our limits. Nevertheless, above all, God has given us free agency to see if we will do His will.

When confronted with the question "Do I believe in God?" then the answer is most certainly, *yes,* because I am directly related to Him. I understand the scriptures that say that concourses of angels will stand around His throne, continuously praising His greatness and glorifying His name for eternity. I have no doubt that He lives, and I know that I can be like Him; after all, I have all His traits and genes. I am a son of God/Adam, and He has given me a small taste of knowing what it is like to be like Him already, by allowing me to create my own family here on the earth. I always think of how I feel about my children. They have all the abilities that I inherited. I wish the best for them. I use my son as a great example. I want him to learn and be stronger, smarter, nicer, and better looking and have all the opportunities in this life that he can manage. I have these desires for him because I love him greatly. For these reasons, I know my heavenly Father loves me, and I can be like Him and return to His presence.

Christ was telling His disciples that if they have seen Him, then they have seen the Father. *"Jesus saith unto him, Have I been so long time with you, and yet has thou not known me, Phillip?* **He that hath seen me hath seen the Father;** *and how sayest thou then, shew us the Father?"* (John 14:9, KJV). It is true that Christ tells them that He is in the express image of His Father (*Hebrews 1:3, KJV*). Seeing Christ is the same as seeing the Father because They look alike, and They are one in purpose, but the most important point is that Christ is also saying that God has already been here on the earth, and that if He hadn't been, then Christ wouldn't be here either because the Father first had to fulfill His part of the mission before Christ could fulfill His.

After Jesus Christ died and rose again and as Stephen was being stoned, *"he, being full of the Holy Ghost, looked up steadfastly into heaven, and* **saw the glory of God,** *and* **Jesus standing on the right hand of God.** *And said, behold, I see the heavens opened, and the* **Son of man standing on the right hand of God"** (Acts 7:55–56, KJV). Both Adam and Jesus Christ have now come to the earth and have returned to Heaven, and we are awaiting the day when They shall return and shout, "Enough!" At least this is what the author imagines the shout will be. The books will then be opened, and Adam will sit down as the Ancient of Days and judge His family. Being our Father gives Him the express right to judge His family and no other. He knows us all better than we know ourselves, He loves us more than anyone else could, and His judgments will be just.

There is a quote by a Mormon prophet named Lorenzo Snow: "As man now is, God once was, as God now is, man may become." We now know that this God is Adam, and because we are His family, we can become like Him, as our children can become like us. Anyone who has the nerve to say they don't believe in God are extremely ignorant on purpose. *"Knowing this first, that there shall come in the last days scoffers, walking after their own lusts, and saying, where is the promise of his coming? For since the fathers fell asleep, all things continue as they were from the beginning of the creation. For this **they willingly are ignorant** of, that by the word of God the heavens were of old, and the earth standing out of the water, and in the water" (2 Peter 3:3–5, KJV).*

To deny the existence of God or hate God and by persecuting and hating God's people makes it easy for selfish, wicked people to justify their own lusts and desires. They reason that they don't need to obey the commandments of God. Therefore, they can whore, thieve, kill, and commit any other evil and depraved desire of their hearts without feeling guilty of their sins. Because they don't want to believe in God, they know that they must think completely opposite to what God wants them to, which causes them to distance themselves from God. They are now heading in the completely opposite direction, into outer darkness. They are going away from the light of Christ. They are in open rebellion to God and bringing about their own judgments on themselves. This is why, when we stand before God/Adam at the last, no one will be able to say that the judgments of God/Adam are not just.

Matthew chapter 21 talks about Christ throwing the money changers out of the temple and how he healed the sick, the lepers, the blind, and the lame. The next morning, he returned to Jerusalem from Bethany. *"And when he was come into the temple, the chief priests and the elders of the people came unto him as he was teaching, and said, by what authority doest thou these things? And who gave thee this authority?" (Matthew 21:23, KJV).*

Christ tells them another parable. A parable is another name for a riddle. In this parable, He is talking about His Father/Adam as planting a vineyard, which represents this earth, and the grapes represent His family/children, whom He wants to return to Him. The husbandmen are the leaders of government and religious leaders, ones He left in authority to govern His people. His servants are the holy men or prophets sent to give instruction and make an accounting, and of course, His Son is Jesus Christ Himself. Adam/God is the householder:

*Hear another parable: there was a certain **householder**, which **planted a vineyard**, and hedged it round about, and digged a wine press in it, and built a tower, and **let it out to husbandmen**, and **went into a far country**: And **when time of the fruit** drew near, he sent his **servants to the husbandmen**, that they might receive fruits of it. And the husbandmen took his servants, and beat one, and killed another, and stoned another. Again, he sent other servants more than the first: And they did unto them likewise. But **last of all he sent unto them his son**, saying, they will reverence My son. But **when the husbandmen saw the son, they said among themselves, this is the heir**; come **let us kill him**, and **let us seize on his inheritance**. And they caught him, and cast him out of the vineyard, and **slew him**. When the Lord therefore of the vineyard, cometh, what will he do unto these husbandmen? They say unto him, He will miserably destroy those wicked men, and will let out his vineyard unto other husbandmen, which shall render him the fruits in their seasons. (Matthew 21:33–41, KJV)*

So if we don't want to believe the words of a man telling you that Adam is our Father in Heaven, then perhaps we can believe Christ when He says it as He has done here in this parable or riddle. Another parable is about the ten talents, which is similar. Christ spoke to Mary just after His resurrection: *"Jesus saith unto her, touch me not; for I am not yet ascended to my Father: but go to my brethren, and say unto them, I ascend unto **my Father, and your Father**; and to **my God, and your God**" (John 20:17, KJV).*

The Pharisees and Sadducees didn't catch on that Christ was talking about them and the Romans as being the husbandmen. In Matthew, Christ explained that He was talking about them. Christ was talking about any people or group of people, institution, or religion that sought to kill or destroy His servants and the prophets and then think to kill the Son of God, with the idea of leaving Christ perpetually on the cross as dead and of stealing Christ's inheritance and power. The Romans carried out this act through the accusations of the Pharisees and Sadducees, who were the political and religious leaders of Israel.

The Catholic Church was organized later after Christ's church, trying to replace it. The Catholic Church had to drive the church of Jesus Christ into the wilderness, which started the Dark Ages. The voices continued to cry from the dust, however, in the form of the Holy Scriptures. The pope emerged as the vicar of Christ, meaning substitute for Christ, thinking to steal the position of Christ, determining that Christ was dead. *"Jesus saith unto them, did ye never read in the scriptures, the stone which the builders rejected, the **same is become the head of the corner**: this is the Lord's doing, and it is marvelous in our eyes? Therefore, say I unto you, the Kingdom of God shall be taken from you, and given to a nation bringing forth the fruits thereof"* (Matthew 2:42–43, KJV).

Christ still lives as does His Father, Adam. Christ's mission is to redeem mankind, if they will believe on His name and seek to obey His commandments, making it possible to return to the presence of our Father. Not everyone will be redeemed because they don't want to do what is right and, therefore, wish to remain ignorant. These people are judging themselves to not be the children of God. *"When the Son of man shall come in his glory, and all the holy angels with him, then shall he sit upon the throne of his glory: And before him shall be gathered all nations: and he shall separate them one from another, as a shepherd divideth his sheep from the goats: And he shall **set the sheep on his right hand**, but **the goats on the left**. Then shall the King say unto them on his right hand, Come, ye blessed of my Father, inherit the kingdom prepared for you from the foundation of the world"* (Matthew 25:31–34, KJV).

Some people don't want to believe that Adam could possibly be our Father in Heaven, and try to pop that theory with a small pin, however. Adam and Eve were given a commandment directly from God. The commandment they were given was: *"And God blessed them, and God said unto them, be fruitful, and **multiply and replenish the earth**, and subdue it: and have dominion over the fish of the sea, and over the fowl of the air, and over every living thing that moveth upon the earth".* *"(Genesis 1:28, KJV)* They were soon after given their second commandment, which was: *"And the LORD God commanded the man, saying, of every tree of the garden thou mayest freely eat: but of the tree of the knowledge of good and evil, thou shalt not eat of it: for in* the day that thou eatest thereof thou shalt surely die." *(Genesis 2: 16-17, KJV)* Satan then came tempting Eve, saying; *"And the serpent said unto the woman, Ye shall not surely die,"" For God doth know that in the day ye eat thereof, then your eyes shall be opened, and ye shall be as gods, knowing good and evil".* *(Genesis 3:4-5, KJV)* Eve, therefore partook of the fruit, and in so doing, violated God's second commandment unto her and her husband, Adam. She fell from God's presence, and therefore was alone. She now could in no way keep God's first commandment, which was to "multiply and replenish the earth", without Adam, her husband.

Adam now had quite a dilemma, as he was still in a godly state, and without his wife Eve, he would never be able to multiply. He had to choose, because God had given them **"free-agency."** God had given Adam two commandments and he could only keep one, he could not keep both. On the one hand, his wife Eve, was now in the world/Hell, and on the other hand, he was still in the presence of God/as God, and he had an important decision to make. Adam could either play it safe and stay where he was at, or he would have to go into Hell to get his wife Eve, and have children and raise a family like he was commanded to from the start. Adam knew what he was doing, and did it willingly to obey God and save his wife, Eve, which he did, when presented with the fruit by Eve.

Adam understood full well the sacrifice it required to return back into the presence of God later on after proving himself here on earth. For the sake of rescuing his wife, and at the same time, keeping the greater commandment of God, to multiply and replenish the earth. He understood that the work and glory of God is "to bring to pass the immortality and eternal life of man". He chose to obey God and seek God's will. He chose to be unselfish, and his act was accounted unto him as righteousness. Adam was blessed of God, and therefore **he did not sin**. *"And Adam was not deceived, but the woman being deceived was in the transgression. Notwithstanding she shall be saved in childbearing, if they continue in faith and charity and holiness with sobriety". (1 Timothy 2:14-15, KJV)* He was zealous for the glory of God, just like Phinehas, who was also zealous for the sake of God when he rose up and slew Zimri who was dishonoring God, and therefore halted a plague that was sent upon the children of Israel. *(Numbers 16:6-9, KJV)*

Even now in the political arena, people are gathering to the right or to the left. They are judging themselves as they choose what side they are on. The

Left's thinking is completely opposite to that of the people on the right. The goat is the symbol of the devil, whereas the sheep is the symbol of Jesus Christ. The left and the right is the dividing line, and when all those who will come from the left go over to the right, then Christ will come, and the end will come with Him. I am eagerly awaiting the day when we see Him coming, and we can be reunited with Christ and our Father.

Even though we are the literal offspring of God, He has set strict guidelines that we must obey to heal the enmity between Him and His children. We must follow His Son, Jesus Christ, and believe in Him and obey His commandments; otherwise, God has no claim on us. God is a perfect being Himself and cannot tolerate sin to any degree. Therefore, we must be drawn back to God through Christ, and that is the only way. We are drawn by accepting the gospel of Jesus Christ and doing it His way.

In the beginning, there was a deal done between God and Satan. The deal was this: God wanted us to be born into this world of sin, into Satan's jurisdiction, to experience life in the flesh. It meant letting Satan have a hold on us, and we belong to him now by rights as, after the age of accountability, we have sinned or, like Adam and Eve, have come under the same contracts that they did. So *justice* is that we are all under the control or jurisdiction of Satan for eternity. God, in His "mercy," however, included in the deal a way that we could break the chains or contracts that bound us to Satan. God wanted us here in this world so that we could experience the bad in the hopes that we could recognize the good and reach out to God, those who would. God's deal was that, to redeem all His children after being on the earth for a while, and when they had learned their lessons, He would send, and offer up His Son, Jesus Christ, into the world to Satan as a sacrifice for us. Being in Satan's jurisdiction, Satan would use this as an opportunity to destroy the Son of God. Satan could now tempt Him, buffet Him, ridicule and humiliate Him, injure Him, and even kill Him to get Christ to commit sin. If Satan succeeded with his plan, then all of us would be Satan's slaves for eternity. If he didn't succeed, then we would all be set free, to leave Satan's jurisdiction of our own free will, those who wanted to leave.

The "World", represents "Justice," and "Mercy" is represented by the "Tree of Life." It is impossible for the mercy of God to rob justice. By Adam and Eve, our first parents, submitting to the jurisdiction of the devil, brought about the enslavement of all mankind. So, **justice** is that all mankind remains slaves to the devil for eternity, without any hope of something better. It was because of the deal made between God and Satan, before the world was, that there also be a plan of **mercy.** In order to obtain the freedom of mankind, a payment had to be made. The payment for our release then was to be made through the sacrifice and death of the Son of God, Jesus Christ. It was stipulated in the agreement for the release of mankind, that the life and death of the Son of God would be a spotless or perfect life up to the death of Jesus Christ. This is the only way that this contract between God and Satan could be finished. Christ, while on the cross said, *"It is finished".* On the other hand, the deal also included the fact that in order for any of us to go free, and act as an outward showing for our support of this plan, was that each of us are required to acknowledge and receive the "gospel of Jesus Christ" and live it. So, this is the only way that **"Mercy"** can pay off **"Justice".** *"And behold, he cometh to* **redeem** *those who will be* **baptized** *unto repentance through faith on his name". (Alma 9:27. Book of Mormon).*

We must rely on Christ for this **"act of Grace".** This is what the scriptures mean when it states: we are "saved by grace". Christ came and paid the price, not because we deserved coming after, or saving. He did it knowingly and willingly. He didn't have to put His neck on the line, but He did it because He wanted to. This was such a huge, gracious act on the part of Jesus Christ. There was no one else from the Godhead that could have done such an act, because Adam and Eve, being mortal, and being within the jurisdiction of Satan when they fell from the Garden of Eden, were also in bondage. Then of course, the Holy Ghost, the third member of the Godhead, is a personage of spirit, and so, he couldn't do it, because the deal required a blood sacrifice. Christs act of mercy paid the price for all mankind, including Adam and Eve, or we were all lost. Everything all hinged on Christ being able to pull this off, as it required the sacrifice of a God, and He was the only one left, not under the jurisdiction of Satan, having the ability to do this. If the lights of understanding can go on in our minds, then we realize just how great the work that Christ did for us, was.

We all know that Christ walked this earth, having a perfect life, not failing in one little thing; and because of this, God was well pleased. This is what the price of our freedom all hinged on, Christ being able to live up to the challenge and meeting the payment for our sins. Now we are free to leave

Satan's jurisdiction if we will accept Christ as our Savior and embrace the truth of the gospel here on the earth. Christ is and was the only one capable of fulfilling this mission, and He did it in style.

To be literal offspring of God is one thing, and to be accepted into God's family is another. There are many of the children or offspring of God who won't have anything to do with Him. They hate Him and downright reject Him. Instead of hearing the truth and living it, they are plugging their ears to it; and instead of going toward Christ, they are going away from Him. This kind of people, unless they repent and have a change of heart, will not be in the family of God, but Satan is their God for eternity.

Christ, when confronting the Pharisees and Saduccees in Jerusalem, told them, *"Ye are of **your father the devil**, and the lusts of your father ye will do. He was a murderer from the beginning, and abode not in the truth, because there is **no truth in him**. When he speaketh a lie, he speaketh of his own: for he is a liar, and the father of it" (John 8:44, KJV).*

So it was in the days of Noah. The people, all except eight, were drowned in the flood because they wouldn't listen to God; and God got tired of their disrespect, stubbornness, and love of lust and violence. He saw they were not going to change, He could see their hearts, and so He quit striving with them. In other words, He lost patience like a good parent eventually would and let them serve the master they chose. He let Satan have them. Even after the flood, people turned from God as they multiplied on the earth, but the Bible talked about those who were "sons of God." *"That the **sons of God** saw the daughters of men that they were fair, and they took them wives of all which they chose" (Genesis 6:2, KJV).* This instance is referring to those who were diligent in obeying God, and therefore, had the right to be called the sons of God.

It was recorded in Job, *"Now there was a day when the **sons of God** came to present themselves before the Lord, and Satan came also among them" (1:6, KJV).* *"Yet the number of the children of Israel shall be as the sand of the sea, which cannot be measured nor numbered; and it shall come to pass, that in the place where it was said unto them, Ye are not my people, there it shall be said unto them, Ye are the **sons of the living God**" (Hosea 1:10, KJV).* The true children of God are the ones who believe in Jesus Christ and seek to do His will. *"But as many as received him, to them gave the power to become the **sons** *of God, even to them that believe on his name" (John 1:12, KJV).*

*"For as many as are led by the **spirit of God**, they are the **sons of God"** (Romans 8:14, KJV).* This is what Paul is talking about when, in Galatians, he mentions the adoption of the believers. Because we believe in Christ and we receive the gospel of Jesus Christ, then it is an acceptance by the Father of us and that now we are His children of the gospel covenant and have earned the right to be called the "sons and daughters of God." *"But when the fulness of the time was come, God sent forth his Son, made of a woman, made under the law. To redeem those that were under the law, that we might receive the **adoption of sons"** (Galatians 4:4–5, KJV).* Even though we are literal offspring of God, we still have to prove that we are worth it to God by believing in His Son and doing the things we have seen and know He has done. We then have the promise of being lifted up at the last day, to be with Him, because we are like Him.

*"That ye may be blameless and harmless, the **sons of God,** without rebuke in the midst of a crooked and perverse nation, among whom **ye shine as lights in the world"** (Philippians 2:15, KJV).* *"Beloved, now are we the **sons of God,** and it doth not yet appear what we shall be: but we know that, when he shall appear, we shall be like him; for we shall see him as he is" (1 John 3:2, KJV).* Not only will we be like God when He appears but we also shall see Him as He is, in His glory. That is such a beautiful promise, but that is not all. It will be glorious, as He has promised it will be, because we will inherit great things. *"He that overcometh shall **inherit all things;** and I will be his God, and he will be **my son"** (Revelation 21:7, KJV).* The Mormons' *Book of Mormon* explains it more clearly. *"Behold, I am he who was prepared from the foundation of the world to redeem my people. Behold, I am Jesus Christ. I am the Father and the Son. In me shall all mankind have life, and that eternally, even they who shall believe on my name; and they shall become **my sons and my daughters"** (Ether 3:14, Book of Mormon).* Christ is saying that He is the "Father" (our Creator) and also the "Son of God" and was prepared to come into the world from the beginning.

This was why Christ talked to the scribes, Pharisees, and Sadducees the way He did; they didn't believe in Him. Therefore, they didn't belong to Him, according to the deal. *Book of Mormon* again said, *"And now, because of the covenant which ye have made, **ye shall be called the children of Christ, his sons, and his daughters;** for behold, this day **he hath spiritually begotten** *you; for ye say that your hearts are changed through faith on his name; therefore, ye are his sons and his daughters"* (Mosiah 5:7, Book of Mormon). The bottom line was what Joseph Smith revealed in the *Doctrine and Covenants*: *"For verily I say unto you, **all those who receive my gospel are sons and daughters in my kingdom"** (section 25:1).*

There you have it; this is how you know whose side you are on, and it is simply by accepting Christ and living His gospel. His gospel is (1) having faith in the Lord, Jesus Christ; (2) repenting or refraining from doing that which Christ deems is not right; (3) being baptized by immersion for the remission of sins; (4) receiving the gift of the Holy Ghost by the laying on of hands; (5) enduring to the end and running a straight race, because man can fall from grace; (6) having faith in the atonement of Jesus Christ and what He did to seal the deal so that you can be free; (7) looking forward to a glorious resurrection because of Christ; and (8) knowing that you will receive a just judgment and that if you repent, God will remember your sins not at all. I am so grateful for the gospel of Jesus Christ, for the hope and peace it has brought into my life, and may it bless yours also. Let us not be like the people talked about by Timothy in the New Testament. *"Ever learning, and never able to come to the knowledge of the truth"* (2 Timothy 3:2, KJV).

CHAPTER 3

The Tree of Life

As I was sitting in a truck stop in Cheyenne, Wyoming, many years ago on a Sunday, I was reading the scriptures and meditating on the meaning of how Christ's government worked and many other things relative to man's government. As I was thinking about the things pertaining to God, trying to understand how it all came together, and wondering how I fit into God's plan, a "scroll" unrolled before my eyes, and I saw a vision. I saw myself sitting on a chair in a veranda of this great and beautiful building. The building had great marble pillars, and the veranda itself was made out of beautiful white marble, and the steps were many leading down to the ground. I was facing out, looking over this big, rugged field, separated from the building with an old, plain, modest fence that was in need of repair. Behind me, I heard a bustle of activities, that of celebration, laughter, music, and loud conversation. I turned and looked behind me, and I saw this beautiful building with huge golden double doors that were opening both ways as people streamed in and out. The people appeared well to do. Many were very wealthy, and it could be seen by their fine attire. The men wore fine, expensive suits, Rolex watches, fine shoes, and the like. The women were dressed in fine gowns and I could see their rings, earrings, and jewels. There was much laughter as they drank their fine wines and flirted with the opposite sex.

Being as it was, me finding myself sitting on the veranda, it was as if the building was hovering in the air. I, in an instant, knew I was out of place and didn't want to be there. I turned back around, and looked out into the large field, and I saw a man standing out there all alone by a lone tree. I looked closely, and I saw that the man was dressed in a bright white robe, and He was motioning for me to come to Him with His arms. Immediately, I had a strong desire to be with him, and so, I jumped up from my chair because I recognized the man as my friend, Jesus Christ. He wanted me to come to Him.

I leaped down the stairs of the veranda, two at a time, to the boundary of the field. It was a rickety old fence, and it had a little narrow gate, which I went through on the run. I ran and ran toward the man in white, but the way began to get harder and harder, and I found I was slowing down as the going became more difficult. Even though I kept my eyes on the man in white, the ground became swampy, and then it got muddy and was beginning to bog me down. I kept falling and getting stuck in the mud, but I kept going. There was nothing I wanted more, than to reach the man in the white robe.

Finally, the water got too deep, and I fell headlong into a muddy, deep pool. I was so tired that I couldn't pull myself out. I was going under, and when I thought I was finished, I saw arms stretched toward me with the sleeves of this white robe, reaching out to me. The man in the white robe pulled me from the muddy swamp. I saw myself sopping wet, splotched with mud spots here and there over my body, I was exhausted, and I had such a great feeling of love and gratitude toward this wonderful man, as I knew who He was.

It was then that the vision ended, and then I understood. This was Christ who was reaching out to me and encouraging me to come to Him and not be afraid because He will save me. After everything I can do for myself, he would do the rest, and I was not to give up and quit the race. I understood that the rickety old fence is the dividing line between the kingdom of Satan and the kingdom of Christ. I understood that the beautiful building is the world with its appeal, temptations, ease, and pride. I understood that the field is the opportunity at life, granted unto each and every one of us, and going through life, with its challenges, hurdles, pitfalls, discouragements, and frustrations. I understood that we must never give up but continue toward the light, for it is after doing everything that we can do, that Christ will take care of the rest. I understood that, because I believed in Christ, He would save me and redeem me from the Fall. The mud splotches represented my personal sins and that I could be washed clean by following Jesus Christ and believing in Him. I knew I was on the right track, and I was not to get discouraged in the race of life.

Then the understanding of government and what was meant by the two trees in the Garden of Eden flooded my mind. I understood that they were, figuratively speaking, two systems of government, and these two trees also represented two churches tied together with those two systems, the church of God and the church of the devil. Just as it was with the tree of knowledge of good and evil, so it was with the tree of life. There is opposition in all things. You choose either that which is good or that which is evil.

The tree of life represents the kingdom of Jesus Christ. It is His church; it is the terrestrial kingdom. Partaking of its fruits or the things of Christ continually will break the bonds of death and the chains of Hell. This kingdom is what the scriptures also refer to as *Zion*, meaning "peace and tranquility." *"**Great peace have they that love thy law**: and nothing shall offend them" (Psalm 119:165, KJV).* "And ***blessed are they that shall seek to bring forth my Zion*** *at that day, for they shall have the gift and the power of the Holy Ghost; and if they endure unto the end they shall be lifted up at the last day, and shall be saved in the everlasting kingdom of the lamb; and **who so shall publish peace**, yea, tidings of great joy, **how beautiful upon the mountains shalt they be**" (1 Nephi 13:37, Book of Mormon).*

These two trees embody all the different denominations of the world. Every church belongs to one of these two, whether because of their beliefs or because of their practices. The people make up the churches and, therefore, are both collectively and singularly liable for their churches' actions and for their own. Everyone, whether an institution or an individual, is categorized into one of these two churches and is liable for themselves and any other organization they support. The people are independently liable for their own actions and even the laws they support. They fall under either the church of God or the church of Satan. Remember, if you love God, then you love your fellow man. Because of this, you are going to do all those things that support and help your country, fellow man, and family; and by doing this, you will honor God, and you all will be blessed by Almighty God. If you hate God, then you are going to be a commandment breaker. You will take advantage of your brother; you will steal, kill, or seek to commit adultery with your brother's wife; you will do anything to gratify your own pleasures, as you are selfish.

*"And out of the ground made the Lord God to grow every tree that is pleasant to the sight, and good for food; the **tree of life** also in the midst of the garden, and the **tree of knowledge of good and evil**" (Genesis 2:9, KJV).* These two trees represent the two systems of government. The tree of knowledge of good and evil represents the devil's kingdom, and the tree of life represents Jesus Christ's kingdom. The *Book of Mormon* says it plainly. *"And he said unto me: Behold, **there are save two churches only; the one is the church of the Lamb of God**, and **the other is the church of the devil**; wherefore, **whoso belongeth not to the church of the Lamb of God belongeth to that great church, which is the mother of abominations**; and **she is the whore of all the earth**" (1 Nephi 14:10, Book of Mormon).* Whether you claim to be Catholic, Mormon, Jehovah's Witness, Lutheran, Seventh-day Adventist, Baptist, Pentecostal, Methodist, Hindu, Buddhist, Mason, universal religion follower, witch, or of any other Christian or pagan religion, they all fall under one of these two churches, both collectively as an organization and as an independent person, corporate or incorporate. The **"Beast,"** as it talks about in the scriptures, is the corporate system.

God loves all of us the same, and He has extended the ability for all of us to repent/change and cast off the chains of Hell and come out of the wilderness/the world. Those of you who are so arrogant to think that you are righteous and have no sin, think again. You do not even know what you are talking about. There are various contracts that all of us have entered into with the devil/corporate system unknowingly and knowingly that chain us down. Laws that we may support put not only ourselves but also our families and our fellow man into bondage and slavery that strips them of their rights. If you are a Democrat and claim to be a Christian, think again. What laws, as a Democrat, do you support? Do you support open borders, abortion/the killing of the innocent, socialism/communism, welfare for all, free education, free health care, and federal income tax, which is a huge lie, or are you supporting a candidate who does? The Democrats support everything completely opposite to what a conservative, who believes in God, supports.

Christ is the head of this terrestrial kingdom/tree of life, and He governs by allowing us, the people, free will/free agency. We the people set up the Constitution by the grace of God, and the law is called common-law jurisdiction. The Constitution embodies the Ten Commandments. If we do not acknowledge the hand of Christ in all things, then we are not of this kingdom. This is a kingdom where if we love God, then we will keep His commandments. *"Jesus saith unto them, did ye never read in the scriptures, The **stone which the builders rejected**, the same is **become the head of the corner**: this is the Lord's doing, and it is marvelous in our eyes?" (Matthew 21:42, KJV).* Christ was the "rock" that was cut out of the mountain without hands, that rolled forth and struck the image in the legs made out of part iron and part clay. This rock has brought down the Roman Empire and scattered the ten kingdoms of Europe.

We the people love the Constitution because we cherish liberty, and by upholding this document, we are serving God. The Constitution of America is a huge part of this "rock." The *Book of Mormon* explains very clearly where we stand when we obey the law of liberty. *"For **how knoweth a man the master whom he has not served**, and who is a stranger unto him, and is far from the thoughts and intents of his heart?" (Mosiah 5:13, Book of Mormon)* Jesus Christ is the rock upon whom we should build. *"And the rain descended, and the floods came, and the winds blew, and beat upon that house; and it fell not: for it was founded upon a **rock**" (Matthew 7:25, KJV).* Our Constitution, which includes the Bill of Rights, embodies the Ten Commandments. This Constitution brings freedom and liberty to all mankind under its banner, regardless of color, rich or poor, and it brings equality under the law. The people's upholding of this great document shows that we love God. Those who try to destroy it show that they hate God and their brother/sister.

***If ye love me, keep my commandments**. And I will pray the father, and he shall give you another comforter, that he may abide with you forever; Even the **Spirit of truth**; whom the world cannot receive, because it seeth him not, neither knoweth him: but ye know him; for he dwelleth with you, and shall be in you. I will not leave you comfortless: I will come to you. Yet a little while, and the world seeth me no more; but ye see me: because I live, ye shall live also. At that day ye shall know that I am in my Father, and ye in me, and I in you. **He that hath my commandments and keepeth them, he it is that loveth me**: and he that loveth me shall be loved of my Father, and I will love him, and will manifest myself to him. Judas saith unto him, Not Iscariot, Lord, how is it that thou wilt manifest thyself unto us, and not unto the world? **He that loveth me not, keepeth not my sayings**: and the word which ye hear is not mine, but the Fathers' which sent me. Jesus answered and said unto him, If a man love me, he* *will keep my words: and my father will love him, and we will come unto him, and make our abode with him. (John 14:15–24, KJV)*

The first four of the Ten Commandments are about first loving God, and the other six are about loving our neighbor/others. Christ has said that the first, greatest commandment is to love God with all of our heart, might, mind, and strength. The second is like unto it: love your neighbor as thyself. *"Master, which is the greatest commandment in the law? Jesus said unto him,* **Thou shalt love God** *with all thy heart, and with all thy soul, and with all thy mind. This is the first and greatest commandment. And the second is like unto it,* **thou shalt love thy neighbor as thyself. On these two commandments hang all the law and the prophets"** *(Matthew 22:36–40, KJV).*

When we love God first, our brother/neighbor will be blessed, especially our families. If we do not love God, we will not love our brother; and if we don't love our brother, then we do not love God. Because we don't love our brother, then we are an enemy to God and are in open rebellion against Him because God's work and glory is to bring to pass the immortality and eternal life of man. When we do things against our brother, then we are fighting against God's work. We show we hate or love our neighbor/brother simply by the laws we uphold, which either put ourselves and our neighbor into bondage or extend to us freedom. It is not just how we treat our neighbor face-to-face and personally but who or what we support.

Our Constitution is a divine document and gives power to the federal government, but also state, county, and city governments unincorporated. It also limits the size of government and provides checks on government. When we support anything that is against this document, then we are rebelling against God and our neighbor.

Other terms for the terrestrial kingdom are preparatory state, republic, and church of the Lord God. It is a preparatory state in which we prepare to meet God. We are promised that if we are diligent in seeking the kingdom of God, He will remember our sins/imperfections no more. As none of us are perfect, this promise should be beautiful to our ears. The line between right and wrong has been drawn since the beginning of Creation, and each of us are compelled to choose between Christ and Satan and between the systems of government they each represent. There is no excuse for people to not know which master they serve, and therefore, when they come before

God to be judged, they are left without excuse. They have each chosen freely which master they will serve. Those who choose Christ and His kingdom are going toward the truth, and those who choose Satan and his kingdom are going in the opposite direction, away from the truth and into outer darkness, and will suffer the "second death." This is a spiritual death, which forever separates us from God.

The churches who have incorporated and joined themselves to the world, have forced the children of their denominations to attend public schools, which puts them in the position of being forced to learn things such as evolution, atheism, and sexual education, and they learn to experiment with both the opposite sex and the same sex, immorality, and depravity of all kinds. They are now in public schools and under severe peer pressure, and because of this, they are encouraged and tempted to participate in all these things, including getting familiar with religions such as Islam and practices done by this pagan religion. They have learned about witchcraft and other forms of Satan worship. God has been taken out of the schools and replaced by theories and ideologies of the kingdom of Satan. The churches, by incorporating and forcing their children to tolerate such teachings, have successfully been driven into the wilderness/world. The Mormons' *Doctrine and Covenants* talks about this: *"Verily, thus saith the Lord unto you my servants, concerning the parable of the wheat and of the tares: Behold, verily I say,* **the field was the world,** *and* **the apostles were the sowers of the seed;** *And* **after they have fallen asleep** *the great persecutor of the church, the apostate, the whore, even Babylon, that maketh all nations to drink of her cup, in whose hearts the enemy,* **even Satan, sitteth to reign—behold he soweth the tares,** *wherefore,* **the tares choke the wheat and drive the church into the wilderness**" *(section 86:1–3).*

These public schools teach our children not only immorality of every kind but also political correctness, disobedience to the law and parents, rebelliousness, disrespect for authority, etc. Even the church leaders show bad examples due to ignorance and lack of understanding, lying to their children because it is the path of least resistance, which is a form of laziness. The leaders of the churches are very hypocritical as they teach about Christ on Sundays and Saturdays but fail/neglect to get involved in issues that will otherwise be checks against bad government and protect our freedoms. The phrase *church and state* was included into our government not to separate God from it but to avoid any one denomination from controlling the government. The Ten Commandments are already embodied in the Constitution, which brings liberty and justice for all and gives everyone the right to life, liberty, and the pursuit of happiness, even the unborn innocent. We all need to be involved in good causes, stand up, and be counted, whether or not the issue is deemed political, because to "separate church and state" is impossible.

The devil is desperately working on separating us from our God by attempting to take God out of government at all levels and replacing God with the devil and his evil religion. The churches, by and in the ignorance of their leaders, have allowed evil people to fool them with lies, which undermines the truth and our Constitution. Instead of being up and resisting evil institutions, they have become doormats for evil laws that they feel compelled to obey, which look on the surface as law but on the inside are evil and violate the Constitution and God's law. One of the evil laws we have is the Sixteenth Amendment. It has made way for the Federal Reserve Bank, the IRS, and the graduated income tax. Another is Planned Parenthood with *Roe v. Wade*, making it easy for the killing of our unborn children. Still another is *Erie v. Tompkins*, which has done away with our common law and replaced it with uniform commercial law. Another is the Emergency War Powers Act, which keeps us in a perpetual state of war.

We, as a people and as Christians, must boycott public schools that are destroying our children through lies and peer pressure. We need home schools and private schools run by good Christian people. The Mormon churches are built with several rooms that can be used as classrooms and turn out constitutional experts and future leaders by the thousands, transforming our great republic into the type of country America is meant to be. The church leaders, who the people depend on to lead them to God, in reality, are leading the people down to Hell because of their ignorance and unwillingness to gain knowledge and act against evil, but they tolerate it. The *Book of Mormon* is very clear, as well as Isaiah in the Bible, on this point. *"Wo unto the wicked for they shall perish; for the reward of their hands shall be upon them. And my people, children are their oppressors, and women rule over them,* **O my people, they who lead thee cause thee to err and destroy the way of thy paths"** *(2 Nephi 13:11–12; compare Isaiah 3, KJV).*

For the love of money and the desire for commerce have the people become willing to give up their freedom. This has been the case from civilization to civilization. This has led the churches to divorce and separate themselves from God, but it is not God who is doing it. It is the lust for money and power by the people and the churches. The churches are the mother of the people, and they have left God. *"Thus, saith the Lord:* **Have I put thee away,** *or have I cast thee off forever? For thus saith the Lord:* **where is the bill of your mother's divorcement***? To whom have I put thee away, or to* **which of my creditors have I sold you***? Behold, for your iniquities have* **ye sold yourselves,** *and* **for your transgressions is your mother put away***" (2 Nephi 7:1, Book of Mormon; compare Isaiah 50, KJV).* The mother is the churches, and the churches have sold themselves into the corporate system under a 501(c)(3) contract with the world.

It is very obvious which master a person serves just by the things that they say and do. There is a great void between the people of God and the people of the devil. There is no such thing as separation of church and state, except for keeping any one denomination from controlling the government. God and Satan are mortal enemies, and if God rules in our republic, then His laws will manifest themselves in our government. If Satan rules, then his laws will manifest themselves in the government. Currently, God's law reigns supreme as His laws are made manifest in our government. However, Satan is working nonstop to undermine the good things of God by trying, through his minions—the liberals/Democrats/communists/socialists—to destroy everything good and bring all people in all countries into subjection to him.

Satan has made great strides in this effort through his minions, through the ten planks of *The Communist Manifesto*, and through the international banking system. It is completely impossible to be a liberal/Democrat and then turn and call yourself a true Christian. A bumper sticker reads "To be liberal is to be 100 percent fact-free." To be liberal, you have to be selfish, ignorant, lawless, dishonest, immoral, anti-God, rebellious, evolutionist, etc. Liberals believe completely opposite to what a Christian/conservative believes. A liberal can be seen one hundred miles away. A liberal comes in a wide variety.

Many believe in political correctness, while others believe in atheism, evolution, and immorality. Others believe in not working and then getting on welfare and having everything free at other people's expense. Everything a liberal does and believes in is to discredit God because they hate God. More examples of liberal institutions are lobbyists, special interest groups, and unions. Liberals think only of themselves, what they want for themselves, and what the country or community can do for them. They just want, and when they don't get, they throw tantrums and fits until they get. They don't care about the consequences, even if it means destroying everything in their paths to get what they want, even at the expense of their own families or of themselves for that matter. Most prove to be as dumb as a box of rocks. They commit crimes to accomplish their goals, from the ones in the gutter to the officials in high offices in the land. Their saying goes "The means justifies the end."

We are always in the positions we are in because of the decisions we make. The Mormon prophet Joseph Smith elaborated on this point in the *Doctrine and Covenants*. *"There is a law, irrevocably decreed in heaven before the foundations of this world, upon which all blessings are predicated—And when we obtain any blessing from God, it is **by obedience to that law upon which it is predicated**" (section 130:20–21).*

When Adam and Eve partook of the tree of knowledge of good and evil, they became subject to the devil and his jurisdiction in his system of government. They made a choice, and now a process of hard knocks of learning and a probationary state was mandatory and imperative before they could go back into the presence of their God. In the beginning, they had to leave the presence of God, like they were leaving home to travel off to college. God had to make it so that they couldn't immediately partake of the tree of life and live forever in their sins. So He placed cherubim and the flaming sword to protect the narrow gate, which led to the presence of God. *"So he drove out the man; and he placed at the east end of the Garden of Eden **cherubims**, and **a flaming sword** which turned every way, to **keep the tree of life**" (Genesis 3:24, KJV).*

God wants born-again and repentant men and women to come back to His presence, not just out of their convenience. He wants them to go through a trial period of education, where they can recognize right from wrong, righteous from evil, good from bad, and God from the devil. He wants them to voluntarily seek Him because they love and prefer God over Satan and his system. He wants the men and women to love Him with their whole beings, with all their hearts, might, minds, and strength. This plan of God, to test mortals after leaving His presence if they love God more than Satan, is ingenious. It gives every intelligence an opportunity to have a body, get experiences here on the earth, and prove who they are willing to follow, God or Satan. *"Know ye not, that to whom ye obey,* **his servants ye are to whom ye obey;** *whether of sin unto death, or of obedience unto righteousness?" (Romans 6:16, KJV).*

Satan's system of government, while mankind is being tested in this probationary state of mortality, has a gate that is wide and waiting with welcome arms to ensnare mortals, not just Adam and Eve but also you and me. Satan uses not just voluntary means, but also threat, duress, and coercion to scare, intimidate, and lie to the people to get them to volunteer, whether knowingly or unknowingly, to the point where the door can be slammed shut, and they are bound to him forever.

On the other hand, Christ calls to us softly by His Spirit, the Holy Ghost. He wants us to be diligent by reading and listening to His voice of truth through experience and hard knocks, long-suffering, patience, and gentle persuasion. He wants us to give up the baggage we carry of the world, including our weaknesses, sins, and things that will weigh us down. He wants us to trust wholeheartedly in Him. His system is completely based on "free agency." When we believe and obey Him and trust in Him, then we are ready to go past the cherubim and the flaming sword with clean conscience before God and enter through that little straight, narrow gate into the kingdom of Jesus Christ, which is like a layover station. This kingdom is the preparatory state, called the terrestrial kingdom. This is a prerequisite and necessary before going back into God's presence. This is what God has sent His Son to do, draw men after Him and have them follow Him back to God. *"Jesus saith unto him,* **I am the way, the truth, and the life: No man cometh unto the Father, but by me"** *(John 14:6, KJV).* That little narrow gate is baptism.

Baptism is talked about by just about every clergyman, including pastors, priests, teachers, ministers, and supposed gospel scholars. They will go into intellectual discourses explaining baptism like how a doctor explains the symptoms of a cold. They can explain that, through baptism, you are in the similitude of Christ's death by going under the water; and then when you come out of the water, you are in the similitude of Christ's resurrection. They explain that you are washed or absolved of your sins because of your willingness to follow Christ. All these things are true, but the bottom line is that baptism is simply the outward showing of your *"swearing of allegiance to the kingdom of God"*. I liken this to a newly naturalized citizen swearing allegiance to the United States of America.

I witnessed the swearing in of my wife, who on March 21, 2019, became a newly naturalized citizen of America. As a new candidate to be naturalized, you go before a judge or person authorized to hear the swearing. This comes after a process of learning about America, the government, Constitution, etc. As a person to be naturalized, you will raise your hand to the square and repeat after the judge or person in authority, under oath, that you will forsake all other countries, governments, and allegiances to any other foreign powers. You, under oath, swear allegiance to the United States of America and that to her only will you be loyal and faithful, and this you must do before you can be declared a citizen of the United States of America. Once you make that declaration and swear in, you are now a different person, with the full rights and privileges of any other citizen of the United States of America and with full protection under its Constitution.

When you accept Christ and follow Him into the waters of baptism, you have just made a deliberate decision to belong to the kingdom of God over that of the kingdom of the devil/world. You have now made an outward showing that you now serve Christ willingly and are now preparing to go back into the presence of your Father/God. This is why the plan of God is so ingenious. It separates the goats from the sheep. The *Book of Mormon* explains this very clearly:

*O then, my beloved brethren, come unto the Lord, the Holy one, remember that his paths are righteous, Behold, the way for man is narrow, but lieth in a straight course before him, and **the keeper of the gate is the Holy One of Israel**; and **he employeth no servant there**; and **there is none other way save it be by the gate**; for **he cannot be deceived**, for the **Lord God is his name**. And whoso knocketh, to him will he open; and the wise, and the learned, and they that are rich, who are puffed up because of their learning, and their wisdom, and their riches-yea, they are they whom he despiseth; and save they shall cast these things away, and consider themselves fools before God, and come down to the depths of humility, he will not open unto them. (2 Nephi 9:41–42)*

Now we go to the New Testament:

"Enter ye in at the strait gate: for wide is the gate, and broad is the way, that leadeth to destruction, and many there be which go in there at: Because strait is the gate, and narrow is the way, which leadeth unto life, and few there be that find it." (Matthew 7:13–14, KJV)

*"Then said Jesus unto them again, verily, verily, I say unto you, **I am the door of the sheep**. All that ever came before me are thieves and robbers: but the sheep did not hear them. I am the door: by me if any man enter in, he shall be saved, and shall go in and out, and find pasture. . ... **My sheep hear my voice**, and I know them, **and they follow me**." (John 10:7–9, 27 KJV)*

*"Thomas saith unto him, Lord we know not whither thou goest; and how can we know the way? Jesus saith unto him, **I am the way, the truth and the life**: no man cometh unto the Father, but by me. **If ye had known me**, ye should **have known my Father also**: and from **henceforth ye know him**, and **seen him**." (John 14:5–7, KJV)*

If we know Christ, then we know that He is in the express image of the Father and that the Father has already been here on the earth. By knowing Christ and what He stands for, we also know the Father and what He stands for. *"For **a good tree bringeth not forth corrupt fruit; neither doth a corrupt tree brings forth good fruit**. For **every tree is known by its own fruit**. For of thorns men do not gather figs, nor of a bramble bush gather they grapes. A good man out of the treasure of his heart bringeth forth that which is good; and an evil man out of the treasure of his heart bringeth forth that which is evil: for of the abundance of the heart his mouth speaketh." (Luke 6:43–45, KJV).*

Then the *Book of Mormon* explains:

*For behold, the time is at hand that whosoever bringeth forth not good fruits, or whosoever doeth not the works of righteousness, the same have cause to wail and mourn. O ye workers of iniquity; ye that are puffed up in the vain things of the world, ye that have professed to have known the ways of righteousness nevertheless have gone astray, as sheep having no shepherd, notwithstanding a shepherd hath called after you and is still calling after you, but ye will not hearken unto his voice! Behold, I say unto you, that the good shepherd doth call you; yea, and in his own name he doth call you, which is the name of Christ; and if ye will not hearken unto the voice of the good shepherd, to the name by which ye are called, behold, ye are not the sheep of the good shepherd, **of what fold are ye**? Behold,*

I say unto you, that the devil is your shepherd, and ye are of his fold; and now, who can deny this? Behold, I say unto you, whosoever denieth this is a liar and a child of the devil. (Alma 5:36–39)

For every fruit of the tree of life, there is an opposite on the tree of knowledge of good and evil. In fact, the opposite of a conservative/Christian is a liberal/Democrat. They think completely opposite to each other. A conservative is anti-abortion, whereas a Democrat is pro-abortion. The language of God is the truth. *"That by two immutable things, in which* **it was impossible for God to lie**, *we might have a strong consolation, who have fled for refuge to lay hold upon the hope set before us" (Hebrews 6:18, KJV).* And the language of the devil is lies. *"Ye are of your father the devil, and the lusts of your father ye will do. He was a murderer from the beginning, and abode not in the truth, because there is no truth in him. When he speaketh a lie, he speaketh of his own:* **for he is a liar, and the father of it***" (John 8:44, KJV).*

The following is a short example of other opposites contained in each of the two kingdoms.

devil's kingdom	Christ's kingdom
public schools	home/private schools
churches incorporated under 501(c)(3)	DBA unincorporated churches
unjust taxation/IRS/land tax	tithing, import, export, and excise taxes
hate	love
unknown contracts	covenant/promise
bonds of death/chains of Hell	word is bond/honesty/integrity
policemen	peace officers
law merchant/admiralty jurisdiction	Constitution/common-law jurisdiction
witchcraft	priesthood of God
wickedness	righteousness
evil	good

compulsion	voluntary
slavery	freedom
justice	mercy
persecuting the poor	helping the needy
death	life
fear	courage
darkness	light
lies	truth
war	peace

It is a constant battle to guard against bad habits, traits, and temptations; but as we learn to love God, we will instantly recognize who is tempting us, whether it be of God or of Satan. We will instantly recognize him, who is the serpent, who has come crawling and slithering into our lives in the form of lies. If our mindset or desire is to be a good person, then it takes practice. So surrounding ourselves with like-minded people is very necessary, desirable, and essential. If I am a conservative, then I will want to surround myself with other conservatives. I will not surround myself with liberals, whose morals are very slim to none. They lie, talk filth about girls, and have no integrity or honor. They believe in abortion, they are atheists and don't believe in God, and they discredit Him. They believe in evolution and are very selfish and dishonest people. Because of their wishing to contradict God and to justify their actions, they will also disrespect the people of God. They hate God because they don't want to feel guilty, and they learn to hate the people of God, who make them feel guilty.

I am continuing to reach out to the ignorance of liberals, hoping to teach them things that I have learned as I once was tempted in different things, which came from lack of understanding. You quickly learn to recognize those who love rebelling against God among those who are innocently ignorant. God has told us all that we can repent/change and serve him, and He will forget and forgive us our sins and rebellion. Only by desiring the truth will this lead us toward God, and that comes from believing in Jesus

Christ, whom God sent to lead us back to His presence. Christ is the only way.

As we align our thinking with that of Christ, we get closer to our Father. If we hate God, then we are going to hate Christ and not believe in Him, and our thinking begins to be completely opposite to those who love God. This causes those who hate God to go in the completely opposite direction. They lose any light they have had and eventually find themselves in outer darkness. Remember that Christ is the Truth, the Way, and the Life, and no one goes to the Father but by Him. The people who hate God are judging themselves.

When God comes to burn the earth, the judgment has already been completed; otherwise, why is Christ coming to burn the wicked? *"When the Son of man shall come in his glory, and all the holy angels with him, then shall he sit upon the throne of his glory: And before him shall be gathered all nations: and he shall separate them one from another, as a shepherd divideth his sheep from the goats: And he shall set the **sheep on his right** hand, but the **goats on the left**. Then shall the King say unto them on his right hand, Come, ye blessed of my Father, inherit the kingdom prepared for you from the foundation of the world"* *(Matthew 25:31–34, KJV)*. We can see the division taking place in the world even as we speak. The liberals are the Left, and the conservatives are the Right. The way that they think is completely opposite to each other. There is a spiritual war going on for or against freedom. Every one of us constantly has to choose between the two masters, of the tree of life or of the tree of knowledge of good and evil.

This telestial kingdom we are in is full of pitfalls and temptations. We were born into this world under the subjection of the devil, enabling us to experience the good and evil in the hope that each of us will choose God/Christ to be our King. Even though we ignorantly make mistakes—and we all have and do—we can change.

*Wash you, make you clean; put away the evil of your doings from before mine eyes; cease to do evil; **Learn to do well**; seek judgment, relieve the oppressed, judge the fatherless, plead for the widow. Come now, let us reason together, saith the Lord: though your sins be as scarlet, they shall be as white as snow; though they be red like crimson, they shall be as wool. **If ye be willing and obedient**, ye shall eat the good of the land. But **if ye refuse and rebel**, ye shall be devoured* *with the sword: for the mouth of the Lord hath spoken it. (Isaiah 1:16–20, KJV)*

In the *Book of Mormon*, God explains it further:

*And **he loveth those who will have him to be their God**. Behold, he loved our fathers, and he covenanted with them, yea, even Abraham, Isaac, and Jacob; and he remembered the covenants which he had made; wherefore, he did bring them out of the land of Egypt. (1 Nephi 17:40)*

*And **blessed are the Gentiles**, they of whom the prophet has written; for behold, **if it so be that they shall repent and fight not against Zion**, and **do not unite themselves to that great and abominable church**, they shall be saved; for the Lord God will fulfill his covenants which he has made unto his children; and for this cause the prophet has written these things. Wherefore, they that fight against Zion and the covenant people of the Lord shall lick up the dust of their feet; and the people of the Lord shall not be ashamed. For the people of the Lord are they who wait for him; for they still wait for the coming of the Messiah. (2 Nephi 6:12–13)*

We are the Gentiles the scriptures are talking about, and we most certainly need to understand, act, and be diligent in the cause of freedom. We have an immediate duty to our God, our country, and our families in that order. By remembering and loving God first, then our country and our families will be blessed. The Mormons, in their book *Doctrine and Covenants*, a revelation by their prophet Joseph Smith, have gotten it together in explaining these important points.

*It is **an imperative duty** that we owe to God, to angels, with whom we shall be brought to stand, and also to ourselves, our wives and children, who have been made to bow down with grief, sorrow, and care, under the most damning hand of murder, tyranny, and oppression, supported and urged on and upheld by the influence of that spirit which hath so strongly riveted the creeds of the fathers, who have inherited lies, upon the hearts of the children, and filled the world with confusion, and has been growing stronger, and is now the very mainspring of all corruption, and the whole earth groans under the weight of its iniquity, It is an iron yoke, it is a strong band; they are the very handcuffs, and chains, and shackles, and fetters of hell. Therefore, it is an imperative duty that we owe, not only to our own wives and children, but to the widows and fatherless, whose husbands and fathers have been murdered under its iron hand. Which* *dark and blackening deeds are enough to make hell itself shudder, and to stand aghast and pale, and the hands of the very devil to tremble and palsy. And also it is* **an imperative duty** *that we owe to all the rising generation, and to all the pure in heart—For there are many on the earth among all sects, parties, and denominations, who are blinded by the subtle craftiness of men, whereby they lie in wait to deceive, and* **who are only kept from the truth because they know not where to find it**—*Therefore, that we should waste and wear out our lives in bringing to light all the hidden things of darkness, wherein we know them; and they are truly manifest from heaven—These should then be attended to with great earnestness, Let no man count them as small things; for there is much which lieth in futurity, pertaining to the saints, which depends upon these things, You know, brethren, that a very large ship is benefited very much by a very small helm in the time of a storm, by being kept workways with the wind and the waves. Therefore, dearly beloved brethren, let us cheerfully do all things that lie in our power; and then may we stand still, with the utmost assurance, to see the salvation of God, and for his arm to be revealed. (Section 123:7–17)*

And **that Law of the Land which is constitutional,** *supporting that principle of freedom in maintaining rights and privileges, belonging to all mankind, and is justifiable before me. Therefore, I, the Lord, justify you, and your brethren of my church, in* **befriending that law which is the constitutional law of the land;** *And as pertaining to law of man, whatsoever is more or less than this, cometh evil. I, the Lord God, make you free, therefore ye are free indeed; and the law also maketh you free. (Section 98:5–8)*

According to the laws and **Constitution** *of the people, which I have suffered to be established, and* **Constitution of this land,** *by the hands of wise men whom I raised up unto this very purpose, and redeemed the land by the shedding of blood. (Section 101:77–80)*

In the kingdom of the devil/Satan, we the people are as chattel on his tree of knowledge of good and evil. We are chattel in a socialist or communist system of government. The very bottom line is that in a system of force, there is *slavery*.

In the Garden of Eden, the tree of knowledge of good and evil represents Satan's kingdom. In Christ's kingdom, we the people are at the very top of the tree of life, just under Christ. In contrast, Washington, DC, the first federal corporation, is at the bottom as the people's servants, and we have told it to stay within its box of ten square miles and within its jurisdiction. The bottom line for us, the people in Christ's system of government under the Constitution, is *freedom*.

When King George's general Cornwallis delivered up his arms to Gen. George Washington, he had his band play the tune "The World Turned Upside Down." Any time a system of force rules the land of any country through a king or a dictator, the devil's/Satan's jurisdiction is prevalent, the people are slaves, and freedom is void. If the people have free will, and there is a choice given in what laws they want to be governed by, then Christ's kingdom is prevalent. This is illustrated through a democratic system of electing officers who carry out the will of the people. America has this free system where the laws are instituted by, of, and for the people; and we elect our officers, such as presidents, senators, and representatives. Our Constitution embodies the Ten Commandments, which gives equality and justice to all people who are citizens of the country. There is a constant battle to protect our God-given rights and freedoms. The people of the devil/left are constantly trying to erode our conservative values through immorality, atheism, evolution, deceit, rebellion, and disrespect for authority and are using our public schools to accomplish their agendas.

There are three degrees of glory as mentioned in the New Testament: *"There are also **celestial** bodies, and bodies **terrestrial**: but the glory of the celestial is one, and the glory of the terrestrial is another"* (1 Corinthians 15:40, KJV). This verse implies that not everyone is going to be in the same kingdom when they die or to meet God again, if ever they do. The Mormon prophet Joseph Smith touched on this point as well: *"For he who cannot abide the law of a **celestial** kingdom cannot abide a celestial glory. And he who cannot abide a **terrestrial** kingdom cannot abide a terrestrial glory. And he who cannot abide a **telestial** kingdom cannot abide a telestial glory, therefore, he must abide a kingdom which is not a kingdom of glory"* (Doctrine and Covenants, section 88:22–24).

There are three separate kingdoms of glory. The first mentioned is the celestial kingdom with a celestial glory. Each kingdom is governed by law, and the celestial kingdom is governed by the law of the priesthood and is back in the presence of Almighty God. The terrestrial kingdom is governed by Christ under common-law jurisdiction, and in the case of America at this time, the name of that law is the Constitution of the United States of America. The telestial kingdom is Satan's jurisdiction of force under admiralty jurisdiction/old merchant law/Uniform Commercial Code in America. Even the devil's kingdom is a system of law but is abused by evil people seeking to get rich, to lie, to kill, and to get power over one another. This system is a system of commerce.

There are some people who won't obey any laws but are the law unto themselves to get gain and power. These people can't be trusted in any way, shape, or form throughout eternity and are cast into outer darkness. We can see some very evil people in society today, but only God, for sure, can make the call on who these people are. He calls such people "sons of perdition."

The *Book of Mormon* and the prophet Lehi give us a picture of what freedom looks like.

*And it came to pass after I had prayed unto the Lord, I beheld a large and spacious field. And it came to pass that **I beheld a tree, whose fruit was desirable to make one happy**. And it came to pass that I did go forth and partake of the fruit thereof; and **I beheld that it was most sweet, above all that I ever before tasted**. Yea, and I beheld that **the fruit thereof was white to exceed all the whiteness that I had ever seen**. And as I partook of the fruit thereof, it filled my soul with exceedingly great joy; wherefore, I began to be desirous that my family should partake of it also; for **I knew that it was desirable above all other fruit**. (1 Nephi 8:9–12)*

Christ and Satan are at perpetual war over our souls. We are not responsible for Adam's transgression, but we are responsible for our own because of Adam's. The bottom line is, Satan brings *slavery*, and Christ brings *freedom*. We have the freedom to choose, and for this reason, not everyone will be redeemed because there are those who have and will choose Satan's system and his kingdom over that of Christ. This is why God's judgment will be just.

You see, both kingdoms are here on earth, right now, at the same time. Christ personally established his kingdom in Jerusalem, when he set up his church. Of course, prior to this, the children of Israel observed feasts, sabbaths, and sacrifices pointing to the day when Christ would come into the world. Satan was already here, because he was cast down to earth, along with a third of the hosts of heaven, as it records in the book of Revelation, in the Bible.

It is beautiful to know that God is such a wonderful, kind, loving, and understanding parent. God has such power and knowledge, yet He chooses to let us make our own decisions and choose freedom or slavery of our own free will. He knows everyone is not the same because He knew us all before we were born, but when we were born on the earth in our physical bodies as babies, we were caused to forget. We then were forced to choose between God and Satan as we grew and gained knowledge. We all learn and grow according to the situations we were born into, the influences crossing our paths, our circumstances, and our environment. You might say, that as we grew from childhood, our true colors were revealed, exposing the characters we had before we were born. God is very intelligent in His plan. He is giving all a chance to change upon our arrival here on the earth just as he did for Cain. The Mormons' *Pearl of Great Price* mentions this: *"For from this time forth thou shalt be the father of his [Satan's] lies; **thou shalt be called Perdition; for thou wast also before the world**" (Moses 5:24).*

In Christ's kingdom, we the people are at the very top of the tree of life, just under Christ. Washington, DC/Satan, the first federal corporation, is placed at the bottom as our servant, and we have told it to stay within its box of ten square miles and within its jurisdiction. You see, Washington, DC, has been planned and set out to resemble the goat's head of Mendes early on, the goat being the symbol of Satan. The streets in Washington, DC, are set out in the form of the five-cornered star. This is where the five-cornered star becomes a circle. The circle is represented by the freeway that circles around Washington, DC.

The federal government is the jurisdiction of the devil, which is a system of force, and it is not all bad and is needful as our forefathers set it up to serve the people for national security purposes. It must not be joined, nor should it be let out of its box by incorporating our businesses or churches into it. The kingdom of Satan is here on the earth under the Uniform Commercial Code. The kingdom of Christ is here on the earth also under common law of the Constitution. The scriptures tell us to be in the world but not joined to it. We are able to move within the world of commerce and still maintain our sovereignty under the Constitution with knowledge. The bottom line for us, the people in Christ's system under the Constitution is *freedom*.

CHAPTER 4

The Tree of Knowledge of Good and Evil

Satan's kingdom represents the telestial glory, represented by the glory or brightness of the stars. *"There are also celestial bodies, and bodies terrestrial: but the glory of the celestial is one, and the glory of the terrestrial is another. There is one glory of the sun, and another glory of the moon, and **another glory of the stars**, for one star differeth from another star in glory"* (1 Corinthians 15:40–41, KJV)

Joseph Smith explains this further:

*And again, we saw the glory of the **telestial**, which glory is that of the lesser, even as the glory of the stars differs from that of the glory of the moon in the firmament. These are they who received not the gospel of Christ, neither the testimony of Jesus. These are they who deny not the Holy Spirit. These are they who are thrust down to hell. These are they who shall not be redeemed from the devil until the last resurrection, until the Lord, even Christ the Lamb, shall have finished his work. These are they who receive not of the fulness in the eternal world, but of the Holy Spirit through the ministration of the terrestrial; And the terrestrial through the ministration of the celestial. And also, the **telestial** receive it of the administering of angels who are appointed to minister for them, or who are appointed to be ministering spirits for them; for they shall be heirs of salvation. And thus, we saw, in the heavenly vision, the glory of the **telestial**, which surpasses all understanding; And no man knows it except him to whom God has revealed it. And thus, we saw the glory of the **terrestrial** which excels in all things the glory of the **telestial**, even in glory, and in power, and in might, and in dominion. And thus, we saw the glory of the **celestial**, which excels in all things—Where God, even the Father, reigns upon his throne forever and ever; Before whose throne all things bow in humble reverence, and give him glory* *forever and ever. They who dwell in his presence are the church of the Firstborn; and they see as they are seen, and know as they are known, having received of his fulness and of his grace; And he makes them equal in power, and in might, and in dominion. And the glory of the celestial is one, even as the glory of the sun is one. And the glory of the terrestrial is one, even as the glory of the moon is one. And the glory of the **telestial** is one, even as the glory of the stars is one; for as one star differs from another star in glory, even so differs one from another in glory in the **telestial** world; For these are they who are of Paul, and of Apollos, and of Cephas. These are they who say are some of one and some of another—some of Christ and some of John, and some of Moses, and some of Elias, and some of Esaias, and some of Isaiah, and some of Enoch; But received not the gospel, neither the testimony of Jesus, neither the prophets, **neither the everlasting covenant**. Last of all, these all are they who will not be gathered with the saints, to be caught up unto the church of the Firstborn, and received into the cloud. These are they who are liars, and sorcerers, and adulterers, and whoremongers, and whosoever loves and makes a lie. These are they who suffer the wrath of God on earth. These are they who suffer the vengeance of eternal fire. These are they who are cast down to hell and suffer the wrath of Almighty God, until the fulness of times, when Christ shall have subdued all enemies under his feet, and shall have perfected his work; When he shall deliver up the kingdom, and present it unto the Father, spotless, saying: I have overcome and have trodden the wine-press alone, even the winepress of the fierceness of the wrath of Almighty God. Then shall he be crowned with the crown of his glory, to sit on the throne of his power to reign forever and ever. But behold, and lo, we saw the glory and the inhabitants of the **telestial** world, that they were **as innumerable as the stars** in the firmament of heaven, or as the sand upon the seashore; And heard the voice of the Lord saying: These all shall bow the knee, and every tongue shall confess to him who sits upon the throne forever and ever; For they shall be judged according to their works, and every man shall receive according to his own works, his own dominion, in the mansions which are prepared; And they shall be servants of the Most High; **but where God and Christ dwell they cannot come**, worlds without end. This is the end of the vision which we saw, which we were commanded to write while we were yet in the Spirit. (Doctrine and Covenants, section 76:81–113)*

The fruit of either of the two trees is not apples or oranges but are benefits as a result of our actions. The benefit could be a blessing or a curse, depending on the tree the benefit is obtained from. If it is obtained from the tree of life, then it is from God and is counted as a blessing. If it is obtained from the tree of knowledge of good and evil, then it could be construed to be a curse. Generally, people blame Adam and Eve for eating the apple from the forbidden tree; but in reality, they have accepted a benefit from Lucifer/Satan. Some benefits that put us into bondage today are things like our churches incorporating under a 501(c)(3) charter, welfare program, Department of Education, Internal Revenue Service, AMA, FDA, United Nations, *Roe v. Wade*, Sixteenth Amendment, Federal Reserve bank, and Emergency War Powers Act. These laws and programs are designed to make slaves out of the people by initiating unknown contracts that bind us to the world/telestial kingdom. These contracts or "chains of Hell" or "chains of death" must be broken by repentance and change.

Adam and Eve's listening to the voice of the devil put themselves into Satan's jurisdiction, and because of what they did, we have to overcome. Our Father in Heaven knew we couldn't break the chains of Hell alone, so He sent His Son, Jesus Christ, to show us how and show us the way back to the presence of our Father. All we simply need to do is look up to Christ, believe in Him, forsake our sins, and follow Him back to God by doing the things we see Him do. *"Those things, **which ye have both learned**, and **received and heard**, and **saw in me, these do**, and **the God of Peace will be with you**"* *(Philippians 4:9, KJV).*

The Mormons' thirteenth article of faith reads, "We believe that men will be punished for their own sins, and not Adam's transgression." So, with this in mind, we the people are also partakers of these same trees/systems of government individually and as churches and as nations, whether we choose evil or good. As stated in the previous chapter, *"And he said unto me: Behold, there are save two churches only; the one is the church of the Lamb of God, and the other is the church of the devil; wherefore, whoso belongeth not to the church of the Lamb of God, belongeth to that great church, which is the mother of abominations; and she is the whore of all the earth"* (1 Nephi 14:10, Book of Mormon)

It is impossible then to look at all the different religions on the earth and not realize that, even if the churches are operating in one jurisdiction or the other, there are only two choices. This is where we need to have the knowledge to recognize them by their fruits. *"**Ye shall know them by their fruits**. Do men gather grapes of thorns, or figs of thistles? Even so every good tree* *bringeth forth good fruit; but a corrupt tree bringeth forth evil fruit. A good tree cannot bring forth evil fruit, neither can a corrupt tree bring forth good fruit. Every tree that bringeth not forth good fruit is hewn down, and cast into the fire. Wherefore by their fruits ye shall know them" (Matthew 7:16–20, KJV)* see the chart "Gospel of Jesus Christ Illustrated").

Each system of government is like a tree:

Satan/Roman Empire	Jesus Christ/King of kings
Law of commerce/admiralty jurisdiction	Common law/common law jurisdiction
International bankers/FRB	We the people/kings and queens
Washington D.C. Incorporated	The Constitution/Bill of Rights
Uniform Commercial Codes	U.S. Treasury/creation of money
State/county/city governments, Inc.	State/county/city govt unincorporated
We the People/chattel	Washington D.C. Incorporated

The tree with the glory of that of the stars/telestial is also the jurisdiction of Satan/Lucifer, and he is the head of it. He is over the law of commerce, with its accompanying jurisdiction. This system has both good and evil but is run through intimidation and lies. We can see these facts by looking at the way the Democrats lie and manipulate to accomplish their agendas. *"But Peter said, Ananias, why hath Satan filled thine heart to lie to the Holy Ghost?" (Acts 5:3, KJV).*

"Even that old serpent who is the devil, who is the father of all lies" (2 Nephi 2:18, Book of Mormon). Satan uses money to buy up people to do his bidding, as he has done with the Democrats, and promises them riches, power, glory, and titles. The *Pearl of Great Price* says, *"Wherefore, because that Satan rebelled against me [God], and sought to destroy the agency of man, which I, the Lord God, had given him, and also, that I should give unto him mine own power; by the power of mine Only Begotten, I caused that he should be cast down; And he became **Satan**, yea, even the devil, **the father of all lies**, **to deceive and blind men**, and to lead them captive at his will, even as many as would not hearken unto my voice" (Moses 4:3–4).*

He uses the banking system to accomplish this task as he did in earlier times. These we know as the international bankers, also the authors of the Federal Reserve bank. The Federal Reserve bank is the evilest institution on the face of the earth as it creates slaves of the people of all nations. This banking system is not a part of the federal government but is a private corporation like the Internal Revenue Service. This banking system robs the people of their labor, their wealth, and everything they own. *"And they come to Jerusalem: and Jesus went into the temple, and began to cast out them that sold and bought in the temple, and overthrew the tables of the **money changers**, and the seats of them that sold doves; And would not suffer that any man should carry any vessel through the temple. And he taught, saying unto them, is it not written, My house shall be called of all nations the house of prayer? But ye have made it a den of thieves"* (Mark 11:15–17, KJV).

The money system incorporates many secret organizations to further an agenda to destroy America and subject the people, heal the wound of the beast, and reunite the Roman Empire as discussed in Daniel. *"These great beasts, which are four, are four kings, which shall arise out of the earth . . . Then I would know the truth of the fourth beast, which was diverse from all the others, exceeding dreadful, **whose teeth were of iron**, and his nails of brass; which devoured, brake in pieces, and stamped the residue with his feet. . . . The fourth beast shall be the fourth kingdom upon earth, which shall be diverse from all kingdoms, and shall devour the whole earth, and shall tread it down, and brake it in pieces"* (Daniel 7:17, 19, 23, KJV). Daniel was speaking of the fourth kingdom of the image that he saw when interpreting the dream of Nebuchadnezzar. The fourth kingdom were the legs of iron, with the feet and toes partly of iron and of clay.

The first kingdom of the image was the Babylonian Empire, the head of gold, under Nebuchadnezzar. The second was the Median and Persian Empire, represented by the shoulders and arms of silver. The third was Alexander the Great and the Macedonian/Greek Empire, represented by waist and hips of bronze. The fourth, of course, was the Roman Empire, represented with the legs of iron, feet and toes partly of iron and partly of clay, and teeth of iron. The Roman Empire refused to let go despite the awful wound it sustained when Christ was born and when Martin Luther began the Reformation period, which is still going on today.

The Reformation basically ended the Dark Ages as the light of Jesus Christ burst through and exposed the truth, which fulfilled the prophecy of the rock cut out of the mountain without hands and rolling forth until it filled the whole earth. *"Thou sawest till that a **stone was cut out without hands**, which smote the image upon his feet that were of iron and clay. And break them to pieces. Then was the iron, the clay, the brass, the silver, and the gold, broken to pieces together, and became like the chaff of the summer threshing floors; and the wind carried them away, that no place was found for them: and the stone that smote the image became a great mountain, and **filled the whole earth**"* (Daniel 2:34–35, KJV). The "**Rock**" is Jesus Christ and the "**great mountain**" is America, And America, with it's Christian beliefs and values, have filled the whole earth. America is a predominantly Christian nation.

The Roman Empire is still very much alive in every country of the world, despite the awful wound it has sustained. Most European countries are still predominantly Catholic, but the leaders of the Catholic Church use lies to keep them as Catholics while its wound has been healing. It uses the money system of international banks, the Federal Reserve system, Democrats, and secret organizations and corporations to exercise power and works toward healing its great wound. It uses the money system to rule with blood and horror on the earth to overthrow all countries and kingdoms. Some of the secret organizations it uses are Knights Templar, Illuminati, Skull and Bones, Masons, Jesuits, Knights of Malta, and many more. However, the secret orders began with Cain.

Cain entered into a secret contract with Satan, swearing allegiance to him when he killed his brother Abel for gain. Also, in the Mormons' *Pearl of Great Price*, it states,

*And it came to pass that Cain took one of his brothers' daughters to wife, and **they loved Satan more than God**. And Satan said unto Cain: **Swear unto me by thy throat**, and if thou tell it thou shalt die; and swear thy brethren by their heads, and by the living God, that they tell it not; for if they tell it, they shall surely die; and this that thy father may not know it; and this day I will deliver thy brother Abel into thine hands. And Satan swear unto Cain that he would do according to his commands. And **all these things were done in secret**. And Cain said: Truly **I am Mahan**, the **master of this great secret**, that **I may murder** and get **gain**. Wherefore Cain was called Master Mahan, and he gloried in his wickedness. (Moses 5:28–31)*

Most of these orders originate from the Catholic Church, whether it be German, Italian, French, or Spanish.

*"After this, I saw in the night visions, and behold, a fourth beast, dreadful and terrible, and strong exceedingly; and it had great **iron teeth**: it devoured and brake in pieces, and stamped the residue with the feet of it: and it was diverse from all the beasts that were before it; and **it had ten horns**" (Daniel 7:7, KJV).* These ten horns were the ten kings of Europe that were under the rule of the Roman Empire—England, Germany, Spain, France, Ireland, Italy, Turkey, Russia, Poland, Hungary, Sweden, Norway, Holland, etc., not necessarily with these names nor in this order, but they were all part of the Roman Empire, whether or not they were individual countries as they are today or part of a kingdom at the time of the Roman Empire (see *The Roman World*).

"[A]nd the stone that smote the image became a great mountain, and filled the whole earth" (Daniel 2:35, KJV). The stone was cut from the mountain without hands on the day that our Savior, Jesus Christ, was born in Bethlehem. The knowledge of Him and by Him, what He did, and who He is spread like wildfire across the world. The Bible is a gathering of documents, letters, translations, revelations, and understandings written down by early prophets, historians, teachers, apostles, and good and holy men. The Bible is a compilation of all these documents that testify and agree with the preceding documents written by earlier prophets. The Bible is literally irrefutable evidence of Christ and the workings of God due to the many witnesses who had seen, heard, and revealed about Christ in many different places, times, and words but were talking about the same thing. The men and women who testified of Christ were real people who really lived and who were of record. No court in the world can discredit this book.

The Bible got into the hands of good men like Martin Luther, who was a Catholic monk living in Germany. Up to that time, the scriptures were protected from the regular people, with the purpose of holding them in ignorance or in the dark about the truth of Christ. Martin Luther translated the Bible into the German language and made it available to the people to read for themselves. The truth quickly spread throughout the known world. This began the Reformation of the Catholic Church, which was the "awful wound" talked about in the Bible. *"And I saw **one of his heads as it were wounded to death**; and his **deadly wound was healed**: and all the world wondered after the beast" (Revelation 13:3, KJV).* For a great reference material on the Catholic Church, everyone should read *The Great Controversy* by Ellen White, the author and the spiritual leader of the Seventh-day Adventist Church.

Because of the Reformation period, the truth of Jesus Christ once again burst into the light, and the Catholic Church was about to be destroyed. Something had to be done for the church to survive, so the leaders at the time got together and decided to make a split in the church. According to the history of the Dark Ages, Constantine's seat of government had been changed from Italy to Turkey. He called his established seat of government in Turkey "Constantinople." The white pope was to remain in Rome, Italy, with its seven hills or seven heads, while the black pope—with the military arm of the Catholic Church—carried on in Constantinople. The military arm of the Catholic Church is the Jesuits. The Jesuits are the so-called missionaries sent out to different parts of the world, recruiting the American Indians, Mexicans, South American people, and any peoples with the purpose of infiltrating. Both white and black popes used, and are using secret orders spoken of earlier, such as Illuminati and Masons.

The knowledge of Constantinople is, as a myth of a time and place that existed once but is nowhere to be found today. It is like a fairy tale, and that is the way it was planned to be thought of by the Catholic Church to fool the people. They didn't change their doctrine at all but just went silent about many things. For instance, Pope Benedict became pope on April 19, 2005, and he was the modern-day leader or authority of the Inquisition, which was responsible for burning apostates at the stake. My great-grandfather Rev. John Rogers of England was burned at the stake. The Catholic Church followed the Pilgrims to America later on to carry on their work of healing the wound of the beast by infiltrating every organization they could, and thinking to destroy America.

The fathers of the church began preaching Christ from the pulpits as if they were Christians, but their hearts were far from Christ. They didn't do the works of Christ as their form of baptism is still by sprinkling, they still worship Mary, and they push paganism in the forms of superstition. They preach the upholding of the rosary of beads and scapulars, the use of Hail Marys, and other forms of God replacements. The pope wears the fish-head hat always, which is a representation of the god, Dagon of ancient Egypt. He calls himself the vicar of Christ, which means Christ's substitute. Christ is displayed in every Catholic Church impaled on the cross in a perpetual representation of His death. The statue of Saint Peter in Saint Peter's Square at the Vatican Basilica is really that of Nimrod, the mighty hunter, immortalized and placed in the sky as clusters of stars or constellations. The alleged Mary and the baby Jesus are really Isis/Semiramis and Horus/Cupid, who died soon after birth, also immortalized into a deity.

Constantinople is still very much alive, but most people don't know where it is located today. Constantinople is the seat of the black pope and the Jesuits, located in Turkey. *"And to the angel of the church in **Pergamos** write; I know thy works, and where thou dwellest, even **where Satan's seat is**: and thou holdest fast my name, and hast not denied my faith, even in those days wherein Antipas was my faithful martyr, who was slain among you, **where Satan dwelleth**" (Revelation 2:12–14, KJV).*

The name *Constantinople* was changed to *Pergamos/Pergamum* to fool the people. However, the city of Istanbul, Turkey sounds similar to Constantinople, and is not far from Pergamon. The Catholic Church teaches about Christ just enough to fool the masses; it lies to them without conscience. The Jesuits flood governments in every country of the world. They are the Democrats or Communist Party. Many Democrats are graduates of Ivy League or Catholic/Jesuit colleges. They send their children to the same colleges and participate in secret organizations and fraternities where they learn what is expected of them. These Jesuits include people from all walks of life, and they are in everything and every organization conceivable. They are determined that the means justifies the end. They are Antichrists and are pro-Satanists. They think completely opposite to what Christ teaches. There is a man called Doc Marquis who had been a Satanist for twenty years before he became born again and says that he could and still can go into any Catholic Church and feel right at home.

The Jesuits are the assassins, harbored by the Catholic Church. John Wilkes Booth, who shot Abraham Lincoln, was one. Abraham Lincoln, a Christian and Republican, saved America not just by freeing the slaves but also by mainly creating money from the U.S. Treasury, which financed the North, instead of going into debt by borrowing from the international bankers/ Federal Reserve. Lincoln created the greenback. He understood that to stay solvent, he could not put the North into debt. It would have destroyed the Union, and the Republic of the   united states of America. The South lost the war because they were borrowing from the same banks that Abraham Lincoln avoided, and they got into extreme debt. The plan was for the Federal Reserve bank to finance both sides and use this debt to destroy America. Through Providence and the wisdom of Abraham Lincoln, he destroyed their plans. Abraham Lincoln was a good man. He saved the Union, and he saved America, with its Constitution, through the sacrifice of so many lives.

John Wilkes Booth, a Jesuit, was not burned in the barn as the history books stated, written by Democrats and liars. Adm. G. W. Baird later identified the body in the barn as the body of Capt. James William Boyd, assumed to be Booth's body. Boyd was, in fact, a Confederate spy who, after being killed, was simply dumped into an arsenal prison sinkhole used for dumping dead horses. According to the book by Finis L. Bates, *The Escape and Suicide of John Wilkes Booth, the Jesuit Assassin of Abraham Lincoln*, edited by the *New York Times*, Booth did escape. Some accounts have him hidden by the Vatican in Rome, being tracked there by the American Secret Service. Booth was a member of Pike's Knights of the Golden Circle. He conspired with Albert Pike, Judah Benjamin, John Slidell, and Admiral G. W. Baird while he was in New Orleans during the winter of 1863–1864 to assassinate Abraham Lincoln.

Adolf Hitler ordered the killing of millions of Jews because they were in opposition to him and because they served a different God. Hitler was a Jesuit, and trying to unite the Roman Empire under the Catholic Church. Before him, Napoleon Bonaparte tried to do the same thing. Before Napoleon, Charlemagne tried to unite the Roman Empire by force.

The man we all know as Pope John Paul II, whose real name is Karol Jozef Wojtyla, worked for Hitler during World War II as a salesman and chemist, supplying poisonous gas used to exterminate the Jews. The company he worked for was IG Farben, which had seven subsidiary companies. When the Nuremberg trials began, the Catholic Church hid him out in the Vatican up to the time he emerged into daylight as Pope John Paul II. These are Jesuits pushing the globalist or communist agenda (see the book *Secret History of the Jesuits* by Edmond Paris).

I can identify a communist, globalist, or Jesuit a million miles away. All they have to do is open their mouths. What they believe is completely opposite to what God is trying to do. For this type of people, lying comes so naturally.

They have no scruples, no morals. Some try to say that they are Christian, but their beliefs and actions tell otherwise.

Obama is a globalist, among many others. Look at Obama's friends and who he hangs out with—Merkel from Germany, Macron from France, Trudeau from Canada—and look at the colleges he and others graduated from. Evil people don't get their evil ideas by accident. He graduated from an Ivy League, a Catholic school like the rest. He has had ties and jobs in Catholic schools of Chicago. His Democratic ties are strong, and his grooming to destroy America is evident, proven by what he tried to accomplish while president of the United States.

Others in America are past presidents, senators, and representatives of the Democratic Party and many more who worked and are now working to bring our great republic down and enslave the American people. They attempt this by eroding morals and freedoms, pushing for communist or socialist programs, pushing the theory of globalism, and pushing lies to accomplish their agendas. All these things totally match those opposite to freedom.

We as a people can withstand evil only by standing with Christ, having an unshaken faith in our Father in Heaven, and being diligent in seeking out good men who believe firmly in Almighty God to entrust with fiduciary positions in government. It is through secret organizations, spoken of earlier, that these Jesuits are in our government, whose job it is to infiltrate and use their influences to bring down governments. Each one attempts to work in a manner so as not to alarm the masses but will just change one thing at a time until the complete idea is changed to suit their agendas. It is like the idea of getting a frog to voluntarily stay in the water while it is being boiled. Turn the heat up so gradually until the frog unknowingly has allowed itself to be boiled instead of hopping out of the pan, when it could have done so at any time. This is how the ten planks of *The Communist Manifesto* were put into place, which has infiltrated our republic with communism.

These ten planks govern the devil's kingdom and are codified into the Uniform Commercial Code, which in turn is codified into state statutes, which are set up to strip the people of their rights under the Constitution. We use them all the time and have since 1938, when *Erie v. Tompkins* was ruled on by the U.S. Supreme Court, which changed our common law under the Constitution to the law of commerce or old merchant law, being the law of the ocean/maritime law. This is the system of force under kings and dictators. All our states have codified, such as Idaho Code, Washington Code, and Florida Code. All states have their state statutes, which abrogate and undermine every constitutional right we have.

Next on this tree is Washington, DC, Incorporated. The Uniform Commercial Code governs Washington, DC. It is spoken of by Isaiah. *"Yea,* **ten acres of a vineyard** *shall yield one bath, and the seed of an homer shall yield an ephah" (Isaiah 5:10, KJV).* Washington, DC, is ten square miles that was given as the seat of the federal government by the adjoining states, Virginia and Maryland. *Federal* also means "corporate" and has the same power as that of a king and has absolute power in Washington, DC, or on a ship. *Bath* refers to a full measure. I believe this scripture was prophetically speaking about the ten square miles of Washington, DC; and when it is joined to, it is being let out of its box, and it will be allowed to get out of control as it is today. Because of the disobedience and unwise decisions of the people, allowing their businesses and churches to join this first corporation will most certainly yield a "full measure."

The power of the federal jurisdiction extends to other needful buildings and facilities, such as post offices, military bases, dockyards, federal buildings, and courthouses. The federal government is important in their place and for its purpose and has been given a box and told to stay there. However, people and businesses have joined them by incorporating their businesses, thus letting the corporate beast out of the box. *"Woe unto them that join house to house, that lay field to field, till there be no place, that they may be placed alone in the midst of the earth" (Isaiah 5:8, KJV).* This is the seat of our federal/corporate government. Washington, DC, is the first corporation, and the corporate system is the beast.

Under the incorporated government of Washington, DC, comes state government incorporated, county government incorporated, and city government incorporated. At the very bottom then of this tree is us, the people as chattels/serfs. This system of government under admiralty jurisdiction neutralizes the people's constitutional rights, replaces them with privileges, and violates every constitutional right we have. Thus, this is how slaves are made. Through federal grants, individuals and states are enticed to incorporate and join themselves to the corporate, federal system. Churches are incorporated under a 501(c)(3) charter, neutralizing what they can teach. They have willingly let the devil out of his box and then wonder what happened. *"Therefore,* **Hell hath enlarged herself***, and opened her mouth without measure: and their glory, and their multitude, and their pomp, and he that rejoiceth, shall descend into it"* *(Isaiah 5:14, KJV).*

Because of the ignorance, the laziness, and the desires of the people to have leisure, luxury, money, power, and immorality, they have chosen to discredit God to cover their whoredoms, do their drugs, and exercise dominion over their fellow man. These are the people who have chosen slavery over freedom and are at the very bottom of the tree of knowledge of good and evil as chattel. This is exactly the way it was back in the Dark Ages under the feudal system.

This is what Christ describes as death and Hell, leading to misery and destruction. This system binds us down with the chains of Hell, or contracts because we seal ourselves to the devil's kingdom and separates us forever from the presence of God. This system is the telestial kingdom. Other modern terms include federalism, democracy, socialism, communism, fascism, and Nazism. Ancient terms include Egypt, Babylon, the world, whore of all the earth, the beast, the great and abominable church, great and spacious building that Lehi saw, and wilderness. This is the state-run religion, the church of the devil, and is our probationary state. All these terms, modern or ancient, mean the same thing.

It was because of Adam's transgression that we were born into this world and kingdom of the devil and now have to make decisions whether to choose the fruit of the tree of life or to remain in the devil's kingdom by choosing the fruit from the tree of knowledge of good and evil. We no longer can blame Adam and Eve for our position here because we have free agency to choose for ourselves. This is meant to be our probationary state, where we prepare to meet God.

This is the exact reason Christ came from His Father, and our Father, to His people, with the plan of helping us and guiding us out of slavery, enabling us to return to the presence of our Father, those of us who will listen and understand and will hate what the devil has to offer. *"**My people are destroyed from lack of knowledge***: because thou hast rejected knowledge, I will also reject thee, that thou shalt be no priest to me: seeing thou hast forgotten* *the law of thy God, I will also forget thy children" (Hosea 4:6, KJV; compare Isaiah 5, KJV).*

*Therefore, **my people have gone into captivity, because they have no knowledge**; and their honorable men are famished, and their multitude dried up with thirst. **Therefore hell hath enlarged herself,** and opened her mouth without measure: and their glory, and their multitude, and their pomp, and he that rejoiceth, shall descend into it. (2 Nephi 15:13–14, Book of Mormon)*

***Because of their pride and wickedness they have all gone astray save it be a few,** who are the humble followers of Christ; nevertheless, they are led, that **in many instances they do err** because they are **taught the precepts of men**. (2 Nephi 28:14, Book of Mormon)*

*And it came to pass that there arose a **mist of darkness**; yea, even an exceedingly great mist of darkness, insomuch that **they who had commenced in the path did lose their way**, that they wandered off and **were lost**. (1 Nephi 8:23, Book of Mormon)* The mists of darkness are the many lies and deceptions told by liberals and democrats, and by those who would put the people into subjection.

*And now **I, Moroni, do not write the manner of their oaths** and combinations, for it hath been made known unto me that **they are had among all people**, and they are had among the Lamanites. And **they have caused the destruction of this people** of whom I am now speaking, and also the destruction of the people of Nephi. And whatsoever nation shall uphold such secret combinations, to get power and gain, **until they shall spread over the nation**, behold, **they shall be destroyed**; for the Lord will not suffer that the blood of his saints, which shall be shed by them, shall always cry unto him from the ground for vengeance upon them and yet he avenge them not. Wherefore, o ye gentiles, it is wisdom in God that these things should be shown unto you, that thereby ye may repent of your sins, and suffer not that these murderous combinations shall get above you, **which are built up to get power and gain**—and the work, yea, even the work of destruction come upon you, yea, even the sword of the justice of the Eternal God shall fall upon you, to your overthrow and destruction if ye will suffer these things to be. Wherefore, the Lord commandeth you, **when ye shall see these things come among you** that **ye shall awake** to a sense of your awful situation, because of this secret combination which shall be among you; or wo be unto it, because of the blood of them who have been slain; for they cry from the dust for* *vengeance upon it, and also upon those who built it up. For it cometh to pass* **that whoso buildeth it up seeketh to overthrow the freedom of all lands, nations, and countries;** *and it bringeth to pass the destruction of all people, for* **it is built up by the devil, who is the father of all lies:** *even that same liar who beguiled our first parents, yea, even that same liar who hath caused man to commit murder from the beginning; who hath hardened the hearts of men that they have murdered the prophets, and stoned them, and cast them out from the beginning. (Ether 8:20–25, Book of Mormon)*

By learning knowledge about the past, present, and future and about our Lord and Savior, Jesus Christ, we can be free and return to our Father in Heaven's presence. *"Then saith Jesus to those Jews which believed in him, If ye continue in my word, then are ye my disciples indeed;* **And ye shall know the truth and the truth shall make you free"** *(John 8:31–32, KJV).*

The bottom line concerning the system of government depicted by the tree of knowledge of good and evil is slavery, but knowing the truth makes it possible to change and come out of the world, because Christ is leading the way. This is why He came into the world, to draw all men, if they would follow, unto Him.

For the **word of the Lord is truth,** *and* **whatsoever is truth is light,** *and* **whatsoever is light is Spirit,** *even* **the Spirit of Jesus Christ.** *And the Spirit giveth light to every man that cometh into the world: and the Spirit enlighteneth every man through the world, that hearkeneth to the voice of the Spirit. And everyone that hearkeneth to the voice of the Spirit cometh unto God, even the Father. And the Father teacheth him of the covenant which he has renewed and confirmed upon you, which is confirmed upon you for your sakes, and not for your sakes only, but for the sake of the whole world. And the whole world lieth in sin, and groaneth under darkness and under the bondage of sin. And by this you may know they are under the bondage of sin because they come not unto me. For whoso cometh not unto me is under the bondage of sin. And whoso receiveth not my voice is not acquainted with my voice, and is not of me. And this you may know the* **righteous from the wicked,** *and that the whole world groaneth under sin and darkness even now. (Doctrine and Covenants, section 84:45–53)*

In the *Book of Mormon,* the prophet Nephi made a plea to the people back in his time and to us to liken the scriptures unto ourselves, which is very good advice because they most certainly apply to all generations. *"O that* *ye would awake; **awake from a deep sleep**, yea, **even from the sleep of hell**, and **shake off the awful chains by which ye are bound**, which are the chains which bind the children of men, that they are carried away captive down to the eternal gulf of misery and woe" (2 Nephi 1:13).*

This was why Christ came into the world, to show those who will, the way to overcome the devil's kingdom, draw us unto Him, and get us back into the presence of our Father.

*For **God** so loved the world, that he **gave his only Begotten Son**, that whosoever **believeth in him** should not perish, but have everlasting life. For God sent not his Son into the world to condemn the world: but that the world through him might be saved. He that believeth on him is not condemned: but he that believeth not is condemned already, because he hath not believed in the name of the only Begotten Son of God. And this is the condemnation, that light is come into the world, and **men loved darkness rather than light**, **because their deeds were evil**. For everyone who doeth evil hateth the light, lest his deeds should be reproved. But he that doeth truth cometh to the light, that his deeds may be made manifest, that they are wrought in God. (John 3:16–21, KJV)*

What we the people need to decide on is, who we want as our master for eternity. Once a person has knowledge and understands the situation, he realizes that the kingdom of God is here already. We just need knowledge of the truth and then act, and you are a slave no longer. Every decision we make is a decision for one side or the other, for God or Satan. If you know something is not constitutional, then resist it; and by doing so, you free yourself from the contracts, chains, and bonds of Hell, all the while having a steadfast faith in God. You not only will gain more knowledge but your faith in God also will grow extensively. This I know is true.

CHAPTER 5

The Roman Empire Holding on with Its "Teeth of Iron"

This chapter will talk further about the dream that Daniel had and about the great image he had seen representing the four great kingdoms that were to be on the earth, including the one he served, the kingdom of Babylon. There have been many books already written about these kingdoms, and so I will not attempt to go into great detail about them, but I will attempt to explain certain parts, trying to put many of the puzzle pieces together. It is my wish to help my brothers and sisters in Christ understand the workings of God to the extent that lights may go on, and we will understand our part in the eternal scheme of things so that we may realize where we are in God's plan. Perhaps we can understand our role in this life and how this life relates to our part in the fight for freedom or our acquiescence to slavery.

There are only two churches or kingdoms. There is no middle ground. We must choose the master whom we will serve. My choice is a kind, wise, powerful, heavenly Father, barring all others.

Thou, O king, sawest, and behold a great image, whose brightness was excellent, stood before thee; and the form thereof was terrible. This image's head was of fine gold, his breast and arms of silver, his belly and his thighs of brass, His legs of **iron**, *his feet part of* **iron** *and part of* **clay**. *Thou sawest till that a* **stone was cut out without hands**, *which* **smote the image** *upon his* **feet** *that were* **of iron and clay**, *and brake them to pieces. Then was the iron, the clay, the brass, the silver, and the gold, broken to pieces together, and became like the chaff of* *the summer threshing floors; and the wind carried them away, that no place was found for them: and the stone that smote the image became a great mountain, and filled the whole earth. This is the dream; and we will tell the interpretation thereof before the king. Thou, o king, art a king of kings: for the God of Heaven hath given thee a kingdom, power, and strength and glory. And wheresoever the children of men dwell, the beasts of the field and the fowls of the heaven, hath he given into thine hand, and hath made thee ruler over them all. Thou art this head of gold. And after thee shall arise another kingdom inferior to thee, and another third kingdom of brass, which shall bear rule over all the earth. And the* **fourth kingdom** *shall be strong as* **iron**: *forasmuch as iron breaketh in pieces and subdueth all things: and as iron that breaketh all these, shall it break in pieces and bruise. And whereas thou sawest the feet and toes, part of potter's clay, and part of iron, the kingdom shall be divided; but there shall be in it of the strength of the iron, forasmuch as thou sawest the iron mixed with miry clay. And as the toes of the feet were part of iron, and part of clay, so the kingdom shall be partly strong, and partly broken. And whereas thou sawest iron mixed with miry clay, they shall mingle themselves with the seed of men: but they shall not cleave one to another, even as iron is not mixed with clay. And in the days of these kings shall the God of Heaven set up a kingdom, which shall never be destroyed: and the kingdom shall not be left to other people, but it shall break in pieces and consume all these kingdoms, and it shall stand forever. Forasmuch as thou sawest that the stone was cut out of the mountain without hands, and that it brake in pieces the iron, the brass, the clay, the silver, and the gold; the great God hath made known to the king what shall come to pass hereafter: and the dream is certain, and the interpretation thereof sure. (Daniel 2:31–45, KJV)*

Even as iron will not mix with miry clay, good people won't mix with evil people, nor will Democrats adhere to conservative views but will always be divided. It is evident that God has written the program concerning His family here on this earth, and He has provided the script on how it is going to play out, and this He has done from the very beginning. Through His power and majesty and greatness, it all comes about because He has spoken it. We are the actors, and the script has been written and made sure. God never ceases to give men and women freedom to choose whom they will serve for the purpose of no one having any excuse; thus, His judgment will be just and sure.

The first kingdom, from the time of Daniel, was the kingdom of Babylon, represented by the head of gold. The kingdom afterward was given to the Medes and Persians, represented by the arms and breast of silver. This kingdom was then overthrown by the third kingdom, represented by the belly and thighs of brass. This kingdom was the Greek/Macedonian Empire under Alexander the Great. The fourth kingdom was/is of the Romans, having the legs of iron and feet partly iron and partly clay. The Romans were strong like iron, but they stood on two feet that were weak because they were ten separate kingdoms, as represented by the ten toes, that were constantly divided and fought against one another because they served a different master. These toes were the ten main kingdoms of Europe: England, France, Spain, Germany, Ireland, Netherlands, Russia, Belgium, Turkey, and parts of Africa. They were predominantly Catholic and strove for wealth and power. These countries were parts of bigger kingdoms, with many of them having names not familiar to us. Read *Book of Daniel* by Taylor Bunch (1950) for some great information on this subject.

In the days of these ten kingdoms, Daniel described a stone cut out without hands that rolled forth and struck the image in the legs and feet, which broke it to pieces. This stone was Jesus Christ. *"And he beheld them, and said, what is this then that is written, The **stone** which the builders rejected, the same is become the head of the corner? Whosoever shall fall upon that stone shall be broken; but on whomsoever it shall fall, it will grind him to powder"* (Luke 20:17–18, KJV). From the time that Christ began His ministry, He organized His church, which grew even more during extreme persecution. The Roman Empire was the system of force and the devil's jurisdiction, wanting badly to crush the Christian movement because they were an opposition and were seen as enemies to complete domination of the world.

God and Satan are mortal enemies and cannot coexist without one wanting to change or destroy the other. One is good, and one is evil. To let the Christian go unhindered or unchecked brings freedom, whereas Satan demands complete servitude and slavery. Therefore, belief and faith in Christ undermines what Satan is trying to accomplish; therefore, there must be a perpetual war against God and the destruction of God's family. Satan's plan is that of exalting himself up in the place of God and on the throne of God.

God's plan is to test us to see whom we will obey or worship willingly. He puts governments in place to rule and leaders in authority over us so that we may use our free will to determine how we will think, act, and decide, all of which are an indication of whom we love, whether it is good or evil.

Christ was the stone cut out without hands, and He did start His church, which did roll forth and broke the Roman Empire to pieces. The scriptures and teachings of Christ got into the hands of good men, such as Martin Luther, who was very instrumental in starting the Reformation by exposing the light and knowledge about Christ, thus ending the Dark Ages. Christ mentions how the darkness will break into light. *"And this is the condemnation, that **light is come into the world**, and men loved darkness rather than light, neither cometh to the light, lest his deeds should be reproved. But he that doeth truth cometh to the light, that his deeds may be made manifest, that they are wrought in God" (John 3:19–21, KJV). "Behold, I am Jesus Christ, the Son of God. I am the same that came unto mine own, and mine own received me not. **I am the light** which shineth in darkness, and the darkness comprehendeth it not" (Doctrine and Covenants, section 6:21).*

Martin Luther was responsible for translating the Bible into German, which allowed all the German people to read the scriptures for themselves (see *The Great Controversy* by Ellen White of the Seventh-day Adventists, which is a great and thorough resource of knowledge and research on the Reformation). From Martin Luther, the truth spread throughout all Europe like wildfire. The Catholic Church was terrified of what the truth of Christ was and what it would do to their organization. The Catholic Church began killing hundreds of thousands of what they called apostates throughout the Inquisition. The Inquisition resulted in the burning of these apostates at the stake. They were tied to a pole, and wood was stacked all around them and lit on fire. Catholic apostates, now Christians, left the Catholic Church by the thousands. Many of them were hunted down and killed, and many more were persecuted for their beliefs and had nowhere to flee.

God, in His wisdom and mercy, had already prepared a place for those who loved Him. The New World was discovered, credited to Christopher Columbus, which we proudly call America. The *Book of Mormon* describes this land as a land of liberty.

Wherefore, I Lehi, prophecy according to the workings of the Spirit which is in me, that there shall none come into this land save they shall be brought by the hand of the Lord. Wherefore, this land is consecrated unto him who, he shall bring, and if it so be, that they will serve him according to the commandments *which he hath given, it shall be a land of **liberty** unto them; wherefore, they shall never be brought down into captivity; if so, it shall be because of iniquity; for if iniquity shall abound, cursed shall be the land for their sakes, but unto the righteous it shall be blessed forever. (2 Nephi 1:6–7)*

The Pilgrims led the way for those who wished to come to America, fleeing religious persecution.

There are vacant, ancient cities located in Central America and southern Mexico. The cities are still standing, but there are no people. They predate the Incas and the Aztecs, but not very many know where the people who used to inhabit these cities came from or where they went. Not everyone wants to give credit to the Mormon prophet Joseph Smith and his bringing forth of the *Book of Mormon*. These cities are remnants of the people called the Nephites before they warred with another faction called Lamanites. The Nephites were allowed by God to be destroyed because of how wicked they had become, despite the knowledge of God they once had. The Nephites ceased obeying the commandments of God. The Nephites and Lamanites all belonged to one family, who were brought to this land because they wanted to worship as they chose, but later allowed the devil to come among them. They chose fruits from Satan's tree and destroyed their civilization. Remnants of these people are the American Indians and South American people.

This was the very exact reason the Pilgrims came to America. It was for "freedom to worship" as they chose. They wanted to flee religious persecution from the Catholic Church. They came from England, Germany, Italy, Ireland, France, Spain, Greece, Denmark, Sweden, etc. They came from all over Europe and settled here because they had a vision for having freedom. This land was set up as a Christian nation, founded on the principles of the Bible.

The Constitution of the United States of America embodies the Ten Commandments, which guarantee liberty, equality, and justice for all.

*But behold this land, said God, shall be a land of mine inheritance, and the Gentiles shall be blessed upon the land. And **this land shall be a land of liberty** unto the Gentiles, and **there shall be no kings upon the land**, who shall raise up unto the Gentiles. And I will fortify this land against all other* *nations. And **he that fighteth against Zion shall perish**, saith God. For **he that raiseth up a king** against me **shall perish**, for **I, the Lord, the King of Heaven, will be their king**, and I will be a light unto them forever, that hear my words. Wherefore, for this cause, that my covenants may be fulfilled which I have made unto the children of men, that I will do unto them while they are in the flesh, I must needs **destroy the secret works of darkness**, and of murders, and of abominations. Wherefore **he that fighteth against Zion**, both Jew and Gentile, both bond and free, **both male and female**, shall perish; **for they are they who are the whore of all the earth; for they who are not for me are against me** . . . Wherefore, I will consecrate this land unto thy seed, and them who shall be numbered among thy seed, forever, for the land of their inheritance; for **it is a choice land**, saith God unto me, above all other lands, wherefore **I will have all men that dwell thereon that they shall worship me**, saith **God**. (2 Nephi 10:10–16, 19, Book of Mormon)*

These scriptures are talking about America, and we are the Gentiles. God has promised that there will be no king here. The Democrats seeking to push their socialist/Satanic agendas are fighting against God's promises. The Democrats are the ones who seek the downfall of America, and from within their ranks, the secret orders of the Jesuits, Illuminati, and every other secret order prosper. Now when you look at many of the Democrats and watch their obstruction of good things and how they pass and try to pass bad laws to the detriment of the country, you can immediately recognize them as the "whore of all the earth." By doing a search on these people, you will also find that they are predominantly Catholic, and they give a bad name to most Catholics who are in general, good people at heart.

The Democrat Party, simply put, is the Communist Party in America. Anyone who lies and loves to tell a lie is a part of that "whore of all the earth." Just recently, we witnessed the attempt to impeach President Trump by the Democrat-led Congress under Nancy Pelosi, Adam Schiff, and Jerry Nadler. First, it was the Russia hoax that proved to be 100 percent false, but that wasn't enough. These Democrats still proceeded with an attempted impeachment by secret meetings and fabricating lies in hopes they would fool the people. These Democrats are an example, and there are many who belong to this "whore of all the earth."

The Gentiles are they, who came from Europe and originated from those countries who were predominantly Catholic and had the blood of the children of Israel flowing through their veins. They only became Catholic through the force of the Roman Empire, when it invaded and brutally conquered those areas. These people from Europe used to believe in the God of Abraham, Isaac, and Jacob before they fled Israel as the Northern Kingdom under King Jeroboam. Europe was the Northern Hemisphere and where the Northern Kingdom, under King Jeroboam fled, to keep from being slaughtered by the Assyrians. Now God was recalling them to change back from being Catholic to that God and the Holy One of Israel, who so much loved them from the beginning. The Gentiles were continually going astray, and the Lord continually gathered them as a hen gathers her chicks because of the promises made through their fathers, Abraham, Isaac, and Jacob.

This great land is a melting pot consisting of Pilgrims, Quakers, Amish, Lutherans, Baptists, Methodists, and Catholics because they could worship as they chose, according to the dictates of their own consciences and not at the whim of some king, president, emperor, or dictator. We are all kings and queens under the Constitution as we are all literal children of God. We are of royal heritage but, under a democracy, are slaves, and everything we have is a privilege instead of a right. Article 3 (First Amendment) of the Bill of Rights of the Constitution of the United States of America guarantees religious liberty. *"Congress shall make no law respecting the establishment of religion, or prohibiting the free exercise thereof; or abridging the freedom of speech, or of the press; or the right of the people peaceably to assemble, and to petition the government for redress of grievances."*

Now an independent country built up by God-loving, freedom-seeking people wounded the Roman Empire and the Catholic Church almost to death.

And I stood upon the sand of the sea, and **saw a beast** *rise up out of the sea,* **having seven heads** *and* **ten horns**, *and upon his horns* **ten crowns**, *and* **upon his heads the name of blasphemy**. *And the beast which I saw was like unto a leopard, and his feet were as the feet of a bear, and his mouth as the mouth of a lion: and* **the dragon gave him his power, and his seat, and great authority**. *And I saw* **one of his heads** *as it* **were wounded to death**; *and his deadly wound was healed: and all the world wondered after the beast. And they worshipped the dragon which gave power to the beast: And they worshipped the beast, saying, who is like unto the beast? Who is able to make war with him?*

(Revelation 13:1–4, KJV)

In Rome, Italy, there are seven hills, which is the center not only of the ancient Roman Empire but also of the Roman Catholic Church. The Roman Empire ruled over ten kings of Europe, also representing ten horns. The pope of the Catholic Church blasphemes Christ by having Christ in perpetual crucifixion, still hanging on the cross, and by declaring himself as the vicar or substitute for Christ. The pope is a pagan actor as he wears a hat on his head that represents the fertility god Dagon from Egypt, another form of blasphemy. The dragon represents Satan, whom the beast/Catholic Church/corporation worships and gets its strength and authority from.

*After this I saw in the night visions, and behold a **fourth beast**, dreadful and terrible, and strong exceedingly; and it had great **iron teeth**: it devoured and brake in pieces, and stamped the residue with the feet of it: and it was diverse from all the beasts that were before it; and **it had ten horns**. . . . Then I would know the truth of the fourth beast, which was diverse from all the others, exceedingly dreadful, whose teeth were of iron, and his nails of brass; which devoured, brake in pieces, and stamped the residue with his feet; And of the ten horns that were in his head, and of the **other which came up**, and before whom **three fell**; even of **that horn that had eyes**, and **a mouth that spake very great things**, whose look was more stout than his fellows. I beheld, and **the same horn made war with the saints**, and prevailed against them. (Daniel 7:7, 19–21, KJV)*

This fourth beast was the Roman Empire; the ten horns were the kingdoms ruled by the Roman Empire under Constantine, the emperor. It was during the fourth century that Constantine tried to Christianize the empire. It was about the beginning of the sixth century that the Catholic Church came to power, and all power was diverted to the pope. The pope symbolized the other horn that rose, had eyes, spoke very great things, and made war with the saints and prevailed until the church was wounded almost to death. The first pope created the Inquisition, declaring apostates must be killed. Thousands of men, women, and children were murdered in many terrible ways and not just by burning them at the stake. The Catholic Church ruled with blood and horror on the face of the world to hopefully stop the spread of Christianity.

To stop the spread of the truth of Christ was impossible because it was better in the minds of the Christians to die right than die wrong if they had to be slaves. So it was better to have a hope in Christ for the promises of freedom than to die as slaves and be bound with chains of Hell for eternity. It seemed that the more people were persecuted, the more they believed in Christ.

So the Catholic Church had to do something quickly. Their slaves were leaving their church by the droves. King Henry VIII of England left the church with his whole kingdom, Martin Luther just translated the Bible into German, and Frederick the Wise issued the order to allow his kingdom to have freedom of worship because the nobles insisted and were about to rebel if he didn't. The gospel of Jesus Christ was spreading like wildfire and threatening the very existence of the Catholic Church.

The Catholic Church was very wealthy then and is very wealthy now. It has control of governments because of its wealth. The name *Rothschild* means "keeper of the Vatican's treasury." This then means that the Catholic Church owns the fiat money system in the form of the international bank and the Federal Reserve system. The pope dresses in white when visiting every country in the world, and every president, queen, or leader of all countries dresses in black to meet him. This is because he is acting as if he is Christ. All these leaders of the world then bow and kiss his ring and give homage to him as if he is God. The pope is the reason why the Democrats/liberals are trying to destroy America. Most of the Democrats are Catholic and, through their colleges, have gotten into secret orders and there have taken secret oaths to destroy America. Their intentions are to hand America back to the Roman Empire, under the control of the Catholic Church, which will entirely heal the wound of the beast as discussed in Daniel. All a person needs to follow to see evidence of this is to understand and know what the ten planks of *The Communist Manifesto* are and how they have been implemented into our society and laws today.

"Abolition of private property." The Democrats accomplished this through instituting the overthrow of our public law, and with their ability to argue constitutional principles in the courts, they had replaced it with the Uniform Commercial Code. This was done in 1938 through the Supreme Court case of *Erie v. Tompkins*. They now were able to use statutes to abrogate the Constitution. These statutes made it a lot easier to be changed and altered in and of themselves. Such statutes allowed for the implementation of the land tax, which makes people serfs on their own property. If they don't pay an annual rent on their property, it can be taken away by fictional foreign government. Actually, the county governments don't take your property for nonpayment of statutory taxes. What they do is appeal to the greed and selfishness of the people by holding a prima facie tax auction. The counties recover their interest in unpaid taxes and offer to the people their support and promise of ownership of their property by holding this unconstitutional land tax sale. The counties rely on the greed and ignorance of the people, who believe they have allegedly purchased your property through this tax sale, to harass and use their own resources to attempt an unconstitutional eviction. The counties won't do it themselves because it is not constitutional. What the counties are really going after are the annual rents, and they care not about the means. This tax is now enforced by statute, in violation of our Constitution. The only way out of this is through adverse possession. This is a method a person may use to continue to live on the land despite the statute and any other claims that are averse to theirs for a certain period, commonly seven years. The distraught landowner just has to endure the stress and harassment if he can for this period. The stress, though, caused by the county officials and the people who have allegedly purchased it, is extreme, but it can be done if you know your stuff, and have courage. Another way is to update a land patent on your property.

"Heavy progressive income tax." Evil Democrats accomplished this through the unconstitutional declaration of the Sixteenth Amendment as law and by the institution of the IRS in 1933 as the collection agency of the Federal Reserve bank, using intimidation, threat, duress, and coercion to collect. This tax is also unconstitutional and can be thwarted if you know your stuff. Chapter 7 talks about the IRS in detail.

"Abolition of all rights of inheritance." This was accomplished by a statute giving a fictional foreign government the right to heap huge inheritance taxes on the deceased's estate, cause questions of probate, and give the ability to every member of a family, whether intentional or unintentional of the deceased, to elect a family representative to determine ownership. If the deceased does not leave a written will or if the deed or property is not given or transferred before the death of the deceased, then the fight is on in the courts; and ultimately, judges and attorneys end up with the whole estate. Also, they declare land patents invalid if the original patent holder is not alive. This also is unconstitutional; all land patents are lawful as they can be passed down to the heirs forever.

"Confiscation of property of all emigrants and rebels." This is now done through statute, through taxation, and through confiscation of all property if the person is/was involved in a crime, thus forcing all people to industry and to labor continually as slaves to support the state.

"Central bank." This happened at the creation of the Federal Reserve bank on December 23, 1913, when Woodrow Wilson signed the Federal Reserve Act into law. This same year, the Sixteenth Amendment appeared to be ratified. This paved the way for making slaves of the people by letting a private corporation unconstitutionally create debt. The creation of money is constitutionally a duty exclusively of the federal government, namely, the U.S. Treasury, and is based on the medium of gold or silver created by God.

"Government control of communications and transportation." By statute, a person must have a driver's license to operate a motor vehicle in commerce. All media is monitored and tracked by government.

"Government ownership of factories and agriculture."

"Government control of labor." Government agencies regulate what can be manufactured, the quality, the safety, etc. Agencies are in place such as the Environmental Agency, OSHA, FDA, and many others that regulate every industrial operation, whether it be food for humans or livestock, mining, factories, sawmills, transportation, health, or any other idea. People have allowed control of government into every aspect of their lives, even in the churches through the 501(c)(3) charters and through the unions.

"Corporate farms and regional planning." This is accomplished through the planning and zoning restrictions in towns, cities, and rural areas. Government has bought up companies and farms in all areas of commerce and food production, thus controlling a huge part of industry.

"Government control of education." This was accomplished through the Department of Education, combining public schools with that of industry. The children are educated only about commerce, getting a job, and fitting into society but are taught nothing about God. They are attacked because of their faith and berated by peer pressure to cave to immorality, drugs, and so many more things that destroy the youth. The following scriptures talk about how governments throughout history, including anciently, have tried to destroy our youth through education, and by taking God out of their schools.

*"And he appointed teachers of the brethren of Amulon in every land which was possessed by his people; and thus the language of Nephi began to be taught among all the people of the Lamanites. And they were a people friendly one with another; nevertheless they **knew not God**; neither did the brethren of Amulon **teach** them anything **concerning the Lord their God**, neither the Law of Moses; nor did they teach them the words of Abinidi; But they **taught** them that they should keep their record, and that they might write one to another. And thus the Lamanites began to increase **in riches**, and began to **trade** one with another and wax great, and began to be a cunning and a wise people, as to the **wisdom of the world**, yea delighting in **all manner of wickedness and plunder**, except it were among their own brethren." (Mosiah 24:4-7, Book of Mormon)*

King John of England, back in 1213, deeded everything that Great Britain owned to the pope or Catholic Church (see the treaty of 1213). He deeded over everything that England owned in the past, the present, and anything they would own in the future. America was part of this bargain as it was first claimed and settled by the British people, and then England beat back the French in the French and Indian War. America today is still part of the British Commonwealth. What our forefathers won from the British king was our independence to govern our own country, but actual ownership is by the British Crown, which is, in turn, owned by the Vatican.

Proof that America is owned by the British is that America uses the same law system, with the courts and judges dressed in the same manner, conducted after the form of British tribunals. The laws are after English law and procedure and are handed down from the same terms. America's money system is the same as the British, including the banking system. It stands to reason that the *banksters* are the house of Rothschilds or the Rockefellers, the Americanized version of Rothschild. The division of property into ranges, townships, sections, and counties is all the same. Anytime the Queen of England has a festival, every commonwealth country is expected to attend, and America is always there.

America is Great Britain's greatest ally and vice versa. The truth of the matter is that America won its independence to govern itself only, but is still a British citizenry. If then we are still British, then the Vatican has legal claim to America, according to the document given to the pope by King John. The truth is that if the people of the Catholic Church were to understand all these things in front of them, they would leave the Catholic Church by the droves.

The Catholic Church in Rome is one of these two horns, and the other is the Jesuit secret order in Turkey, making up the two horns that came up in Revelation. *"And I beheld **another beast** coming up out of the earth; and he had **two horns like a lamb**, and **he spake as a dragon**. And he exerciseth **all power of the first beast** before him, and causeth the earth and them which dwelleth therein **to worship the first beast**. Whose deadly wound was healed"* (Revelation 12:11–12, KJV). The Catholic Church pays to have all types of national figures stand up and do their bidding, from popes to presidents, politicians, Hollywood actors/actresses, dictators, and teachers who are willing to lie, cheat, steal, and kill to forward the goal of the Roman Empire in taking control of the whole world forever, ruled by Satan, thus subjecting the whole world into slavery.

Constantine started on the road leading to the takeover by the Catholic Church by getting the idea from Jesus Christ and the example He showed by beginning His church. He saw how effective it was to have the people in a common bond based on a common belief. Christ's method was that of freedom, but Satan's method is that of force. Constantine needed something like this to hopefully bind his empire together; after, he brutally conquered a people. He was continuously having to put down revolts. Constantine never joined his own church until he was on his deathbed.

The Roman Empire under Constantine is the first beast, and the other beast with the two horns like a lamb and who spoke as a dragon is the church separated into two factions, one in Rome under the white pope and the other in Turkey under the black pope. Hitler was a Catholic, and he killed Jews because they opposed his doctrine, for they refused to believe in the pagan gods and goddesses represented by the Catholic Church.

There was Nimrod, the mighty hunter, killed by his uncle Seth because of his wickedness. Nimrod was immortalized as the sun god and was placed in the night sky by the people in the form of a constellation and outside the Vatican's Basilica in Rome. The statue there is surely not Peter. Other titles of Nimrod are Baal, crescent moon, Eucharist, and sunset. Eucharist is the Catholic sacrament. Nimrod's wife, Semiramis or Isis, got pregnant, and she had a baby named Horus or Tammuz. Other names for Semiramis are Astarte, Ishtar, sunrise, and Easter. Horus died soon after but also was immortalized by the pagans and also placed in the sky in constellations. Another name for Horus is Cupid. Today the Catholic Church worships Mary, Mother of God, but who they are really referring to is Isis and her baby Horus and not Mary and the baby Jesus.

The Catholic Church thrives now around the world, even in America, as if the wound has been healed. The Catholic Church claims to be unchangeable. Because they don't want to alarm the people, causing them to apostatize, the church allows clergy to preach Jesus from the pulpit and neglect to follow Christ down into the waters of baptism by immersion. Most Catholics remain Catholic because of tradition. Their parents were Catholic, and their grandparents were Catholic. They weren't alive to see firsthand the deprivation and horror heaped on the nonbelievers when people were being burned at the stake but would just as soon be ignorant. *"Knowing this first, that there shall come in the last days scoffers, walking after their own lusts, And saying, where is the promise of his coming? For **since the fathers fell asleep, all things continue as they were from the beginning of creation. For this they are willingly ignorant of,** that by the word of God the heavens were of old, and the earth standing out of the water and in the water"* (2 Peter 3:3–5, KJV).

To be Catholic is not Christian. Many Catholics have godly qualities, but they refuse to submit to the gospel of Jesus Christ and follow Him only. What they represent and who they serve is the key. *"**My people are destroyed for lack of knowledge**: because **thou hast rejected knowledge, I will also reject thee**, that thou shalt be no priest to me: seeing **thou hast forgotten the law of thy God, I will also forget thy children**"* (Hosea 4:6, KJV).

To be Christian is to follow Christ and do the things that we have seen Him do. *"**My sheep hear my voice**, and **I know them**, and **they follow me**"* (John 10:27, KJV). *"For even hereunto were ye called: because Christ also suffered for us, **leaving us an example, that ye should follow his steps**"* (1 Peter 2:21, KJV). *"And also, the voice came unto me, saying: He that is baptized in my name, to him will the Father give the Holy Ghost, like unto me; wherefore,* *follow me, and **do the things which ye have seen me do**" (2 Nephi 31:12, Book of Mormon).*

Christ set the example of baptism by Himself going down into the water and being baptized by John the Baptist and then being immersed under the water. Christ has set the standard for how people are to enter His kingdom. Baptism is the outward showing of swearing allegiance to the kingdom of God. There is no other way to enter in but by the narrow gate of baptism. ***"Many will say to me in that day,** Lord, Lord, **have we not prophesied in thy name?** And in thy name have cast out devils? And **in thy name done many wonderful works?** And **then will I profess unto them, I never knew you:** depart from me,** ye that work iniquity" (Matthew 7:22–23, KJV).*

If anyone thinks to enter into the kingdom of God by any other way than what Christ has said, knowing full well what He has said, they will not get in because they reject knowledge. This goes for the Catholics. There are many fine people among the Catholics, but they are going to have to get rid of their traditions, humble themselves, and do it the way that Christ has spoken. It was like the children of Israel who were bitten in the desert by poisonous snakes. All they had to do to be healed from the snake bites was to look up to a snake on a pole, and they would be healed, but because of the easiness thereof, many refused to do it and died instead. They didn't just die physically, but they forfeited their opportunity to the Kingdom of God.

The Roman Empire is forging ahead by subtlety and secret orders—Jesuits, Masons, Skull and Bones, Illuminati, Knights Templar, Knights of Malta, Knights of Columbus, and many others. Even the Muslims are working hard to bring about the slavery and domination of all mankind in every country and destroy the free agency and work of God. Look at how world leaders such as Germany and France are allowing Muslims to overrun their countries, thus harming their own citizens. The Muslims are just like the Catholics in principle. They are a system of force and go like hand in glove with the Catholic/Roman agenda. The Jesuits and secret orders are among the Muslims also.

The churches all over the world have all been infiltrated by the Masons, and the Masons have been infiltrated by the Illuminati/Jesuits. To infiltrate an organization, one only needs to change one simple thing at a time, which will entirely change the meaning of a sentence, a paragraph, a book, a ceremony, an ordinance, a creed, a law, a religion, etc. Most churches have been infiltrated by joining the World Council of Churches and by incorporating under the 501(c)(3) charter. Others have gone to more extremes and are entirely different organizations.

There was a man who stated in his video that the signal that all the churches had been infiltrated would be when the first president of the United States gave his inaugural address while standing outside, facing the Washington Monument. Ronald Reagan was that president, and he did it on January 20, 1981. Ronald Reagan also appointed the first ambassador to the Vatican. This occurrence had never happened before.

Before and after Reagan, past and future presidents have been chipping away at the freedoms of the American people. Before him were presidents like Woodrow Wilson, responsible for the Federal Reserve bank and for pushing through the Sixteenth Amendment, which directly relates to the evil IRS. Neither the Federal Reserve nor the IRS is a government agency, but they are private corporations. After Reagan are presidents like George Bush Sr. and Jr., Bill Clinton, Obama, and many others. George Bush Sr. personally talked about and supported the new world order. He supported and covered up the assassination of John F. Kennedy. George W. Bush was behind 911. Bill Clinton was responsible for the Oklahoma City bombing and the Waco genocide. Obama, a member of the Muslim Brotherhood, tried to destroy our country by bringing in all the Muslims we have today and bankrupting the nation. He had it set up for Hillary Clinton to become president and finish America off. These and many, many more have sought to destroy the morality and financial and military ability of the nation. These people have done their part, whether knowingly or unknowingly, in the healing of the wound of the beast.

And I saw one of his heads as it were wounded to death; and his deadly wound was healed: and all the world wondered after the beast. And they worshipped the dragon which gave power unto the beast: And they worshipped the beast, saying, who is like unto the beast? Who is able to make war with him? And there was given unto him a mouth speaking great things and blasphemies; and power was given unto him to continue forty and two months. And he opened his mouth in blasphemy against God, to blaspheme his name, and his tabernacle, and them that dwell in Heaven. And it was given unto him to make war with the saints, and to overcome them: and power was given him over all kindreds, and tongues, and nations. And all that dwell upon the earth shall worship him, whose names are not written in the Book of Life of the Lamb slain from the foundation of the world. If any have an ear, let him hear. (Revelation 13:3–9, KJV)

All the evil going on in the world is organized and planned with the purpose of fighting against God and His people. You can rest assured that if the people in our government are fighting to bring our country down, then they belong to one of these secret orders, such as the Jesuits, and they are the whore of all the earth. The Bushes belonged to the secret order of the Skull and Bones. This country of America is a Christian nation. Because of it, has wounded the beast almost to death. To the Jesuit, it has to fall. You look at the crazed antics of the Left and how they obstruct everything good that President Trump is trying to do for us as Christians, and our wonderful country. It could only be someone who has a deliberate mission or agenda to want to undermine our country and our freedom.

These people are absolutely godless, immoral, criminal minded, and selfish on purpose. What so many Democrats/liberals are trying to do is not by accident. They are deliberately corrupt; they have no consciences. A corrupt tree cannot bring forth good fruit, and a good tree cannot bring forth corrupt fruit. *"Wherefore, for this cause, that my covenants may be fulfilled which I have made unto the children of men, that I will do unto them while they are in the flesh, I must needs destroy the **secret works of darkness,** and of murders and abominations. Wherefore he that fighteth against Zion, both Jew and Gentile, both bond and free, both male and female, shall perish; for **they are they who are the whore of all the earth**; for they who are not for me are against me"* (2 Nephi 10:15–16, Book of Mormon). It is pretty clear who and what is the whore of all the earth. Those who work at destroying the freedom of America, whether it is an organization or an individual, and who are in opposition to God's work or against the Christian values most certainly are the *whore* of all the earth.

We must not however, call any man good, but just remember that President Trump is still only a man, and any man, because they are human, may let you down at some time. There are things recently that President Trump has done that make me raise my eyebrow, especially to do with how he has handled the Covid-19 scam-demic. There is too much theater being played out here, especially since conservatives-Christians understand the scriptures and are very watchful, in order not to be deceived. This scripture could be talking about a leader of a country or a church, but only time will tell.

*"And in the latter times of their kingdom, when the trangressors are come to the full, a king of fierce countenance, and **understanding dark sentences**, shall stand up.""And his power shall be mighty, but not by his own power; and he shall **destroy wonderfully**, and shall prosper, and practice, and shall destroy the mighty and the **holy people**.""And **through his policy**, also he shall cause craft to prosper in his hand; and he shall magnify himself in his heart, and **by peace shall destroy many**: he shall also stand up against the Prince of princes; but he shall be broken without hand".*

God has given the people of this nation of America another chance to heal their land by raising up a leader who is unselfish and has the good of the country at heart, at least it appears so. I personally have prayed for several years, since a young man, that God will raise a leader of integrity. I am sure that many, many others have prayed the same prayer. I am absolutely certain that our prayers have been answered for a short time, through Donald John Trump. President Trump has been a man of his word up to a point. He has gone about revitalizing our land through job growth, stronger regulation on immigration policies, a greater military, and much, much more. I pray for him at least twice a day for protection, for health and strength, and for wisdom and knowledge and that he will be encircled by good people.

The people must remain vigilant, committed to freedom, and keep our eyes on Christ as our only Savior. We must be active in voice and by using our talents and resources to search and spread information of the gospel, because everything good requires a sacrifice. If we don't remain diligent, it is like comparing ourselves to the parable/riddle of the ten talents.

For the kingdom of heaven is as a man traveling into a far country, who called his own servants, and delivered unto them his goods. And unto one he gave five talents, to another two, and to another one; to every man according to his several ability; and straightway took his journey. Then he that had received the five talents went and traded with the same, and made them other five talents. And likewise he that had received two, he also gained other two, But he that had received one went and digged in the earth, and hid his lord's money. After a long time the lord of those servants cometh, and reckoneth with them. And so he that had received five talents came and brought other five talents, saying, Lord, thou deliveredst unto me five talents: behold, I have gained beside them *five talents more. His lord said unto him, Well done, thou good and faithful servant: thou hast been faithful over a few things, I will make thee ruler over many things: enter thou into the joy of thy lord. He also that had received two talents came and said, Lord, thou deliveredst unto me two talents: behold, I have gained two other talents beside them. His lord said unto him, well done, good and faithful servant; thou hast been faithful over a few things, I will make you ruler over many things: enter thou into the joy of thy lord. Then he which had received the one talent came and said, Lord, I knew thee that th**afraid,**, and went and hid thy talent in the earth: lo, there thou hast that is thinou art an hard man, reaping where thou hast not sown, and gathering where thou hast not strawed: **And I was** e. His lord answered and said unto him, Thou wicked and slothful servant, thou knewest that I reap where I sowed not, and gather where I have not strawed: Thou oughtest therefore to have put my money to the exchangers, and then at my coming I should have received mine own with usury. Take therefore the talent from him, and give it unto him which hath ten talents. For everyone that hath shall be given, and he shall have abundance: but from him that hath not shall be taken away even that which he hath. And cast ye the unprofitable servant into outer darkness: there shall be weeping and gnashing of teeth. (Matthew 25:14–30, KJV)*

If we have talents[knowledge], we must use them to the betterment of ourselves and others, by teaching them the "Gospel of Jesus Christ" and bringing them into the fold of Christ. However, the keywords here are, **"And I was afraid"**. *So nothing got done.* This is what this riddle is talking about. If we give up or get sidetracked, we are only going to hurt ourselves, and our families. We can't afford to be lethargic or complacent because if we quit, the devil wins, and we lose our freedom. We must pray unceasingly and then do what we know is right. The only way Satan beats us is if we, as Christians, give up and quit believing in Christ and doing His will. The war has already been won, but what we, as God's people, need to do is endure and keep the faith and do everything we can do within our power. We must resist and teach the Left, not join them.

There is a time when all people will have to stand before God and be judged according to their works. All nations collectively will also stand and be judged according to what the people themselves allowed and tolerated to be put in place. If you look very closely, God is not happy with America entirely because of the immorality, the murders of babies, the Satan worship, the deceits and lies, the Democrats/liberals, the fraud and corruption that goes on, the growing amount of people turning to witchcraft.

America has erected symbols of Satan boldly, which offends God. America is supposed to be a Christian nation, but it has huge images standing as affronts to what a people of God will least be expected to tolerate. *"And there followed another angel, saying, Babylon is fallen, is fallen, that great city, because she made all nations drink of the wine of the wrath of her fornication"* (Revelation 14:8, KJV).

America, with its city of New York and Rome, Italy, both are competing for the label of this Babylon being talked about here. Which one is the most evil? They both will fall together.

*But these two things shall come to thee in a moment in one day, the loss of children, and widowhood: they shall come upon thee in their perfection for the multitude of thy **sorceries**, and for the great abundance of thine **enchantments**. For thou hast trusted in thy wickedness: thou hast said, None seeth me. Thy wisdom and thy knowledge, it hath perverted thee; and thou hast said in thine heart, I am, and none else beside me. Therefore shall evil come upon thee; thou shalt not know from whence it riseth: and mischief shall fall upon thee; thou shalt not be able to put it off: and **desolation** shall come upon thee suddenly, which thou shalt not know. Stand now with thine enchantments, and with the multitude of thy sorceries, wherein thou hast laboured from thy youth; if so be thou shalt be able to profit, if so be thou mayest prevail. Thou art wearied in the multitude of thy counsels. Let now the **astrologers**, the **stargazers**, the monthly **prognosticators**, stand up, and save thee from these things that shall come upon thee. Behold, they shall be as stubble; the fire shall burn them; they shall not deliver themselves from the power of the flame: there shall not be a coal to warm at, nor fire to sit before it. Thus shall they be unto thee with whom thou hast laboured, even thy merchants, from thy youth: they shall wander everyone to his quarter; none shall save thee. (Isaiah 47:9–15, KJV)*

France is predominantly a Catholic nation, pagan, and superstitious. America accepted a statue representing a pagan goddess, Ishtar, who is a harlot/whore, also named Libertas (Statue of Liberty). This is the idol that the Catholics are worshipping in their rosary when praying to Mary, Mother of God. Ishtar is the whore of the Catholic Church, with the ten horns on her head as talked about in Revelation and Daniel. By accepting this image and erecting it in America, we have offended God and have broken the first commandment: "Thou shalt have no other Gods before me." Besides this image, we have allowed other pagan religions to come to America and build their pagan churches and temples. Unless we address these problems and change, the judgments of an indignant God is hanging over America.

God talks about Rome, Italy, and the Catholic Church as Babylon, the great mother of harlots:

*And there came one of the seven angels which had the seven vials, and talked with me, Come hither; I will shew unto thee the judgment of **the great whore that sitteth upon many waters**. With whom the kings of the earth have committed fornication, and the inhabitants of the earth have been made drunk with the wine of her fornication. So he carried me away in the spirit into the wilderness: and **I saw a woman sit upon a scarlet coloured beast**, full of names of blasphemy, **having seven heads and ten horns**. And the **woman was arrayed in purple and scarlet colour**, and decked with gold and precious stones and pearls, **having a golden cup in her hand full of abominations** and **filthiness of her fornication**: And upon her forehead was a name written, "MYSTERY, BABYLON THE GREAT, THE MOTHER OF HARLOTS AND ABOMINATIONS OF THE EARTH." And **I saw the woman drunken with the blood of saints**, and **with the blood of martyrs** of Jesus: and when I saw her, I wondered with great admiration. And the angel said unto me, wherefore didst thou marvel? I will tell thee the mystery of the woman, and of the beast that carrieth her, which hath the seven heads and ten horns. The beast that thou sawest was, and is not; and shall ascend out of the **bottomless pit**, and **go into perdition**: and they that dwell on the earth shall wonder, whose names were not written in the book of life from the foundation of the world, when they behold the beast that was, and is not, and yet is. And here is the mind which hath wisdom. The **seven heads are seven mountains, on which the woman sitteth**. And there are seven kings: five are fallen, and one is, and the other is not yet come; and when he cometh, he must continue a short space, And the beast that was, and is not, even he is the eighth, and is of the seven, and goeth into perdition. And **the ten horns** which thou **sawest are ten kings**, which have received no kingdom as yet; but receive power as kings one hour with the beast. These have one mind, and shall give their power and strength unto the beast. These shall make war with the Lamb, and the Lamb shall overcome them: for he is Lord of lords, and King of kings: and they that are* *with him are called, and chosen, and faithful. And he saith unto me, The waters which thou sawest, where the whore sitteth, are peoples, and multitudes, and nations, and tongues. And the ten horns which thou sawest upon the beast, these shall hate the whore, and shall make her desolate and naked, and shall eat her flesh, and burn her with fire. For God hath put in their hearts to fulfill his will, and to agree, and give their kingdom unto the beast, until the words of God shall be fulfilled. And the woman which thou sawest is that great city, which reigneth over the kings of the earth. (Revelation 17:1–18, KJV)*

Verse 9 describes Rome, Italy, where the Vatican and the Catholic Church sit on the seven hills. There is no mistake.

America has made a great start by electing Donald Trump to be their president, but we must defeat the evil Democrats. The Democrats are simply the Communist Party in America. They obstruct all that is good. They are evil and selfish and seek the downfall of America. They are the "natural man" spoken of in the scriptures, they are in open rebellion against God, and they fight against Him. I have often said that if you don't love God, then it is impossible to love your fellow man. If you don't love your fellow man, then it is impossible to love God. We must vote all liberals out of our government but still continue to hold the gospel out to them to the end.

The Democrats/liberals are the breeding grounds for evolutionists, anti-God groups, gays, unions, welfare recipients, or any other special interest group or those seeking special favors from government. They are immoral people who want something for nothing. And all fit into a stereotype of what a liberal is and where they can be found.

Many liberals are changing as the Spirit of God enlightens their minds. This is because they are looking and paying attention. There has been a great awakening of minds as the WalkAway movement is underway, that is, walk away from the Democrats to the Christian/conservative side, from the left to the right. Everything a person believes in is made manifest in their actions. The line has been drawn in the sand. You are either on the right or on the left. There is no middle ground. *"And he shall set the **sheep on his right hand**, but the **goats on the left**" (Matthew 25:33, KJV).*

Rome, Italy is that Mystery Babylon spoken of in Revelation 14:8, and it is also mentioned in Jeremiah: *"O thou that **dwellest upon many waters**,* *abundant in treasures, thine end is come, and the measure of thy covetousness"* *(Jeremiah 51:13, KJV).* Revelation 18 is talking deliberately about New York, as well as Rome, as the described Babylon. There is Mystery Babylon (Rome), and then there is Babylon (New York City/America), depicting the woman sitting on the waters (Statue of Liberty), the ships and ship masters, and the merchants and commerce. New York City is the center for this world trade and commerce. It is to be cast into the ocean as the angel throws the millstone into the sea. The Lord is calling all good people who believe in God to come out of New York City so that it can be cast into the ocean.

*And after these things I saw another angel come down from heaven, having great power; and the earth was lightened with his glory. And he cried mightily with a strong voice, saying, **Babylon the great is fallen**, is fallen, and is **become the habitation of devils**, and the hold of every foul spirit, and a cage of every unclean and hateful bird. For **all nations have drunk** of the wine of the wrath **of her fornication**, and the kings of the earth have committed fornication with her, and the merchants of the earth are waxed rich through the abundance of her delicacies. And I heard another voice from heaven, saying, **Come out of her, my people**, that ye be not partakers of her sins, and that ye receive not of her plagues. For her sins have reached unto heaven, and God hath remembered her iniquities. Reward her even as she rewarded you, and double unto her double according to her works: in the cup which she hath filled fill to her double. How much she hath glorified herself, and lived deliciously, so much torment and sorrow give her: for she saith in her heart, I sit a queen, and am no widow, and shall see no sorrow. Therefore shall **her plagues** come in one day, **death**, and **mourning**, and **famine**; and she shall be **utterly burned with fire**: for strong is the Lord God who judgeth her. And the kings of the earth, who have committed fornication and lived deliciously with her, shall bewail her, and lament for her, when they shall see the smoke of her burning, Standing afar off for the fear of her torment, saying, Alas, alas, that great city! For in one hour is thy judgment come. For in one hour so great riches is come to nought. And every shipmaster, and all the company in ships, and sailors, and as many as trade by sea, stood afar off, And cried when they saw the smoke of her burning, saying, What city is like unto this great city! And they cast dust on their heads, and cried, weeping and wailing, saying, Alas, alas, **that great city**, wherein were made rich all that had ships in the sea by reason of her costliness! For in one hour is she made desolate. Rejoice over her, thou heaven, and ye holy apostles and prophets; for God hath avenged you on her. And a **mighty angel** took up a **stone like a***

great millstone, *and* **cast it into the sea**, *saying, Thus* **with violence shall that great city Babylon be thrown down**, *and* **shall be found no more at all**. *(Revelation 18:1–10, 17–21, KJV)*

We have watched as the mayor of New York City has, through city government and state legislators, passed and signed legislation approving pro-abortion laws, urging on the killing of our unborn children. We have watched as the anti-God sentiment and lethargy has risen greatly. We have witnessed the violence and crime escalate; the Satanism, the witchcraft, and so much more increase in New York City. It is the center of commerce for the world. The world stock market and even the center for the United Nations is found there. It has become a literal sewer for depravity of every kind. It is much worse than Sodom and Gomorrah.

America has been provoking God to anger for many years. The Left has become so evil, and it shows in the laws enacted such as pro-abortion laws, *Roe v. Wade*, the thinking of the mainstream media, the lying, the murders, the special interest organizations, the robbing, the gay agenda, the evolution beliefs, the growth in fraud perpetrators, the growing Satanism, the witchcraft, the removal of God from schools and all public facilities, the growing violence and making gods out of sports, and Hollywood. Crime is rampant, the open borders and immigration are out of control, and the Left is trying to destroy our country from within.

God has given our country another chance to repent/change, and it has been through the God-believing people, those who call themselves Christians who are stepping up and appealing to God for help in their time of need. We have watched our country deteriorate under each president and then really go downhill under Barack Obama. We now have a good, solid chance, so let's not waste it.

If we don't take advantage of our blessings, then God will judge America very harshly as spoken of in Jeremiah:

The burden of Babylon, which Isaiah the son of Amoz did see. Lift ye up a banner upon the high mountains, exalt the voice unto them, shake the hand, that they may go into the gates of the nobles. I have commanded my sanctified ones, I have called my mighty ones for mine anger, even them that rejoice in my highness. The noise of a multitude in the mountains, like as of a great people; a tumultuous noise of the kingdoms of nations gathered together: the Lord of hosts mustereth the host of the battle. They come from a far country, from the end of heaven, even the Lord, and the weapons of his indignation, to destroy the whole land. Howl ye; for the day of the Lord is at hand; it shall come as a destruction from the almighty. Therefore shall all hands be faint, and every man's heart shall melt: And they shall be afraid: pangs and sorrows shall take hold of them; they shall be in pain as a woman that travaileth: they shall be amazed one at another; their faces shall be as flames. Behold, the day of the Lord cometh, cruel both with wrath and fierce anger, to lay the land desolate: and he shall destroy the sinners out of it. For the stars of heaven and the constellations thereof shall not give their light: the sun shall be darkened in his going forth, and the moon shall not cause her light to shine, And I will punish the world for their evil, and the wicked for their iniquity; and I will cause the arrogancy of the proud to cease, and will lay low the haughtiness of the terrible. (Isaiah 13:1–11, KJV; compare *2 Nephi 23:1–11, Book of Mormon*; see *Alive after the Fall* by Alexander Cain as a good resource material).

America is this Mystery Babylon. *"A sound of battle is in the land and of great destruction. How is the **hammer of the whole earth** cut asunder and broken! How is **Babylon** become a desolation among nations! I have laid a snare for thee, and thou art also taken, O Babylon, and thou wast not aware: thou art found, and also caught, because thou hast striven against the LORD"* (Jeremiah 50:22–24, KJV).

When Christ comes again, the wicked are to burn as stubble. You see, everyone has been judged already; or else, why will God tell us that when He comes, the wicked will be burned? We are judging ourselves by the adherence we give or do not give to Christ's words. We are being judged in everything we say and everything we do and by the intents of our hearts, which only God can see entirely. Those who are filthy will be filthy still, and those who are clean will be clean still. *"He that is unjust, let him be unjust still: and he which is filthy, let him be filthy still: and he that is righteous, let him be righteous still: and he that is holy, let him be holy still"* (Revelation 22:11, KJV).

The plans of the wicked will go awry because God has His own plans and will do it His way. He has already written the end of the play. God is the author of the book. How arrogant of men/women to think that they can exalt themselves above God, thinking that they can enlist the help of such a one as Satan to get power and glory and honor. No wonder the scriptures talk about God sitting back and laughing at the futility of man. *"**They that shall see thee shall narrowly look upon thee**, and consider thee, saying, **Is this the man that made the earth to tremble, and did shake the kingdoms; God laughs at the arrogance of man**, for **after they are learned they think they are wise"** (Isaiah 14:16, KJV). "For the **wisdom of the world is foolishness** with God. For it is written, **He taketh the wise in their own craftiness"** (1 Corinthians 3:19, KJV). "**The Lord shall laugh at him**: for he seeth that **his day is coming**" (Psalm 37:13, KJV).*

The following is by Albert Einstein, when he humiliated a college professor while he was attending the university. This is very profound and true. (The author of this is unknown.)

Does Evil Exist?

The university professor challenged his students with the question, "Does evil exist? Did God create everything that exists? A student bravely replied, "Yes, He did!"

"God created everything?" The professor asked. "Yes, sir," the student replied.

The professor answered, "If God created everything, then God created evil since evil exists and, according to the principle that our works define who we are, then God is evil."

The student became quiet for a moment contemplating the implications of such an answer. The professor was quite pleased with himself and boasted to the students that he had proven once more that the Christian faith was a myth.

Another student raised his hand and said, "Can I ask you a question, professor?" "Of course," replied the professor.

The student stood up and asked, "Professor, does cold exist?"

"What kind of question is this? Of course it exists. Have you never been cold?" The students snickered at the young man's question.

The young man replied, "In fact sir, cold does not exist. According to the law of physics, what we consider cold is, in reality, the absence of heat. Everybody and every object is susceptible to study when it has or transmits energy, and heat is what makes a body or matter have or transmit energy. Absolute zero (-460 degrees F) is the total absence of heat; all matter becomes inert and incapable of reaction at that temperature. Cold does not exist. We have created this word to describe how we feel if we have too little heat." The student continued, "Professor, does darkness exist?"

The professor responded, "Of course it does."

The student replied, "Once again you are wrong sir. Darkness does not exist either. Darkness is, in reality, the absence of light. Light we can study, but not darkness. In fact, we can use Newton's prism to break white light into many colors and study the wavelengths of each color. You cannot measure darkness. A simple ray of light can break into a world of darkness and illuminate it. How can you know how dark a certain space is? You measure the amount of light present. Isn't this correct? Darkness is the term used by man to describe what happens when there is no light present."

Finally, the young man asked the professor; "Sir, does evil exist?"

Now uncertain, the professor responded, "Of course, as I have already said. We see it every day. It is in the daily example of man's inhumanity to man. It is in the multitude of crime and violence everywhere in the world. These manifestations are nothing else but evil."

To this the student replied, "Evil does not exist sir, or at least it does not exist unto itself. Evil is simply the **absence** of God. It is just like darkness and cold, a word that man has created to describe the absence of God. God did not create evil. Evil is not like faith, or love, that exist just as does light and heat. Evil is the result of what happens when man does not have God's love present in his heart. It's like the cold that comes when there is no heat or the darkness that comes when there is no light."

The professor sat down. The young man's name—**Albert Einstein.**

CHAPTER 6

The Infiltration of the Churches, i.e., the Mormon Church

Joseph Smith, the prophet of the Mormon Church, was, and is, a very great man. He was a true prophet of God, even as Moses, Elijah, Isaiah, and Jeremiah were prophets of God. He touched on every subject about God, including government, who we are, where we came from, why we are here, and where we are going for eternity. He became very educated about the things that pertained to the salvation of mankind. He truly did speak to God, and he truly did see our Father, Adam, and His Son, Jesus Christ, in real life, face-to-face as the prophets of old. I am sure that if Joseph Smith were alive today, he would identify the Father as being that same Adam who was in the Garden of Eden.

Joseph Smith was told by God, when he was about thirty, that if he lived to be to the age of eighty-five, he would see Christ and His Father return in Their glory, bringing the New Jerusalem with Them and restoring it back to the earth. Joseph Smith had done many wonderful things in the furtherance of knowledge for mankind. He translated the gold plates into what we now have as the *Book of Mormon*. He re-translated certain parts of the Bible, giving us greater understandings of key elements of concern regarding the scriptures. He had brought forth the *Pearl of Great Price* and the *Doctrine and Covenants*. He had sacrificed his time and energy to reestablish the true church of Jesus Christ on this earth, with the *"fullness of the gospel"*. He got involved in government and laid down his life for the truth and against corruption.

Through all this, the evil forces have continually, been fiercely at work, attempting to destroy the work of God and contradict the truth, which is Christ. When Joseph Smith and Oliver Cowdery were translating the *Book of Mormon*, evil men set about to steal the records and get in the way of God's work. Joseph Smith was tarred and feathered in an attempt to stop him. He had parts of his translations stolen, while they were in the possession of Martin Harris, to contradict the work of Joseph Smith and hinder his progress. The stolen transcript was done by a man called Solomon Spalding, who was a member of the Baptist Church.

Joseph Smith established the city of Nauvoo, Illinois, by draining a swamp and making a beautiful city. He had done countless things too innumerable to list. He even decided to run for president of the United States, which was probably what ultimately led to his death. He had begun surrounding himself with men who were envious and who were seeking his downfall for one reason or the other. He joined the Masons to get information they had about the ancient temple ceremony and received the first degree, but as what the church history disclosed, he was sorry he joined the Masons and discussed the need to repent for what he had done. However, because of the amount of members who supported him in it, he swiftly rose in ranks, along with his father, Joseph Smith Sr., and his elder brother, Hyrum Smith.

Joining the Masons or any other secret order is like joining a gang. Once you are sworn to secrecy and you learn all the organization's secrets, the only way out after that is feet-first. It was made known to Joseph Smith by God that he would be killed. *"I am going like a lamb to the slaughter; but I am calm as a summer's morning; I have a conscience void of offense towards God, and towards men. I SHALL DIE INNOCENT, AND IT SHALL BE SAID OF ME—HE WAS MURDERED IN COLD BLOOD"* (Doctrine and Covenants, section 135:4). Joseph Smith sealed his mission with his blood, like other prophets of old had done because they stood up for what they knew to be true.

Up to this time, Joseph Smith had talked about traitors and tyrants in and out of the church. Many members were excommunicated for failure to support the prophet due to a failed banking venture within the Mormon Church. Some of the members, who were also businessmen, had gotten it into their minds of riches and great success. They figured that they had a monopoly on knowing what the future held because they had in their midst a prophet of God who would tell them. I guess they were trying to use Joseph Smith as their private crystal ball to foretell the future. They staked everything on the idea and went forward, hounding Joseph about starting the bank until he gave in; and when their greedy plans didn't pay off, they either left the church or were excommunicated for apostasy. The cry went up that a prophet had fallen. That is the way liberals act. When they don't get their way, they throw tantrums, spin the truth, and accuse others of the exact thing that they either did or are doing themselves.

The Mormon Church had grown to be quite a good size by this time and was still growing by leaps and bounds. Surrounding neighbors had a hard time competing with the church in business dealings and therefore became offended, jealous, and envious, and some were scared. Joseph Smith made many unjustified enemies because of this, both inside and outside the church. There began to be much more persecution than usual. Rumors and lies began to spread, and propaganda was rampant, like it is today with fake news.

Joseph Smith was able to talk to God, he was a strong conservative, and he stood for freedom, so when he decided to run for president of the United States, he was a marked man. He almost assuredly would have won. Satan could not get anything past him while he was alive, and you can rest assured that the corruption at that time was just as dominant to the people then as it is in this time to us. If Joseph Smith had become president, it would have set the international bankers and the Roman Empire back forever, and the Left was not going to let that happen. Andrew Jackson, being elected in 1829–1837, set them back seventy-five years, and Garfield was killed in 1881 for promising to do the same, to keep the Federal Reserve bank from getting a foothold. This move meant everything to the Jesuits. So unless Joseph Smith was dead, this was the sort of thing that was going to happen. If Joseph Smith had been allowed to run for president, he would have followed Andrew Jackson's example in exactly the same mindset and belief in God, but he was killed in 1844 by the secret conspiracies to keep this from happening.

Here is a writing by Gerrit Dirkmaat in August 2017. He is talking about information gathered from some Council of Fifty notes:

By mid 1842 Joseph seemed to be gravitating towards the Whig Party, and the Whig party candidate, Henry Clay. Clay was a very well-known politician, the Great Compromiser, and he was seen as someone who was willing to defend the rights of the minority. I think Joseph had really put a lot of eggs into his basket. At any rate he decided to abandon the Democratic Party, I know it's really hard to believe, but almost every Mormon in the 1830s and 40s was a Democrat. This movement away is captured a little bit, you see a little bit of Joseph's angst, in probably the greatest quote ever given by Joseph Smith, but also the one that now all of you are going to misuse in a High Priest Group. As he was giving this interview to David Nye Wyler of the Pittsburgh Weekly Gazette, he says:

"I have sworn by the eternal gods that I will never vote for another Democrat again; and I intend to swear my children, putting their hands under the thigh, as Abraham swore Isaac, that they will never vote a Democratic ticket in all their generations. It is the meanest lowest party in all creation . . . the lowest, most tyrannical beings in the world. They opposed me in Missouri, and were going to shoot me for treason, and I had never committed any treason whatever." . . . Joseph wrote to all the people that had at least expressed interest in running, or people who thought they were running, and one by one, they all responded back to him—not all of them, but the ones that did respond—told him that they would not help the Mormons at all if they were to be elected. Finally, one of the ones he received was from Henry Clay. So Joseph goes from thinking he could support Henry Clay as a candidate for President, and Henry Clay said in a very high-minded way, very sympathetic, "oh, I felt so badly to see what has happened to your people, but as President there is nothing I could possibly do to help you out."

After this, Joseph Smith will declare himself to be a candidate for President, earning him the undying hatred of both the Whigs and the Democrats, so it probably wasn't the best move politically for the Mormons. But it is in this context, that Joseph is going to create the Council of Fifty. He has already declared himself a candidate for President, but at the same time, he knows that the Church is unlikely to find respite anywhere in the United States. It appears that Joseph Smith had plenty of enemies, who could not afford to let him live, whether for personal or political reasons.

On the morning of June 27, 1844, Joseph Smith, Hyrum Smith, John Taylor, and Willard Richards were incarcerated in Carthage, Illinois. The charges were manufactured—like the liberals do today, lying and deceiving to get their result—with the full intention of killing Joseph Smith. Only a few others accompanied the prophet to Carthage, but there was no indication that they stayed to guarantee his safety until a trial was held. You would reasonably believe that if they had suspicion that he would be killed, they would hang around to at least be witnesses. They may have been threatened with their lives or bribed, but either way, they were not there. These doubts would make a reasonable person believe there were many conspirators in the church itself.

That same night of being incarcerated, a mob stormed the Carthage Jail. Joseph Smith and his men were attacked by men using guns, and they were firing deadly rounds into the jail. Hyrum Smith was shot in the head as he slammed the door shut after Joseph fired through it, upon it being opened by an assailant. Joseph Smith killed one of his attackers, but he himself was shot several times before falling out a second-story window to the ground, where immediately some men in the mob emptied their guns into him. They wanted to make sure he was dead. There were five indicted for the murders, but none were convicted. It just goes to show that it is much easier to hide in a mob and then stack the jury, and you have a perfect murder.

I am convinced that this is the handiwork of the Jesuit order, like it is done time after time. As for the other two who accompanied Joseph Smith to Carthage, they were left cowering in the room. The mob didn't want them; they only wanted Joseph. It was a politically motivated killing. There was a representative from every government agency—including state, county, and local—in that mob. Some were politicians, some were military, and some were Masons—and there for the oath's sake. This mob was not just a bunch of lawless, ignorant drunken bums. These men in the mob were all deliberately and knowingly there for a specific purpose that had been calculated carefully. The secret orders of Satan were already in place in America to destroy it, and they didn't want some good man getting in the way, so they took this as an opportunity to get rid of him. The plan of Satan to destroy the freedom of man has been going on before the world began. The Jews, during Christ's time, did the same thing to Christ, thinking they were putting out the light of freedom and stealing His inheritance, but the light of freedom always flares up somewhere else.

I watched a DVD put out by a Seventh-day Adventist pastor. I could not recall his name, but I learned of the signal to be given by the Illuminati when all churches worldwide were to have been infiltrated by them. The sign to be given for the secret orders to recognize was when, for the first time ever, a president of the United States was to stand outside the capitol, facing the Washington Monument, giving his inaugural address. This happened on January 20, 1981, at the inauguration of Ronald Reagan as the fortieth president of the United States. He did it on the west front lawn of the United States Capitol in Washington, DC. This was the first inauguration to be held on the building's west side. So I asked myself, *If it is true that all the churches worldwide have been infiltrated by secret orders and the Illuminati, then how has the Mormon Church been infiltrated without noticing it?* Remember that it only takes changing small subtle things to change the whole meaning of something.

I have been a member of the Church of Jesus Christ of Latter-day Saints all my life. I fulfilled a mission for the church in Hong Kong, China, from 1977 to 1979. I would not have believed it then that the church could be infiltrated or has, but after being involved in government all these latter years, learning about the Constitution, and being active and watchful for our liberty in America, I discovered many ways that men and women in the past had been very subtle in treachery by their lies and deceits. I learned that it only takes changing little things, one at a time, to change a meaning or a direction of something good or bad. I had noticed subtle changes in doctrine of other churches, such as the Lutherans, Methodists, and Catholics. These all belong to the World Council of Churches, of course led by the Catholic Church. I would never have believed this about the Mormons as they were led by a prophet of God. I believed it to be impossible. I had a very hard time believing such a thing could happen without noticing it. I decided that if the church was really infiltrated by the Illuminati, then it must have been done early on, but they had to kill the prophet Joseph Smith to do it.

One day I received from my sister Radine a publication titled "The Death Bed Confessions of John Doyle Lee." It was in his own handwriting, and I still have it in my possession today. It was a confession by him about his part in the Mountain Meadows Massacre. He was admitting his involvement and that he carried it out at the order of Brigham Young, the Mormon prophet at the time, and outlined the involvement of many other men from the church. He talked about the murders of a whole wagon train on their way from Arkansas to California. It told how the Mormons, under the orders of Brigham Young, stirred up the Paiute Indians to attack the wagon train. He also outlined how the Mormons planned to make it look like they were rescuing the wagon train members by telling them to give up their arms so that the Indians wouldn't bother them.

Each male, accompanied by his wife and children, if any, from the wagon train would be accompanied by a male member from the church, walking alongside him through the Indians. The wagon train agreed to this proposal, thinking they had no other choice and trusting the members of the Mormon Church. It was planned between the Mormon members that, upon a signal by one of their designated leaders, they were to pull their guns and shoot the male member of the wagon train next to them. They then commenced killing every woman and child down to the age of eight. This was exactly what happened, but many children were killed below the age of eight; in fact, very few children were left.

Brigham Young then ordered the confiscation of all the cattle, money, and property belonging to people of the wagon train and made it disappear within the Mormon church. Any children remaining were farmed out to families in the church to be raised as one of their own, with the idea that these children would be too young to remember anything about the atrocity and that no one would miss them. However, the U.S. Army came later and ordered the investigation into the matter and the release of the remaining children. The army demanded answers, and so to save his own hide, Brigham Young offered up John Doyle Lee, who was shot by a firing squad as the only perpetrator.

In his account of this massacre, John Doyle Lee described that—after the killings—Brigham Young ordered all the men involved to the Salt Lake Temple for a special session, and there, were sworn to secrecy, to never divulge what had transpired. John Doyle Lee sealed his testimony with his own blood, while the many other Mormon men walked free. There was not one single case of excommunication. Brigham Young made sure he, himself, was hundreds of miles away so as to appear innocent. He was very intelligent and also very ambitious. One must first get the mindset of Brigham Young before one can believe that he would be capable of such treason and dastardly actions.

Here is another account of Brigham Young by a John G. Turner:

Turner is on the side of good history, and he generally negotiates the many "trip wires in the saint's history." For example, he unflinchingly recounts the notorious 1857 Mountain Meadows Massacre, in which Mormons and their Paiute Indian allies killed a group of emigrants from Arkansas. While he writes that Young encouraged the Indians to attack the wagon trains, Turner allows that no document directly links him to the horrific murders of 120 men, women and children. Turner notes that Young cynically billed the federal government for $3,527 worth of gifts supposedly distributed to "sundry bands of Indians near Mountain Meadows." The gifts— steers, clothing and butcher knives—had in fact been plundered from the slaughtered settlers. What Turner calls "the dark stain, the Mountain Meadows Massacre" left on Young's reputation remains to this day.

. . . Turner elucidates 19th century Mormon theology with sympathetic intelligence. He makes no secret of Young's espousal of "blood atonement," the "chilling perversion of the golden rule," which allowed Mormons to kill sinners before they were able to forsake salvation. "Will you love that man or woman well enough to shed their blood?" Young asked. "That is what Jesus Christ meant."

"Brigham Young was as tough as nails . . ." "Gold will sink a man to hell," he preached, "but he was something of a frontier dandy who ordered a bespoke watch from a London craftsman with the letters of his name substituted for the 12 hours." In 1859, he boasted to the newspaperman, Horace Greeley that he was worth $250,000, perhaps $7 million today. Brigham cruised the famously broad boulevards of Salt Lake City in a magnificent carriage imported by his eastern business agents, along with a dozen pairs "of best French kid gents gloves (goatskin, not sheepskin)" and opera glasses "nicely cased in roan calf instead of patent leather."

Brigham Young was also responsible for the organization called the Danites, who went about terrorizing the early Mormons in Utah, forcing them to his will. All this being true, then how can one say that Brigham Young was saved in the kingdom of God when King David fell because he conspired against only one of his captains, Uriah, to have him killed?

Brigham Young was a Mason before he ever joined the Church of Jesus

Christ of Latter-day Saints. He was already in the higher degrees of the Scottish rite of the Masons before he joined. That means that he knew all about the special signs and tokens and the execution of the penalties used by secret orders to accomplish works of darkness, and he still had many contacts in the east that helped him with his business dealings, making plenty of money, while most of his constituents in Utah were poor as church mice. Brigham Young demonstrated a coldness toward anyone, unless he wanted something from them. I believe that Brigham Young put these morbid signs and penalties in the temple ceremony, which served him and the others well when swearing them all to secrecy.

I grew up in the church being bombarded with the phrase or slogan "Follow the prophet" and going to the temple. I am thankful for the knowledge of what the church offers, as it is so rich. We, however, should never let someone think for us. Most members staple their salvation on the sleeves of one man, and that is the so-called prophet. We put ourselves in the same position as John Doyle Lee put himself in, willing to do someone's bidding, despite the dictates of their own consciences, and then get the shaft because of misplaced trust in some leader. This is what the Catholics do with the pope. They won't think for themselves and, because of this, are being led down to Hell. *"And my people, children are their oppressors, and women rule over them. **O my people, they who lead thee cause thee to err** and destroy the way of thy paths"* (2 Nephi 13:12, Book of Mormon; compare Isaiah 3, KJV). *"The ancient, he is the head; and the **prophet that teacheth lies**, he is the tail. For **the leaders of this people cause them to err; and they that are led of them are destroyed**"* (2 Nephi 19:15–16, Book of Mormon; compare Isaiah 9, KJV).

Finally, the day came that I was to leave on a mission for the Church of Jesus Christ of Latter-day Saints; but first, I was to attend the temple to get my "endowments." It was a great experience, I understand why these things are done, and I agree with the principle. There is nothing that goes on in the temple that is secret, but what goes on in the temple is special, except for what is called the "oath and execution of the penalty."

I went through three different rooms in the course of this session. Each room symbolized a degree of glory or kingdom. The first kingdom represented Satan's kingdom or the telestial glory/Hell, which is also a representation of the world. After the visit into each kingdom, we were told to stand and copy the attendee in administering the sign and token for that part of the session, swearing the oath to never divulge what we had learned in the temple that day, and then showing the execution of the penalty of what would happen to us if we were to do so.

Those of us in the room were told to hold our right hand in a certain position and repeat after the attendee that "I swear to never divulge what I learned in the temple that day," and at the same, I was to draw my right thumb across my belly in the symbology of disembowelment. The second room represented Christ's kingdom or the terrestrial kingdom. The sign was a hand at the appropriate position and drawing the right thumb across my breast or heart. The third room represented the presence of God or the celestial kingdom. The sign was the right hand to the square and drawing my right thumb across my throat while I was swearing to never divulge what I learned in the temple that day. Drawing the thumb across the throat is a representation of having the throat cut or losing one's head.

John Doyle Lee's mistake was to trust Brigham Young. He made his report to Brigham Young throughout the massacre, in writing, at Young's request. Brigham Young had calculated the need for this in the future as his ace in the hand, to be used if necessary to get his own neck and the others' necks off the chopping block.

Since April of 1990, the offering of the oath and penalty have been discontinued by one of the only other people I would have considered as a prophet, and that was Ezra Taft Benson. Ezra Taft Benson was the Mormon prophet from 1985 to 1994. These things being so morbid, it is a wonder that anyone would want to continue the temple ceremony when they saw where it was going. I still wonder about Ezra Taft Benson mysteriously losing his ability to speak toward the end of his life, and for that matter, Spencer W. Kimball lost his as well. Who was their doctor at the time? Both of them had the same doctor.

As discussed earlier, Joseph Smith joined the Masons to get knowledge of the ancient temple ordinances of Solomon's Temple. The temple ceremony was then adapted by Joseph Smith for the Nauvoo Temple in 1842 but was further developed by Brigham Young after Joseph Smith was gone, which would have been just after Joseph Smith was murdered in 1844. Heber J. Grant then revised the endowment in 1919. The endowment has even seen more change through Thomas S. Monson.

These signs and executions of the penalties used are the same symbols the Masons use, both Scottish and York rites. Bear in mind that the Masons have all been infiltrated by the Illuminati, which is a devilish organization of the Catholic Jesuits. These signs and tokens of the priesthood are one thing, but the execution of the penalties is another and added without any rhyme or reason except to be the small change to the temple ordinance to direct the people subtly into the devil's jurisdiction, and I believe that Brigham Young did that.

For the temple ordinance to be similar to the Masons' ritual is understandable as all Masons will trace their beginning to the days of King Solomon, who was responsible for building the first permanent temple. His temple was built around 587 BC. To do this, he contracted a person or master mason of stone named Hiram Abiff. Hiram knew about the temple ceremony, symbols, etc.; and from the Temple of Solomon, others tried to pervert and steal the secrets and proceedings, wanting to get to Heaven without obeying any commandments. In essence, too many people want a shortcut to everlasting life without any merit. Hiram Abiff was killed in the Temple of Solomon by other stoneworkers/masons because he wouldn't disclose secrets or sacred ceremony proceedings in relation to sacred temple ordinances.

Solomon employed many Phoenician bricklayers and stoneworkers to build the temple. Hiram Abiff was an Israelite from the tribe of Naphtali. There is mention of a Hiram in 1 Kings 7. One thing for sure is that the temple ordinances then most definitely predated the Masons today. Then, masons were a guild of a craft or trade; now a mason is still a trade but also gives connotation to a secret order. The Masons today are heavily infiltrated by the Illuminati and pollute our government, churches, and most businesses.

Most obviously, God revealed his proceedings in the Temple of Solomon's day in the ordinances placed there by holy men. It is very realistic then that instead of revealing it again, God just had to tell Joseph Smith where to find the information lost from the temple in Solomon's day. Therefore, it is understandable for Joseph Smith to join the Masons to get the knowledge and reinstate it into the temple of God. I also know that Joseph Smith talked about repenting and leaving the Masons, recorded in the church history. I have no doubt that Joseph Smith is and was a prophet of God.

Through the centuries, since Solomon's Temple, the ordinance has been perverted by unbelievers. It is like the Muslims butchering the five books of Moses to end up with the Koran. The Bible predates the Koran by far, just as the real or genuine temple ordinance predates the Masonic ceremony. So also, the Catholics perverted the tree and used it as a pagan symbol, but the tree in its pure form is a creation of God. They decorated it to symbolize worship to Satan, whereas the Christian sees the tree through different eyes and worships God in Heaven and His Son, Jesus Christ. The Masons stole the information they have from God or the people of God and not the other way around and then perverted it.

Joseph Smith, now accused of divulging the Masonic rituals to the members of the Mormon Church, made many enemies among the Masons and not just the Whigs and Democrats through politics. There were very many now who wanted him dead; in fact, there were many Masons involved in the killing of Joseph Smith, whether members of the church or those outside the church. The signs or penalties of death are evil, and this is the change in the ordinance of the temple. The members of the Church of Jesus Christ of Latter-day Saints are warned in their own standard works that these actions of swearing and showing of penalties by your hand going across the throat, as if to slit the throat or cut off the head or any part of their bodies, are evil and that the swearing to secrecy is a work of darkness and from the devil.

*And it came to pass that Cain took one of his brother's daughters to wife, and they loved Satan more than God. And Satan said unto Cain: **swear unto me by thy throat**, and **if thou tell it thou shalt die**; and **swear thy brethren by their heads**, and by the living God, that they tell it not; for if they tell it, they shall surely die; and this that thy father may not know it; and this day I will deliver thy brother Abel into thine hands. (Moses 5:28–29, Pearl of Great Price)*

*And it came to pass that they all sware unto him, by the God of Heaven, and also by the heavens, and also by the earth, **and by their heads**, that whoso should vary from the assistance which Akish desired, should lose his head; and whoso should divulge whatsoever thing Akish made known unto them, the same should lose his life. And it came to pass that thus, they did agree with Akish. And Akish did administer unto them the oaths which were given by them of old who sought power, which had been **handed down even from Cain**, **who was a murderer from the beginning**. (Ether 8:14–15, Book of Mormon)*

This is not in accordance with church teachings to do such things. The Church teaches as the Bible talks about:

*Again, ye have heard that it hath been said by them of old time, Thou **shalt not forswear thyself**, but shalt perform unto the Lord thine oaths: But I say unto you, **Swear not at all**; neither by heaven; for it is God's throne: Nor by the earth; for it is his footstool; neither by Jerusalem; for it is the city of the great King. Neither shalt thou **swear by thy head**, because thou canst not make one hair white or black. But **let your communication be**, **Yea, yea; Nay, nay**: for whatsoever is **more than this cometh of evil**. (Matthew 5:33–37, KJV)*

It struck me as very odd that the first time I entered the temple, I would encounter such a thing as swearing by my belly, my chest, and then my throat that I would never divulge what I learned in the temple when there was absolutely nothing to hide.

Soon after Joseph Smith's death, Brigham Young—the head of the twelve apostles—appeared in Nauvoo, Illinois, in a conference of the church to decide the direction of the Church of Jesus Christ of Latter-day Saints. The main concern was who would be the one to carry on where Joseph had left off. Since Brigham Young was the head of the apostles, he was chosen for this purpose while someone in the congregation seconded it by claiming that Brigham Young sounded like Joseph Smith. One would have to question this, knowing the craftiness of men. It had been done before where an individual or a group, having an underlying agenda, had one person openly state the idea, and one or two people in the group would then support it by an affirmative agreement. This somehow persuaded many people to ignorantly accept the original idea as gospel truth. This was a very slick way of deception, to put a man in there who could go about unhindered with the intent of subtly destroying the work of God and in such a way that would obscure the truth for generations. Granted, he did very much good for the church, but at what expense to the people?

Now knowing the character of Brigham Young, I would have to believe his being a prophet was a deception, as God has used His enemies many times to accomplish His goals. Brigham Young was calculating and intelligent and also devious. Joseph Smith often talked about traitors among the church members, and I am leaning in the belief that Brigham Young was one of those. *"They were innocent of any crime, as they had often been proved before,* and were only **confined in jail by the conspiracy of traitors and wicked men**" *(Doctrine and Covenants, section 135:7)*. Brigham Young was very clever, and we will probably never know for sure until we stand before God, and all our sins, if not repented of, will be shouted from the rooftops. There are many crimes committed by people that, even though you are sure they did it, you will never be able to prove.

Brigham young, as mentioned before, was a Mason before he joined the church. (See the "

Conjecture of the Origin of Mormon Violence; Brigham Young and De Smet). He was in the highest degree of the "Scottish Rite." The 33rd degree is linked to the Jesuit Order, which is the military arm of the Catholic Church. 33 symbolizes "The Great Work" which aids in Luciferian Worship. The Scottish Rite also controls Islam of the Muslims, and the Vatican City ultimately controls the Scottish Rite. The Jesuit soldier, (Peter) Pierre-Jean De Smet SJ, a good friend of Brigham Young, was in contact with Brigham Young, and he, through the Jesuit Order, influenced Brigham Young to move to the then, territory of Utah. Peter De Smet was a prominent Jesuit agent, one of many, who protected the Roman Catholic Pope's political and religious power throughout the world since the 1500's. ("Conjecture of the Origin of Mormon Violence; Brigham Young and De Smet")

Brigham Young's being linked to the Jesuit order was why he got off from the Mountain Meadows Massacre, and John Doyle Lee was served up as the stool pigeon. The change, made in the Church of Jesus Christ of Latter-day Saints, could only have been made by Brigham Young. Was it possible that the church had been infiltrated by him because he saw a way to get power and glory of man? The church could be infiltrated by simply changing the ordinances in the temples, by implementing the oath and execution of the penalties. Since then, these oaths and execution of penalties were administered to everyone who entered the temple up to 1990, when Ezra Taft Benson had them removed and discontinued. The members of the Church of Jesus Christ of Latter-day Saints, because of these signs and execution of the penalties, had been made into a bunch of traitors to the kingdom of God; therefore, Hell hath enlarged her mouth.

*Therefore **my people are gone into captivity**, because they **have no knowledge**: and their honourable men are famished, and their multitude dried up with* *thirst. Therefore **hell hath enlarged herself**, and opened her mouth without measure: and their glory, and their multitude, and their pomp, and he that rejoiceth, shall descend into it. (Isaiah 5:13–14, KJV)*

*The earth also is defiled under the inhabitants thereof; because **they have transgressed the law, changed the ordinance, broken the everlasting covenant**. There-fore hath **the curse devoured the earth**, and they that dwell therein are desolate: therefore **the inhabitants of the earth are burned**, and **few men left**. (Isaiah 24:5–6, KJV)*

Satan worship and witchcraft have escalated within the church, along with many other depraved practices, such as wife swapping, homosexuality, and lesbianism. The church has experienced a decline in membership due to young people losing their way because of peer pressures from the public school system. The church should be utilizing their beautiful church buildings with all their several classrooms to conduct private or home schools, thus boycotting the public schools.

The Mormons have become lethargic, lazy, and dependent on their leaders to guide them. They are no longer a "peculiar people" but are into the cares and sins of the world when, in reality, most of the leaders are guilty of the same sins themselves. The people insist on guaranteeing their salvation upon the advice and beliefs of a man who wants to be a one-man rule when the people should know for themselves. This kind of ignorance is destroying the next generation and turning them toward the liberal agenda, thus making slaves out of them.

So many members, both old and young, don't know how to act for themselves, thus unknowingly fighting against God. The church has allowed thieves and robbers to have temple recommends, as they claim to be worthy members of the church, such as IRS agents, Democrats, socialists, and bankers of the fiat money system. These people uphold and support our slavery, so how can they claim to be worthy members of the church? These are some of the very people who support the undermining of our freedoms of this great country.

The Church of Jesus Christ of Latter-day Saints, which I love, has literally been driven into the wilderness. *"And **the woman fled into the wilderness**, where she hath a place prepared of God, that they should feed her there a thousand two hundred and threescore days"* (Revelation 12:6, KJV). *"Hath **a nation** *changed their gods, which **are yet not gods**? But **my people hath changed their glory** for that which doth not profit . . . For **my people have committed two evils; they have forsaken me** the fountain of living waters, and hewed them out cisterns, broken cisterns, that can hold no water" (Jeremiah 2:11, 13, KJV). "Verily, thus saith the Lord unto you my servants, concerning the parable of the wheat and of the tares. Behold, verily I say, **the field was the world**, and **the apostles were the sowers of the seeds**; And after **they have fallen asleep** the great persecutor of the church, the apostate, **the whore, even Babylon**, that maketh all nations to drink of her cup, **in whose hearts** the enemy, even **Satan, sitteth to reign**—behold **he soweth the tares**; wherefore, **the tares choke the wheat** and **drive the church into the wilderness**" (Doctrine and Covenants, section 86:1–3).*

There are those leaders and members who believe and teach that the church of God cannot be destroyed, but that is not true. Every blessing or judgment we receive is dependent on our actions. Alma, in the *Book of Mormon*, says the church of God can be destroyed: *"Nevertheless, he cried again saying: Alma, arise and stand forth, for why persecutest thou the Church of God? For the Lord hath said: This is my church, and I will establish it; and nothing shall overthrow it, **save it is the transgressions of my people**"* (Mosiah 27:13).

Since Brigham Young, other changes had taken place in the temple. For instance, when I last attended the temple, the play describing the devil talking to Peter, James, and John discussed how he would rule the world. The actor was quoted as saying, as the devil that he, Satan, "will buy up popes and priests, and rule with blood and horror upon the face of this earth." This statement had now been changed to "I will buy up tyrants." Even Joseph Smith exposed who the real Antichrist is, even the pope of the Catholic Church; but now to be politically correct, Thomas S. Monson had made it tyrants. This helped subvert knowledge and leave the people in ignorance. Was this act done out of ignorance, or was it a knowing, deliberate action?

Thomas S. Monson, at the peak of uncovering Obama's forged birth certificate, and proving that Obama was born in Kenya, saved his bacon by presenting Obama with his genealogy, On July 20, 2009, and giving him an out. Harry Reid, who at that time was the senate majority leader, being a member of the LDS Church, a Democrat, certified that Obama was qualified to run for president.

Brigham Young started the decline in the Mormon Church, and many other alleged prophets afterward have contributed to it. I love the Church of Jesus Christ of Latter-day Saints, but I have learned to question everything, even if the church is led by prophets. Most of these alleged prophets are simply presidents of the corporate church/CEOs of a large corporation. Each one has run the church as a business and has caused a steady deterioration to the detriment of the people and the church collectively.

For instance, Brigham Young stated in the *Journal of Discourses* that "[Adam, a.k.a. Michael] is our Father and our God, and the only God with whom we have to do." I know this statement is true because it can be proven by the Bible. However, Joseph Fielding Smith—another alleged prophet—wrote a book called *Answers to Gospel Questions*. In this book, he stated that "Adam is not God." You would think that if he truly was a prophet, as alleged, then his knowledge would agree with that of Brigham Young's.

Members of the church lean on every word that an alleged prophet speaks, but now who do they believe? They can't believe both. Joseph Fielding Smith also is the author of section 138 of the *Doctrine and Covenants*. This is an alleged vision of Joseph Fielding Smith, where he sees our Father, Adam, and Brigham Young and others. He makes it appear that Brigham Young will be in the kingdom of God, but I seriously doubt it, knowing what I know about him. Such things give way to the steady change of everything Joseph Smith has instituted and the dismantling of the church from within.

Wilford Woodruff issued the "Manifesto of 1890", that ended the church from practicing plural marriage. The "Right to Religion" is protected under the Constitution, in the Bill of Rights, Article three [1st Amendment]. So, why are the leaders afraid to exercise their rights and recognize only Christ, instead of fearing what man can do? Where is their faith in Christ, instead of tucking tail and running at the first hint of trouble? They were not interested in being an example for the Truth, but were more interested in keeping their own hides out of conflict and out of jail.

Because of this action, and the support of the majority of the members of the church, the "Fullness of the Gospel" has been removed from among them, with the leaders now just going through the motions, building temples as monuments to what they have accomplished, while the temples remain empty, as compared to what they could be used for, if the church was honoring their Priesthood covenants, and was doing what is right for the benefit of everyone, other than themselves. Therefore they have sinned against the gospel of Jesus Christ, when they had received such great light.

"And thus commandeth the Father that I should say unto you: At that day when the Gentiles[LDS Church] shall sin against my gospel, and shall reject the fulness of my gospel, and shall be lifted up in the pride of their hearts above all nations, and above all the people of the whole earth [thinking they are better than others], and shall be filled with all manner of lying, and of deceits, and of mischiefs, and all manner of hypocrisy, and murders, and priestcrafts, and whoredoms, and of secret abominations; and if they shall do all those things, and reject the "Fullness of my Gospel", behold, saith the Father, I will bring the "fulness of my gospel [priesthood covenant & new and everlasting marriage covenant]" from among them. [authority of the priesthood, and the New and Everlasting covenant/Plural marriage] (3 Nephi 16:10-12, Book of Mormon)

"Woe unto them that decree unrighteous decrees, and that write grievousness which they have prescribed;" "To turn aside the needy from judgment, and to take away the right from the poor of my people, [violate their oaths of office/join with the beast/corporate system] that widows may be their prey, and that they might rob the fatherless!" (Isaiah 9:1-2 KJV)

There are many young ladies in the church who really believe in the teachings of the church, but they are left holding to a hope that some good man will come along and want to marry them and take them to the temple and be married for time and all eternity. There appears to be more good women than men who wish to be obedient to God's commandments, who really want to believe, and are seeking to obtain the "*Celestial Kingdom*" and return again to the presence of their Father in Heaven. The reason for plural marriage was because of this thing. Women could be sealed to one good man, thus making it possible for every believing woman to have a family in this life, and be able to live the law upon which the principles of the Celestial Kingdom is predicated.

Where are all of the righteous young men who are "*Valiant*" *in the* faith of Jesus Christ? Doesn't Christ say in the New Testament, that no one is either given or taken in marriage after this life? "*For when they shall rise from the dead, they neither marry, nor are given in marriage; but are as the angels which are in heaven." (Mark 12:25, KJV) Also see (Matthew 22:30, KJV).*

What Wilford Woodruff had done, has "*Changed the ordinance and has broken the Covenant*" of the "Law of the Priesthood". "*The earth is also defiled under the inhabitants, because they have transgressed the laws, Changed the ordinance, Broken the "everlasting covenant." Therefore the curse has devoured the earth, And those who dwell in it are desolate. Therefore the inhabitants of the earth are burned, And few men are left." (Isaiah 24:5, KJV)*

When are the people, especially the good women who truly believe, going to realize that they are being lied to understand, then do what Isaiah has talked about? "*And in that day seven women shall take hold of one man, saying, we will eat our own bread, and wear our own apparel: only let us be called by thy name, to take away our reproach." (Isaiah 4:1, KJV)* The problem is that there are so few courageous men with knowledge of the Constitution and the things of God, that are stumbling blocks for good women. *Such* things have contributed to the steady change of everything Joseph Smith has instituted and the dismantling of the church from within.

*"Therefore shall the Lord, the Lord of hosts, send among his fat ones leanness; and under his glory he shall kindle a burning like the burning of a fire.""And the light of **Israel shall be for a fire,** and his **Holy One for a flame;** and it shall burn and devour his **thorns and his briers[world] in one day;**""And it **shall consume the glory of his forest[church],** and his **fruitful field, both soul and body:** and they shall be as when a standard bearer fainteth.""And the **rest of the trees of his forest shall be <u>few, that a child may write them.</u>**""And it shall come to pass in that day, that the remnant of Israel, and such as are escaped of the house of Israel,and such as are escaped of the house of Jacob, **shall no more again stay upon him[Satan/corporate system] that smote them;**but **shall stay upon the Lord, the Holy One of Israel, in <u>truth.</u>**"(Isaiah 10:16-20, KJV)compare 2 Nephi 20, Book of Mormon.*

Ezra Taft Benson wrote a book called *An Enemy Hath Done This.* He talked about what was happening within the church. Maybe he was talking too much, so all of a sudden, he ended up not being able to speak anymore. Was that coincidence? How about Spencer W. Kimball, who all of a sudden lost his speech?

There was an apostle in the church who addressed the students at Brigham Young University in a speech in 1994 at the Freedom Festival. He told them at that time that there was nothing to be alarmed about within our government. He encouraged the people to not be concerned about things going on in our government but to be a good citizen; one only needed to get involved in things like scouts and other civic activities. He said that in all his twenty-five years as an attorney, he had not seen anything in our government for the people to be alarmed about. Meanwhile, every Democratic president and senator and representative is spewing their lies, putting into place bad laws and programs that destroy our freedoms, such as the IRS, United Nations, the North American Free Trade Agreement, the Iran deal, welfare, and the Federal Reserve bank, not to mention the ten planks of *The Communist Manifesto*. The list goes on and on. The church leaders cause much lethargy and ignorance among the members, and no wonder, they support the Democratic Party. The members fall in line behind their leaders, because they think that their leaders would never lie to them. They pick up the chant, "follow the prophet".

He didn't tell the young people to watch out for the lies or deceits by the Left. He told outright lies himself, or he was truly asleep like so many of them. It seems as if the leaders are deliberately steering the people away from the truth when the truth is right in front of them. It seems that if the leaders were up to much, they would be telling the young people about current events, about bad laws and programs, who to support, what to watch out for, about homeschooling their children. They won't tell them these things because the church is incorporated through the 501(c)(3) charter, making it a state church, and the leaders may themselves be liberal-minded people or Jesuit agents. They don't want to lose their preferred tax status; therefore, the churches have become politically correct and very charismatic about important political issues. Many of the leaders themselves—including alleged prophets, apostles, and bishops—have had questionable behavior and actions, which do not inspire faith in the leaders.

The 501(c)(3) is an infiltration by the Illuminati into the church in and of itself. On top of all that, the alleged prophet is the CEO of the Corporate Church, and he receives a salary (living allowance) yearly of up and around $120,000.00 per year, supposedly from business investments of the church and not taken from the tithing. (See The Salt Lake Tribune January 26,

2017). Others in the first presidency make close to the same, as they are also executive officers of the corporation. They wouldn't want to lose their salaries by telling the truth, about the IRS, or other government entities. It appears that the leaders are using the Church as a front, at the people's expense to run a *"tax exempt racket"* for creating wealth for themselves.

So, here is the tradeoff between the IRS and the leaderships of all incorporated churches. The leaders get to pay themselves all of the money they wish and be "tax exempt", but they must keep their congregations/the masses, silent and ignorant to the facts about government, including the IRS, in order to maintain their *"tax exempt status"*. Anyone who steps up with truth and knowledge about government, are immediately silenced in the churches and seen as contentious and rebellious, and they are avoided. Therefore, those who would stand up for theirs, and others Constitutional Rights are shunned in one way or another and discredited.

You can put any label on the money received by leaders from their incorporated businesses(church), but to be incorporated you must make contract with the IRS. When you hold hands with the devil, and rely on his permission to operate, then it is he to whom you are subject to. No matter how you look at it, this is *"priestcraft"*. It perhaps would be better that the church leaders get paid from the *"Tithing"* In order for the people to show their charity, rather than depend upon the <u>world</u> for their employ. From *"Sole Proprietorship", small "LLCs", to small to big corporations,* you must sign the documents that make contract with the IRS, and you agree to be compliant with them. You can be unincorporated and still have the right to do business. The *"DBA" (Doing Business As)* entity is all you need. This type of business is unregistered and protected under the *"Article 11"*[ninth amendment] of the Bill of Rights, of the Constitution. All people, including men, women, and children, have the **<u>right to life, liberty, and the pursuit of happiness.</u>** You have the right to do business just because you can.

*"He commandeth that there shall be **<u>no priestcrafts</u>**; for, behold, **priestcrafts** are that men preach and set themselves up for a light unto the **<u>world</u>**, that they may **get gain and praise of the <u>world</u>**; but they seek not the welfare[freedom] of Zion." Behold, the Lord hath **forbidden** this thing; wherefore, the Lord God hath given a commandment that all men should have **charity**, which **charity is love**. And except they should have charity they were nothing. Wherefore, if they should have charity they would not suffer the laborer in Zion to perish."*

*But the laborer in **Zion shall labor for Zion; for if they labor for <u>money</u> they shall perish.**" (2 Nephi 26:29-31 , Book of Mormon)* Compare: *"Feed the flock of God which is among you , taking the oversight thereof, **not by constraint[contract], but willingly; not for filthy lucre,** but of a ready mind;"(1 Peter 5:2, KJV)*

All of these things, which are only a few examples, cause the church of God to slow down in its progress. The church claims a lot of membership, but how many of its members are actually active, and how many are members in name only? No one is perfect, but to lie and to deceive at the cost of our brothers and sisters also offends God, destroys His work, and neutralizes its effectiveness, causing confusion and disparity.

*"Yea, for thus saith the Lord: Have I put thee away, or have I cast thee off forever? For thus saith the Lord: where is the bill of your mother's divorcement? To whom have I sold you? Behold, **for your iniquities ye have sold yourselves,** and for your transgressions **is your mother put away**" (2 Nephi 7:1, Book of Mormon). see (Isaiah 50:1, KJV)*

This is talking about the corruption in the church and selling themselves into the corporate system. The leaders themselves are interested in making a lot of money, but do not encourage the **Freedom** that is endowed upon the people by God.

*And my people, children are their oppressors, and women rule over them, O my people, **they who lead thee cause thee to err** and destroy the way of thy paths. . .. Therefore, **my people are gone into captivity,** because **they have no knowledge;** and their honorable men are famished, and their multitude dried up with thirst. Therefore, **hell hath enlarged herself,** and opened her mouth without measure; and their glory and their multitude, and their pomp, and he that rejoiceth, shall descend into it. . .. They wear stiff necks and high heads; yea, and because of pride, and wickedness, and abominations, and whoredoms, **they have all gone astray save it be a few,** who are the humble followers of Christ; nevertheless, they are led, that in many instances they do err because they are taught the precepts of men. (2 Nephi 13:12, 15:13–14, 28:14, Book of Mormon)*

Joseph Smith warned the leaders of the church about the judgments to come on the church in the latter days. The revelation was directed at Thomas B.

Marsh, who at that time was the president of the Quorum of the Twelve Apostles of the Church of Jesus Christ of Latter-day Saints (the Mormons). Thomas B. Marsh was not long after this, excommunicated. In this section, God told him how judgments would come on the church but first among the leaders of the apostles at the top.

*In as much as they shall humble themselves before me, and abide in my word, and hearken to the voice of my Spirit. Verily, verily. I say unto you, **darkness covereth the earth**, and gross darkness the minds of the people, and **all flesh has become corrupt** before my face. Behold, **vengeance cometh speedily upon the inhabitants of the earth**, a day of wrath, a day of burning, a day of desolation, of weeping, of mourning and of lamentation; and as a whirlwind it shall come upon all the face of the earth, saith the Lord. And **upon my house shall it begin**, and **from my house shall it go forth**, saith the Lord. **First among those among you**, saith the Lord, **who have professed to know my name and have not known me**, and **have blasphemed against me in the midst of my house**, saith the Lord. (Doctrine and Covenants, section 112:22–26)*

I can honestly say that most members who have attended any temple and made covenants there before the Lord have broken every single covenant they have ever made. Covenants are promises you make before God. At baptism, we covenant with God to do three specific things: (1) we promise to take upon ourselves the name of Jesus Christ by swearing allegiance to Him and His kingdom; (2) we promise to obey His commandments, listening to Him only; and (3) we will carry each other's burdens, and we will love our fellow man. That means that we will only support righteous laws.

After making these promises, it is easy to then go on with life not thinking about what this means. At the moment, we made vain promises because it takes a lifetime to live up to these promises. Ask yourself, "What laws do I uphold? Do the laws I support or the desires I have for myself honor God or Satan? Do the laws I support or fund, help me and my fellow man, or am I supporting slavery and oppression of myself and my fellow man, such as *Roe v. Wade*, which is a law supporting abortion?"

What are you doing about it? Are you part of the silent majority and complacent about it, thus giving it a yes vote? Or are you up and doing something about it, raising your voice in objection, helping fund pro-life movement groups? What about other unconstitutional laws like the Sixteenth Amendment? What about land taxes, also unconstitutional? What about *Erie v. Tompkins*, which destroys our common law and replaces it with commercial law? What about the Emergency War Powers Act, which keeps America in a perpetual state of war, among others? These are many of those that violate the freedoms we hold dear. What about *The Communist Manifesto*, which threatens every freedom we hold dear?

An apostle in the church, referring to the income tax, and other issues, said there was nothing in all his twenty-five years as an attorney that we needed to be concerned about. That apostle was Dallin Oaks. Do you believe him after having knowledge of these things and more? There are no gray areas. Every area is either black or white; there is no middle ground. The line has been drawn and is right in front of us. All laws either grant or destroy our freedoms, and we need to choose. We need to educate ourselves about the Constitution and the scriptures so that we know for ourselves what side of the line we are on. We need to ask ourselves, "Are the laws constitutional or not? Does the law violate God's law or not? Do land taxes oppress or give freedom? Does the IRS bless you and your brother or oppress?" Both answers are oppression because they are unconstitutional.

The people take it for granted that their leaders won't lie to them, but that is what they do in very subtle ways until you are bound with the chains or contracts of Hell through the corporate system. I always tell people that I can see a liberal/communist/socialist a mile away. They just need to open their mouths or do some act. Satan's people are very selfish, so much so, that they can readily be seen for who they are. They are the evolutionists, the atheists; they are deep in the LGBT groups, but not all are liberal because there are many who are just simply ignorant and don't know what they are until they have knowledge and able to make an educated decision. There are the unions, which are breeding grounds for liberals because they are only interested in benefits.

Liberals are anti-God; they are always ready to contradict God, as they want to cover their selfish actions. Liberals are immoral and usually 100 percent fact-free and ignorant. They are also lazy and mean, and many are on welfare and favor government handouts. They want everything free. Liberals include Democrats who take up space in Congress and obstruct, and they want to give everything away free; they want high taxes to do their welfare programs. They do crimes readily such as voter fraud, embezzlement, and pedophilia, and they are involved in organized crime and agents for foreign countries. They are traitors and liars. Democrats appear to have no honor and integrity. They manipulate, scheme, and even kill if they can get away with it, and some do, especially those who have power and money. At least they get away with it for now, but since they don't believe in God or just outright reject God, they aren't giving any consideration to the fact that someday they are going to still stand face-to-face with our Father in Heaven, and their sins will be shouted from the rooftops.

Leaders of the church have embraced the world, and as Spencer W. Kimball, also a former president of the church, once said, "The members of the Church are no longer a peculiar people." How can they be within the public school system?

Gordon B. Hinckley, a former president of the church, during the Winter Olympics, in Utah, in 2002, shook hands with the secretary of the United Nations in a Masonic handshake and said what a fine man he was. I had a bishop who bragged to my wife how he and his wife invited the first councilor and his wife over on Mondays to their home for family home evening and then spent the evening playing the Ouija board together. Thomas S. Monson was sighted at the opening ceremonies of the London Summer Olympic Games on television with Pope Benedict by my son and another family friend, but soon after was nowhere to be seen again. The opening ceremonies constituted the crusade for pro-abortion.

Just recently, March 9, 2019, Pres. Russell M. Nelson met with Pope Francis inside the Vatican and later to the media was exclaiming, "What a most cordial, unforgettable experience! **His Holiness,** he was most gracious and warm and welcoming."

He continued, "What a sweet, wonderful man he is, and how fortunate the Catholic people are to have such a gracious, concerned, loving and capable leader." Seriously? The president of the Mormon Church, supposedly holding Christ in the highest esteem, turned and called a pagan "His Holiness?" putting him on the same pedestal as Jesus Christ.

Back in the Reformation period, in the Dark Ages, the Catholic Church viewed the Christians or conservatives as liberal. Here is a partial oath the

Jesuits take to be inducted into their brotherhood. As you read this, ask yourself if it sounds like someone you know.

I do further declare that the doctrine of the churches of England and Scotland, of the Calvinists, Huegonots, and others of the name Protestants or liberals to be damnable and they themselves damned who will not forsake the same.

I do further declare, that I will help, assist, and advise all of any of **his Holiness**' agents in any place wherever I shall be in, Switzerland, Germany, Holland, Denmark, Sweden, Norway, England, Ireland, or **America**, or in any other kingdom or **territory** I shall come to, and do my uttermost to extirpate the heretical Protestants of Liberals' doctrines and to destroy all their pretended powers, regal or otherwise.

I do further promise and declare, that notwithstanding I am dispensed with, to assume my religion heretical, for the propaganda of the Mother Church's interest, to **keep secret** and private all her agents' counsels from time to time, as they may entrust me and **not divulge**, directly or indirectly, by word, writing or circumstance whatever; but to execute all that shall be proposed, given in charge or discovered unto me, by you, **my ghostly father,** or any of this **sacred covenant**.

I do further promise and declare, that I will have no opinion or will of my own, or any mental reservation whatever, even as a corpse or cadaver (perinde ac cadaver), but will unhesitatingly obey each and every command that I may receive from my superiors in the **Militia of the Pope** and of Jesus Christ.

That I may go to any part of the world withersoever I may be sent, to the frozen regions of the north, to the burning sands of Africa, or the jungles of India, to the center of civilization of Europe, or to the wild haunts of the barbarous savages of **America**, without murmuring or repining, and will be submissive in all things whatsoever communicated to me.

I furthermore promise and declare that I will, when opportunity presents, make and wage relentless war, secretly or openly, against all heretics, Protestants and Liberals, as I am directed to do, to extirpate and exterminate them from the face of the whole earth; and that I will spare neither age, sex or condition; and that I will hang, waste, boil, flay, strangle and bury alive these infamous heretics, rip up the stomachs and wombs of their women and crush their infant's heads against the walls, in order to exterminate forever their execrable race. That when the same cannot be done openly, I will secretly use the poisoned cup, the strangulating cord, the steel poniard or the leaden bullet, regardless of the honor, rank, dignity or authority of the person or persons, whatever may be their condition in life, either public or private, as I at any time may be directed so to do by any agent of the Pope or Superior of the Brotherhood of the Holy Faith, of the Society of Jesus.

In confirmation of which, I hereby dedicate my life, my soul, and all my corporal powers, and with this dagger which I now receive, I will subscribe my name written in my own blood, in testimony thereof; and should I prove false or weaken in my determination, may my brethren and fellow soldiers of the Militia of the Pope cut off my hands and my feet, and my throat from ear to ear, my belly opened and sulphur burned therein, with all the punishment that can be inflicted upon me on earth and my soul be tortured by demons in an eternal hell forever. (See "Conjecture of Origins of Mormon Violence; Brigham Young and De Smet, Exmormon.org)

The Mormon Church has become polluted and has been so for a long time and is becoming steadily worse. The prophet Mormon, in the *Book of Mormon*, has something to say about this.

*Behold, the Lord hath shown unto me great and marvelous things concerning that which must shortly come, at that day when these things shall come forth among you, Behold, **I speak unto you as if ye were present**, and yet ye are not. But behold, **Jesus Christ hath shown you unto me and I know your doing**. And I know that ye do walk in the pride of your hearts; and there are none save a few only who do not lift themselves up in the pride of their hearts, unto the wearing of very fine apparel, unto envying, and strifes, and malice, and persecutions, and all manner of iniquities; and **your churches**, yea, **even every one**, **have become polluted** because of the pride of your hearts. For behold, ye do love money, and your substance, and your fine apparel, and the adorning of your churches, more than ye love the poor and the needy, the sick and the afflicted. O **ye pollutions**, **ye hypocrites**, **ye teachers**, **who sell yourselves** for that which will canker, **why have ye polluted the Holy Church of God**? Why do ye not think that greater is the value of an endless happiness than that misery which never dies—because of the praise of the world? (Mormon 8:34–38, Book of Mormon)*

Ask yourselves, just who are the teachers Mormon is talking about? They are the ones we depend on for guidance and direction. They are the alleged prophets and apostles, that Mormon is talking about. *"The ancient and honourable, he is the head; and the prophet that teacheth lies, he is the tail"* (Isaiah 9:15, KJV).

When a member of the Mormon Church goes to the temple, there, he/she makes a covenant that he/she will build up the kingdom of God, even if it means sacrificing his/her own life, if necessary, but it is just lip service only. The moment they leave the temple, that covenant has already been broken. This covenant goes deeper than just words. Christ was asked, "What is the greatest commandment?" He replied, "First, love God with all your heart, might, mind, and strength. And the second is like unto it: love your neighbor as yourself. On these two hangs all the commandments." Simply put, if you love God first, then your neighbor/fellow man will be blessed; and if you love your neighbor/fellow man, then you and your family will be blessed, and it shows that you love God. If we can simply remember these two things, then we are automatically going to support laws that bring freedom to one another. If we are selfish and want to discredit God, then we will uphold laws that oppress our neighbor/fellow man, to hide our own sins.

The bottom line is this: When the leaders go about with a blind eye to things, and are themselves comfortable in their own servitude, and deny that anything is happening, then they are showing a bad example to the people. If things are happening and they don't see it or don't want to see it, then it is very hard to put any faith on these leaders. There were several instances in the past where members were excommunicated from the LDS Church for not cooperating with the IRS, when even the blindest of them all could see that the IRS is a huge lie.

The leaders choose instead, to persecute their own and live a great, big lie. Will you respect such leaders who walk around blind, trying to lead those that see? Only the blind will follow such leaders, for when the blind lead the blind, then they all fall in the ditch. Leaders from all churches can sure teach a good sermon, but either their knowledge of the lies has escaped them or they are like an ostrich and bury their heads in the sand. If the leaders really lead, then Satan won't get any foothold. *"Let them alone: they be blind leaders of the blind. And if the blind lead the blind, both shall fall into the ditch"*

(Matthew 15:14, KJV).

I believe the answer to why the churches cover for the wickedness of the government is 501(c)(3) charters. They have joined themselves to the beast or corporate system, thus muzzling the clergy about what can be said in church and what points must be discouraged to the members. The churches are selling out their own people.

The leadership of the Church of Jesus Christ of Latter-day Saints was the first church to shut down at the beginning of the alleged coronavirus pandemic, beginning March 12, 2020. The church doesn't plan on reopening again until after Labor Day in September, 2020. President Trump came out on May 22, 2020 and called on governors to allow the churches to reopen now. *"I call on governors to allow our churches to open right now".* It shows that despite President Trump telling the churches to open, instead of Russell M. Nelson, and the first presidency supporting him, they chose to follow after the liberal agenda, by keeping the Church closed long after May, and are not decided if, and when it will reopen in September. Where is the exhibition of faith in the priesthood, so freely spoken of by the Church of Jesus Christ of Latter-day Saints? By what the leaders of the Mormon Church are doing, is a clear indication of where their allegiance lies, and it is with the Democrats, whose agenda it is to disrupt the November, presidential election if they can.

*"And let us consider one another to provoke unto love and to good works," **Not forsaking the assembling of ourselves together,** as the manner of some is, but exhorting one another: and as **much the more**, as ye see the day approaching."* (Hebrews 10:24-25, KJV)

It showed how willing the big incorporated churches were to give up their God-given rights. Even when the leaders of government such as several liberal governors began making executive orders restricting gathering for worship to our Heavenly Father, they shut down the right to travel; they shut down the ability of the people to work. Businesses closed their doors; people lost their jobs that they depended on to feed their families. Even when government leaders were wrong, the leaders of churches quoted from the Bible, Romans 13. This was exactly what Hitler did to get the Christians' support before the Holocaust. Do you suppose the Christians back then will have any sins to answer for?

If and when martial law will be declared and enacted because of some alleged pandemic, orchestrated so subtly by the Left, families will be separated at the behest of government officials; and the clergy, whom we are supposed to trust, will be used to comfort the family members by putting great emphasis on Romans 13 and twisting it to suit their purposes. You can see how dangerous it is to follow leaders blindly, especially in these incorporated churches where there is a one-man rule.

While Obama was president, he instituted the National Defense Authorization Act. This act has the ability to take U.S. citizens into custody for any reason and hold them indefinitely without being charged of a crime (section 1022, subsection [c][1]). Pastors are to be used as "calmers" and "informants" on their own congregations.

Secretly, government officials and church leaders from various organizations started what is known as the "clergy response team". A religious leader by the name of Walt Mansfield helped pioneer the clergy response team, where thousands—as many as twenty-eight thousand—of 501(c)(3) church leaders had signed up to help government officials in times of emergency. When he realized what this was, he came forward and became a "whistle blower" to get the people's attention. Mark Taylor says now, that there is over a million church leaders willing to do the bidding of so-called government officials.

According to the Daily Caller, in 2012, Representative Cleaver—then the head of the Congressional Black Caucus—headed up a meeting with black clergy from the Conference of National Black Churches at the U.S. Capitol, along with representatives from ACLU, the IRS, and Eric Holder, the secretary of state under Obama. Cleaver clearly stated that the purpose of the meeting was to equip the religious leaders with what they need to know about what they can and cannot say in the churches that will violate their 501(c)(3) status. This should not come as a great surprise to many of us, who for many years have wondered why the leaders of the churches don't shout the truth from the pulpits, but instead, are hush-hush about what government, Democrats, and GOP allies are doing. What I have realized is that if we want to remain a free people, then we need to do what is right, despite church leaders who are selling us out.

In about 1995–1996, I wanted to tell the people all around me about the lies being told by our government, especially about the IRS. I was in the church house in the hallway, one Sunday, in the Rathdrum Ward of the Church of Jesus Christ of Latter-day Saints. I was talking about government to a member, and another member overheard us speaking privately. She immediately went to the Bishop at the time, and He called us both into his office. He clearly told me specifically and the other member I was speaking to that we were not to talk about government or politics in the church. I reacted by telling him that what I talked about to another member privately was my business and that whenever someone asked me a question or wanted to know about a certain issue, then I was going to spill my guts, and no one was going to tell me otherwise. So rather than go to church to fight the people there every Sunday, because that was what it was beginning to feel like, my family and I simply quit going. We dreaded going someplace where the people would rather believe lies and there was a spirit of contention.

Here are some facts that I have talked about for many years as the pollution of the churches by incorporating under the 501(c)(3) charter. Going to Worldslastchance.com, this person has hit the nail on the head about how the 501(c)(3) charter destroys the freedom of our churches. "To submit to government oversight, is to submit to government control." He goes on to say:

"When a church accepts the 501(c)(3) status, that church: 1) waives its' freedom of speech. 2) waives its' freedom of religion. 3) waives its' right to influence legislators and the legislation they craft. 4) waives its' Constitutionally guaranteed rights. 5) is no longer free to speak to the vital issues of the day. 6) becomes controlled by a spirit of fear, that if it doesn't toe the line with the IRS, it will lose[revoke] it's tax-exempt status. 7) It becomes a State Church."

"When the church incorporates under the 501(c)(3) rules suggests that the primary function of a tax-exempt organization is to act on behalf of the government in carrying out governmentally approved policies. When a church incorporates as a 501(c)(3) entity with the government, it agrees to be bound by all the rules and laws governing the 501(c)(3) corporations. A church which has filed a 501(c)(3) application has agreed to forego its Constitutional right to practice religion without government interference."

There you have it, and we should be paying attention to what our leaders are and are not saying. In the Church of Jesus Christ of Latter-day Saints specifically, the ones who help the enemy because of their precious 501(c) (3) tax status are not only the first presidency but also every level of the church, throughout the stakes, wards, branches, quorums, priesthood, and ladies' organizations etc.. The people have become so brainwashed that they don't want, or are afraid to speak the truth, even when it is as important as their freedom, for fear of being called on the carpet by the leaders. This goes on in every religion in America.

So where is the faith in doing things that are right, because the people know they are right, and not because a leader gives them permission to speak or do right? Where is the great faith we should have in Christ, enabling us to stand up for truth and right? Isn't Christ the source of all truth, and right? Christ tells us that He is the way, the truth, and the life. Because some leaders say something, doesn't mean they are speaking the truth. The members must know the scriptures for themselves, so they will know if they are being told the truth. They need to know laws, government, history and current events, since theirs' and other's freedom depends on it, throughout all eternity. Christ tells us: *For the **word** of the Lord is **truth**, and whatsoever is **truth is** light, and whatsoever is **light is Spirit, even the Spirit of Jesus Christ.** " (Section 84:45, Doctrine and Covenants)* It takes faith to love all truth [Christ], and not just some of it, because it is convenient or comfortable.

Christ gives an example of great faith when recounting the story of a Roman Centurion: *"And when Jesus was entered into Capernaum, there came unto him a centurion, beseeching him,""And saying, Lord, my servant lieth at home sick of the palsy, grievously tormented.""And Jesus saith unto him. I will come and heal him .""The centurion answered and said, Lord, I am not worthy that thou shouldest come under my roof: but speak the word only, and my servant shall be healed.""For I am a man under authority, having soldiers under me: and I say to this man, Go, and he goeth; and to another, Come, and he cometh; and to my servant, Do this, and he doeth it.""When Jesus heard it, he marvelled, and said to them that followed, Verily I say unto you, **I have not found so great faith**, no, not in Israel.""And I say unto you, **That many shall come from the east and the west, and shall sit down with Abraham, Isaac, and Jacob, in the kingdom of heaven.**""But the **children of the kingdom shall be cast out into <u>outer darkness:</u>** there shall be weeping and gnashing of teeth.""And Jesus said unto the centurion, Go thy way; and as thou hast believed, so be it done unto thee. And his servant was healed in the selfsame hour." (Matthew 8:5-13,*

KJV)

I love the church, but I love the **truth [Christ]** more, and we must open our eyes, think, act for ourselves, get involved,and walk by ourselves and choose from either of the two trees. There are those who don't want you to know the truth [Christ], instead they limit your access to the truth [Christ]. Yes, I mean even well-meaning leaders in all churches, who also need to be taught about the truth [Christ] Which will your choice be, the tree of life or the tree of knowledge of good and evil? When we die, we will be restored eternally to the actions and mindsets we had at the time of death. The above verses from Matthew are talking about *"the children of the kingdom"*. All Mormons believe that the Kingdom of God on earth is the Church of Jesus Christ of Latter-day Saints, this means that Christ is talking about them. They have been given more knowledge, and instead of being humble, they are arrogant, thinking because of their knowledge that they have got it made.

Here is another Riddle that Christ left with us before He left this earth for a time. It is the *"Parable of the talents"*. *"For the kingdom of Heaven is as a man traveling into a far country, who called his own servants [priesthood holders/ children of the kingdom], and delivered unto them his goods." And unto one he gave five talents[responsibilities/charges], to another two, and to another one; to every man according to his several abilities; and straightway took his journey." Then he that received the five talents went and traded [was diligent in the work of his lord] with the same, and made them other five talents [abilities/ warning others]." And likewise he that received two, he also gained other two." But he that had received one went and digged in the earth, and hid his lord's money [was lazy and rejected knowledge, cared not about his neighbor]." After a long time the lord of those servants cometh, and reckoneth with them." And so he that had received five talents came and brought other five talents [children/converts into the fold], saying Lord, thou deliveredst unto me five talents[charges]: behold, I have gained beside them five talents [children of the kingdom] more." His lord said unto him, Well done, thou good and faithful servant: thou hast been faithful over a few things, I will make thee ruler over many things: enter thou into the joy of thy lord." He also that had received two talents came and said, Lord, thou deliveredst unto me two talents[charges/responsibilities]: behold, I have gained two other talents beside them." His lord said unto him, well done, good and faithful servant; thou hast been faithful over a few things, I will make you ruler over many things: enter thou into the joy of thy lord." Then he which had received the one talent[charge] came and said[making excuses for being lazy and thoughtless], Lord I knew thee that thou art an hard man, reaping where thou hast not sown, and gathering where thou hast not strawed:" And I was __afraid,__ and went and hid thy talent[responsibility] in the earth:[so he did nothing at all to help his fellow man]: lo, there thou hast that is thine.""His lord answered and said unto him, thou wicked and slothful[selfish and lazy] servant, thou knewest that I reap where I sowed not, and gather where I have not strawed:[he new before he made covenant/agreement]:""Thou oughtest therefore to have put my money[into doing something good, and helping those who are doing good things], and then at my coming I should have received mine own with usury[interest on someone elses' labors]. ""Take therefore the talent from him[ability and any truth and knowledge] from him, and give it unto him which hath ten talents.""For unto every one that hath[diligent in growing the kingdom of God] shall be given, and he shall have abundance[blessings, more knowledge and light]: but from him that hath not shall be taken away even that which he hath[light/truth and knowledge]""And cast ye the lazy, lying liberal etc.] unprofitable servant into outer darkness: there shall be weeping and gnashing of teeth."(Matthew 25:14-30, KJV)*

From those who have been given much, much more is expected: *"And that servant, which knew his Lord's will, and prepared not himself, neither did according to his will, shall be beaten with many stripes." But he that knew not, and did commit things worthy of stripes, shall be beaten with few stripes. For __unto whomsoever much is given, of him shall be much required:__ and to whom men have committed much, of him will they ask the more." (Luke 12:47-48, KJV)*

*"Therefore, to him that __knoweth to do good,__ and __doeth it not,__ to __him it is sin. (James 4:17, KJV)"*We must be up and warning our neighbor and learn knowledge so that we can teach our families, friends, neighbors wherever they are, even the whole world if possible. Obeying the laws of the kingdom we hope to obtain. By teaching our countrymen brings peace to that nation, that is the charges given to all Christians.

God has said that if you are filthy, you will be filthy still; and if your works are good and clean, then you will be clean still.

O, my son, this is not the case; but the meaning of the word __restoration__ is to bring back again __evil for evil__, or carnal for carnal, or devilish for devilish—

good for that which is good; *righteous for that which is just; merciful for that which is merciful. Therefore, my son, see that you are merciful unto your brethren; deal justly, judge righteously, and do good continually; and if ye do all these things then shall ye receive your reward; yea, ye shall have mercy restored unto you again; ye shall have justice restored unto you again; ye shall have a righteous judgment restored unto you again; and ye shall have good rewarded unto you again. For that which ye do send out, shall return unto you again, and be restored; therefore, the* **word restoration** *more fully* **condemneth the sinner**, *and justifieth him not at all. (Alma 41:13–15, Book of Mormon)*

We shouldn't wait for others to take care of us or fight our battles for us. We should be up and doing something for a good cause, if we want to be part of cleaning up the institutions of the churches and see the secret orders done away with as God requires. President Trump can't do everything. He needs our support by simply doing things we know are right. He needs our voice and our monetary support. We need to be helpful in electing good people in every facet of government who love God and who support our president as long as he is upright and doing that which is right in the sight of God.

Vote for good, strong, and committed conservatives that defend liberty. We need to teach through our examples and through our courage. We must look the devil in the eye every time and eradicate the evil liberal agendas. This is a spiritual war here on the earth. We already know how it is going to end, with or without us, so let's get in the fight for freedom. Let's question everything and everyone.

Even though this chapter is talking mainly about the Mormon Church in particular, keep in mind that all churches are just as guilty, if not more so. All churches have been infiltrated in one way or another. Many have become downright charismatic in their teachings, being afraid to offend, because they rely on the people for their employ. It appears that, in many instances, religion has become a big business.

To become a pastor, reverend, father, or doctor of divinity, in almost every other church, other than the Mormons, you must have a college degree signed by some person supposedly qualified to give such titles. These such qualified persons are themselves just men/women who are just as blind as the person they are giving the degree to. The only real qualification a man/woman needs is to read, study, and put callouses on their knees in continual prayer before God and then get up and lead by example.

I am in no way, shape, or form belittling the Mormon Church but am using them as an example because I am familiar with it the most. I love this church, as I know that the knowledge gleaned from it is so rich, thanks to Joseph Smith. We need to remember one very important thing, and it is this: Joseph Smith didn't create a church on his own. The Church of Jesus Christ of Latter-day Saints is a *restored church* by God from the time when Christ first established His church in Jerusalem, when He called His twelve disciples, as well as from ancient times, dating back to the time of the children of Israel in the wilderness. Christ himself, personally established his kingdom when he walked on earth in Jerusalem, and organized His church. The truth of the matter is this: If the church wasn't the Lord's church, it would have been destroyed long ago by ignorant leaders, leaders in denial, leaders who don't want to rock the boat and choose instead to be blind, or even those leaders with hidden agendas. Only Christ knows, and He is perfectly capable of managing His church without taking away free-agency. No matter what we think about a leader, doesn't take away the facts of the truth, about this being Christ's Church.

The people in all Christian churches have gone to sleep, while the devil and his minions forge ahead with their lies and deceits to fool the people. We must wake up and put on the full armor of God. When the leaders remember to not worry about what men think so much and unincorporate the churches, then they will obtain the blessings from Heaven and there will begin again to be *prophets in the land*. It is my prayer that this church and all churches will come forth out of the wilderness and be clean again.

"Remember all thy church, O Lord, with all their families, and their immediate connections, with all their sick and afflicted ones, with all the poor and meek of the earth; that the kingdom, which thou hast set up without hands, may become a great mountain and fill the whole earth;" **That thy church may come forth out of the wilderness of** *darkness,-- and shine forth fair as the moon, clear as the sun, and terrible as an army with banners."(section 109:73-74, Doctrine and Covenants).*

"Therefore, let every man stand or fall by himself, and not for another. Or not trusting another. Seek unto my Father, and it shall be done in that very moment what ye shall ask, if ye ask in faith, believing that ye shall receive.""and if thine

eye which seeth for thee, him that is appointed to watch over thee, to show thee light, become a transgressor and offend thee, pluck him out. It is better for thee to enter into the Kingdom of God with one eye than having two eyes to be cast into hell fire. For it is better that thyself should be saved than to be cast into Hell with thy brother." (Mark 9:44-48. J.S.T. KJV)

Despite the questions raised in this chapter of what Brigham Young may, or may not have done, he still was a man of wisdom and did many great things. He warned the people about putting too much trust in a single man. The following is a couple of quotes by Brigham Young:

"I am more afraid that this people have so much confidence in their leaders that they will not inquire for themselves of God whether they are led by him. I am fearful lest they settle down in a state of self-security, trusting their eternal destiny in the hands of their leaders with a reckless confidence that in itself would thwart the purpose of God in their salvation and weaken that influence they could give to their leaders, did they know for themselves, by the revelations of Jesus, that they are led in the right way. Let every man and woman know, by the whispering of the Spirit of God to themselves, whether their leaders are walking in the path the Lord dictates or not," (page 209, Journal of Discourses of Brigham Young).

"Those who suffer themselves to be led entirely by another person, suspending their own understanding, and pinning their faith upon another's sleeve, will never be capable of entering into the celestial glory, to be crowned as they anticipate; they will never be capable of becoming Gods...who will? Those who are valiant and inspired with the true independence of Heaven." (1:312, J.D. Of B.Y.)

Joseph Smith gives all people, sound advice about learning knowledge: *"Search the scriptures, search the revelations which we publish, and ask your Heavenly Father, in the name of His Son Jesus Christ, to manifest the truth unto you, and if you do it with an eye single to His glory, nothing doubting, He will answer you by the power of His Holy Spirit. You will then know for yourselves and not for another. You will not then be dependent on man for the knowledge of God." (page 11-12, Teachings of the Prophet Joseph smith).*

CHAPTER 7

The agencies of the corporation, i.e., Internal Revenue Service

Upon getting married to my second wife in 1992 and settling down to raise my second family, I got involved with a group called the Concerned Citizens for Constitutional Government of Idaho. Growing up as a young man, my dad was very conservative and had a love of God. He took his children to church every Sunday almost without fail, unless something happened beyond his control, such as a sickness or car breaking down. The ones I looked up to were my elder brothers, who had some knowledge but not a lot about what was happening in our government, such as how elected officials were deviating from the Constitution and attacking our unalienable rights. They knew enough to notice the erosion of morality and the enhanced oppression being perpetrated a little at a time by left-leaning elected officials, who were many. They regularly voiced their concerns and opinions, and I listened to the best of my ability because these things interested me as I was trying to gain knowledge and grow physically and spiritually.

As it were, being raised on sound principles of the gospel, I learned to not take someone's opinion as always the truth, but I learned to question everything until I was satisfied I had arrived at the truth. Wanting to make a difference for God and for my country, I decided to join this group, learn about our Constitution, and understand it. The group's intent was to educate the public about the erosion of constitutional rights being perpetrated by elected officials, including presidents, congressmen, judges, mayors, and governors. I began to see that we the people were being lied to consistently in a deliberate manner and that there were very few elected officials in fiduciary positions that the people could trust.

There are many seriously bad laws put into place by liberal presidents and congressmen and women trying to, little by little, destroy America from within. The purpose of this chapter is to expose the fraudulent IRS and explain who and what they represent. There have been a lot of books and literature written, related to the fraudulent nature and practices of the Internal Revenue Service or the IRS. My goal is to simplify the person's understanding of why the IRS exists and how it exists but, most importantly, why we the people let them exist. If the people simply wake up and show some fortitude, the IRS will not exist.

The IRS is, simply put, the muscleman of the Federal Reserve bank. The Federal Reserve bank is the evilest institution that ever has existed on the planet Earth. The money system throughout history, when corrupted, has caused the destruction of all nations after enslaving the people and causing misery and bankruptcy. When private business and people control the creation of money, which is to serve as the exchange of goods and services, then it is easy for conflict of interest, selfish ambition, bribery, and control of the populace to take place. The Federal Reserve has extended its power across the globe, even controlling governments.

America is the "little horn" that wounded the beast almost to death, and it has been plotted by Satan for hundreds of years, if not thousands of years, to heal the wound of the beast by destroying America. It is no accident that the Democrats are busy attempting to obstruct President Trump from making America great again. One of the primary means for doing this and ruling the world is the creation of the Federal Reserve bank. Mayer Amschel Rockefeller stated, "Permit me to issue and control the money of a nation, and I care not who makes its laws." Make no mistake about it; these evil people care not about America, but they care only about power.

The problem for these evil, anti-America, and anti-God people is that America is filled with freedom- and God-loving patriots who have knowledge, are armed, and will stand up and fight aggressively and fearlessly if they have to, committed to the cause of freedom. I am one of them, and I am going to reveal the truth and simplicity of the evil IRS.

Up to 1992, I was ignorant of the IRS's fraud until I was presented with a videotape by a man named Stewart. This video showed a man named Carter and his fight with the IRS. It struck me so hard to find out how blatantly the IRS would lie to rob this man of his money and then cover up a lie. They were caught with their hands in the cookie jar, and ever since, I have refused to file or pay the IRS one red cent. I haven't filed since 1993, and when your lights finally go on, you will never file again either.

Most people today suffer from a terrible disease called ignorance. This disease can be accidental or on purpose. Most people are ignorant because they don't get involved in politics or government, where they will learn what it means to be a good citizen, by learning constitutional principles. The rest claim they are smart but won't get involved because either they are trying to cover their own selfish lusts or desires or they would much rather play the stupid card because they are afraid.

The Constitution allows for three lawful taxes only, and they are import taxes, export taxes, and excise taxes. That means that income tax is not lawful. In 1913, Colonel House—while under the Woodrow Wilson administration—stood before Congress and announced, "It appears that the Sixteenth Amendment has been ratified." The wording is *it appears*. This is how magicians deceive others, making others believe something that is not real, appear real. It is sleight of hand or deception. This was what Colonel House did, to get the people to believe that the Sixteenth Amendment was made law. Would you honestly believe a lying Democrat? That is all the language the Democrats know how to speak. They speak the language of the devil, and that is lies.

The following is taken from the *Federal Civil Judicial Procedure and Rules*, 1997 edition: "Article XVI of the Constitution: "The Congress shall have power to lay and collect taxes on **incomes**, from whatever source derived, without apportionment among the several States, and without regard to any census or enumeration." Further included are historical notes and proposal and ratification. *"The Sixteenth Amendment, set out in 36 Stat. 184, was proposed to the legislatures of the several States by the Sixty-First Congress, on July 12, 1909, and was declared, in a proclamation by the Secretary of State, dated February 25, 1913, to have been ratified."* One needs to notice the wordplay *incomes*. The word *income* is something foreign earned. Also, notice the wordplay on "from whatever source derived." From whatever foreign source, they failed to explain.

The Sixteenth Amendment was just declared as appearing to be ratified by a bully Democrat-led Congress, just like when the Congress tried to push through the impeachment of Donald Trump. If you are a naturalized or natural-born citizen and not receiving foreign-earned income, then the Sixteenth Amendment does not apply to you. If your employment is with a corporation within the United States and you are a natural-born or naturalized citizen of the United States, it still does not apply to you because the money you earn is "remuneration," where you are trading your assets (your labor) for value in like kind as exchange. Further, it does not apply to you because they offer a fraudulent form for you to fill out (1040), which carries a penalty of ten years in prison for mail fraud, and they can't force you to commit a felony. Therefore, you have no "incoming" source of remuneration. Even though it may appear to some people that the states ratified the Sixteenth Amendment, since to tax your source of remuneration is not constitutional, then all they can do is tax foreign-earned incoming monies from whatever source; and even then, it is a "voluntary compliance" system.

A man named Bill Benson wrote a book called *The Law That Never Was*. He went to every state in the Union, did the research, and learned that not one single state ratified the Sixteenth Amendment. He documented the results, put them together in this book, and published his findings. Not one single state ratified the Sixteenth Amendment. At least it was not ratified by "we the people". Some people try to say that some states ratified it but that it wasn't done properly. The important point to remember is that if the Sixteenth Amendment wasn't ratified properly, well then it wasn't ratified. It wasn't ratified properly because it's not constitutional. The Sixteenth Amendment, therefore, is not positive law but only prima facie law. This means it is law until proven otherwise. Bill Benson just proved otherwise.

The steps to remember in understanding the IRS are these:

- If the Sixteenth Amendment is not really law, then filing income taxes is not enforceable by law. Anything then that the Federal Reserve and the IRS throw at you is 100 percent not legal but is a fraud. It is a law on appearance only until proven otherwise; everyone has to walk on their own two feet to claim his/her freedom. On Friday, March 4, 1994, Judge David Hagen of the federal district court in Reno, Nevada, issued the following: "Declaratory Judgment that: a) The 16th Amendment was and is invalid: b) The Federal Reserve Act of 1913, is declared Unconstitutional as it was and is applied to State Citizens: c) The Gold Reserve Act of 1934 to be a fraud on its surface and to be declared Unconstitutional: d) Title 26 USC (the Internal Revenue Code) to apply to the Federal United States, (not to the citizens of the fifty states) and all other implications to be fraud and therefore declared Unconstitutional" *(Ronald L. Jackson v. United States, et al., Case No: CV-N-93-401-DWH).*

- If you dig further into the IRS, you begin to realize and uncover the fact that Title 26 USC, the Internal Revenue Code, only pertains to immigration, including nonresidents, permanent residents, resident aliens, illegal aliens, federal residents, and corporations of the federal United States of America. It does not apply or include natural-born citizens or naturalized citizens under the Constitution of the several united states of America. These constitutional citizens are exempt from any federal or state income tax. The "remedy in law" is the Uniform Commercial Code 1-207/1-308 and 1-103. This remedy can be used very effectively when signing your Form W-2 or W-4 when being employed by an employer. I simply write in my name, my address, and my social security number, nothing else, except down at the bottom, the form asks if you are exempt: "I claim exemption from withholding for (year), and I certify that I meet **both** of the following conditions for exemption." Both of these conditions are: "Last year I had a right to a refund of **all** federal income tax withheld because I had **no** tax liability, **and** This year I expect a refund of **all** federal income tax withheld because I expect to have **no** tax liability." Even though you didn't file or have in the past, now that you have the knowledge, you can honestly say that you have the right to receive the return of all income taxes paid. This is simply because you are a natural-born citizen or a naturalized citizen, and income taxes don't apply to a citizen under the Constitution. I then write in the box at the bottom right "exempt," and then I sign it at the bottom left. Before I sign it, however, I write just above where my signature will be "Not Liable! UCC 1-207/1-308 and

UCC 1-103." What I am saying is this: I refuse to be forced to perform under any unknown contract that I have not entered into knowingly, and I also refuse the liability of the compelled benefit. The income tax is an unknown contract. Since 1938, our common law has been replaced by commercial law, and most of us today were not in 1938, even a twinkle in our daddy's eye. We were not alive or of age at the time of this contract, so it is unknown to us and is covered by the remedy of UCC 1-207/1-308. UCC 1-103 means that I refuse to be liable for the compelled benefit. This is the fiat money system. The money is not real, and this fake money is IOUs, once again another unknown contract. UCC 1-103 is our remedy for not being liable for this fake money since we were not around or of age to agree to it. Any document pertaining to demand of money by any government agency—such as court fees or fines, jail fees, and booking fees—can have this remedy when used. I have a good buddy who rather than go to the trouble that I did, simply wrote to the IRS and requested their form to claim exemption to filing the income tax. Leonard has not filed for about as long as I have.

- There are no implementing regulations attached to the Sixteenth Amendment compelling or requiring the constitutional/natural-born/naturalized citizen to file income taxes. Any positive law is accompanied with implementing regulations, compelling performance, and a penalty for nonperformance. Any regulation associated with Form 1040 is referenced to alcohol, tobacco, and firearms.

- The income tax is a "self-assessment and voluntary compliance system." According to the *Handbook for Special Agents: Criminal Investigation Intelligence Division Internal Revenue Service*, "'Agents . . . Our tax system is based on individual self-assessment and **voluntary compliance . . . the material contained in this handbook is confidential in character . . . and must not under any circumstance be made available to persons outside the service.'—Mr. Mortimer Caplin, Internal Revenue Service, Commissioner**." The IRS does not personally send you or anyone you know any form through the mail, unless explicitly requested in writing and signed by you. Instead, they want you to voluntarily go to any library, courthouse, or post office and pick one up. They then expect you to fill it out or pay to have it done with your own name and social security number, sign it with your signature, put your own stamp on the envelope, seal the envelope yourself, address it, and then drop it in the mail to send to them. You have just sent a demand or request to the IRS with the intention of receiving a monetary benefit. What the IRS doesn't tell you is that you have just requested this monetary benefit on a fraudulent form and sent this request through the mail, committing mail fraud.

- Form 1040 is a fraudulent document. The IRS would not send it to you in the mail, but you send it to them, demanding payment for money, and now you have just committed mail fraud. The masses are committing mail fraud every year unknowingly, but the IRS keeps quiet about it because they are able to rob the people because of the people's ignorance, and they are serving their master, the Federal Reserve bank. Though the IRS doesn't want to alarm the masses, they prey on those who do act like they know, and if those who know cause trouble for them by trying to educate others, they will try to frame such a person by lies and deceit to show that the person has committed mail fraud and tax evasion. These are two separate felonies, with the penalties being ten years in prison each. Title 26 CFR 602.101 fails to cross-reference the IRS form 1040 (OMB control number 1545-0074) for the purpose of collecting information from the public, necessary to enforce CFR 1.1-1.

- The IRS is not part of the federal government but is a private corporation since 1933, when they were first incorporated in the state of Delaware. They are now headquartered in the federal territory of Puerto Rico. Title 26 IRC itself supports the fact that the term *United States* is being used in the geographic sense and thus refers only to the District of Columbia and territories over which the federal government has exclusive jurisdiction but not the several states (see IRC 770(a)(9)-(10); see also *Caha v. United States*, 152 U.S. 211, and *Foley Brothers v. Filardo*, 336 U.S. 281 [1948]). It has also been stated by the Supreme Court that each of the several states is a foreign country, as to the District of Columbia, and thus maintains exclusive jurisdiction within its geographic area. This is why the IRS is no longer quartered in the States but in Puerto Rico, a territory. They have no jurisdiction within the several states unless you give it to them.

- The IRS works as a collection agency for the Federal Reserve bank, which is also a private corporation and also not a part of our federal government. This is another deception by the use of the word *federal*.

- There is no law requiring a person to file Form 1040 or any income tax for that matter. For the IRS to try to force someone to file Form 1040 is the same as attempting to force the person to commit a felony. They want the person to file the form voluntarily.

- Filing income taxes does not apply to natural-born or naturalized citizens under the Constitution of the United States, and the commercial remedy is UCC 1-207/1-308 and UCC 1-103. Remember, income is for those who make money from without the several states of the republic. Foreign-earned income is what is taxable. It is incoming money from a foreign source. A sovereign citizen under the Constitution is in one country. A corporation of the United States of America is in another or a foreign country. The IRS does not want to explain the term *income*, but this is what it is. They do not want to have to tell you, their meaning; otherwise, it will reveal the truth. If you are a sovereign citizen, then the proper term to use is *remuneration*.

- The IRS is a system of threat, duress, and coercion, so much so that companies and corporations are intimidated into acting as collection agents to their employees by withholding from their paychecks. The businesses and corporations are not agents and not under any law to act as collection agents for the IRS. All that is required for the businesses or corporations to qualify their actions is to give each employee a W-4 or W-2 to voluntarily fill out with any exemptions they assess themselves as having, send the completed W-4 or W-2 to the IRS, and at the end of the year furnish to the employee a 1099 or with the statement of the employee's earnings for the year, and that is all.

- The IRS has no police or law enforcement powers. They can only lie, threaten, intimidate, misrepresent, and deceive people into doing their dirty work. They scheme and watch for a crime to be committed, such as setting a person up for mail fraud or tax evasion, and then they make a complaint to the correct authorities and have you indicted or arrested, tried, and convicted, but they and their evil agency have no police power.

So you see, the IRS has no power at all, unless you give them the power over you. They have no jurisdiction over a natural-born or naturalized citizen of the United States of America-Republic. For the IRS to have jurisdiction over you, you must be in the water with them, where they can harm you. A letter from Harry Reid, on a U.S. Senate letterhead, replying to an inquiry to a Mr. Tolotti said, "I consulted the legal and tax divisions of the Congressional Research Service to answer your question. They found no tax on an 'occupation of Common Right.'"

There are two systems of government. When growing up and in school, we as children were taught about the Constitution of the United States of America, about our rights under it, and how we are protected because of this special, sacred document. I have made comparison of the Constitution as representing dry land or common-law jurisdiction. Another system not explained to the people, is the laws under maritime law or old merchant law. This maritime law is the law of the sea. On the ocean, in a ship, the captain is the dictator, with absolute authority and control. What he says goes in the way he manages his ship, which is an extension of his federal government of the country he represents.

In Washington, DC, or the District of Columbia, this same jurisdiction is prevalent. This is called admiralty jurisdiction. Incorporating our businesses and churches has brought this system onto dry land and out of the District of Columbia, where it was told to stay. The oceanic laws/Uniform Commercial Code had replaced common law back in 1938 under *Erie v. Tompkins*. In the respective states, they have been codified into state codes, such as in Wisconsin, where they are Wisconsin Code, and in Idaho, where they are Idaho Code. So, because of this maritime law on the land, we need the remedy in UCC 1-207/1-308 and UCC 1-103 to maintain our common-law rights under the Constitution. In any system, the people of God must have a choice with whom they wish to serve. Though the commercial law is intimidating, free choice must also be made available. The evil Democrats or agencies won't tell us where the remedies are; therefore, we must read, study, find, and understand for ourselves where the key is that unlocks the door of our freedom.

The Federal Reserve money system makes slaves of the people worldwide. The fiat or fake money is made by it, and it is a private corporation. The Federal Reserve owns these IOUs, and you are in debt just by having it in your possession, and it must be paid back with interest; and to make sure you pay it back, it sends its collection agency to intimidate, threaten, coerce, and deceive—whatever it takes. Because the IRS is out of the sea of commercial law and on dry land, under constitutional law, it is completely powerless. We all need to understand that, in America today, the Constitution is the "supreme law of the land" and is a representation of God. When close to God, we are safe; but when we partake of that other system of government/ fictional foreign system, or maritime law, we come under another foreign jurisdiction. Admiralty jurisdiction is its name, among others. It is contract law. Other names already mentioned earlier are federal, corporate, king, dictator, fascist, socialist, communist, or democracy. Other biblical or ancient terms are Babylon, Egypt, the world, whore of all the earth, and great and abominable church. These are all different terms, but they all mean the same thing.

Another analogy is this: Imagine the IRS as a gigantic octopus. In Puget Sound, Seattle, there are some huge ones. In old times, there were old stories handed down about sea monsters attacking ships. Some of the pictures show huge tentacles wrapped around the ships, threatening to capsize their boats. As long as those octopuses stay in the water, they are very scary monsters. Now take that monster-sized octopus and drop him on dry land, and you have nothing but a big blob of slimy, writhing tissue that is completely helpless and powerless. The water represents the law of the sea or admiralty jurisdiction. The land represents the Constitution or common-law jurisdiction. The octopus represents the scary, monstrous IRS, and when you take this evil agency out of the water and drop it under the Constitution, on the land, it becomes helpless and powerless, and it will eventually die. This is really how simple it is.

Each tentacle of the octopus is a representation of what makes up the authority of the beast.

- The Sixteenth Amendment wasn't ratified of, for, and by we the people.

- There are no implementing regulations

- Title 26 of the Internal Revenue Code applies only to immigration or federal agencies of the District of Columbia and not the several united states.

- The system is a voluntary compliance system.

- There is no law requiring a person to file.

- Form 1040, used for gathering information from the public, is fraudulent.

- A natural-born or naturalized citizen is not required to file.

- The IRS is not part of the federal government but is a private corporation.

- The IRS is a system of intimidation.

- The IRS has no police or enforcement powers.

So knowing all these things just causes any authority the IRS appears to have to just up and melt away when it is overshadowed by the Constitution. The IRS is a system of threat, duress, and coercion.

The United States of America is the correct styling of the name of our great republic. There is another corporate name given by evil people seeking to bring about the downfall of our republic, and that is *the United States of America*. This sleight of hand or deception was made deliberately by the Democrats/liberals trying to turn our republic into a communist/socialist country under admiralty jurisdiction. You can hear Nancy Pelosi or any of the liberals talking about their "democracy" and how they are trying to protect our democracy. What they aren't telling you, and what they really mean is that when they use this word or title loosely, they are claiming a socialist government and are trying the deception trick to get Americans to buy into it; after all, it does resemble a democratic form of government. However, *democracy* and *democratic* are two different things.

Democratic is the form of government where the people are able to elect their own representatives, whether it is a democracy or a republic. The difference here is that a republic election is by the people, for the people, and of the people; any and everyone has equality and justice under the law of the Constitution; and anyone can run for office. In a democracy, the only choices you have for elected representatives are from among the rich people. Only the rich rule and are allowed to elect their leaders or masters, thus making the poor and ordinary people chattel, like it was during the feudal system.

I have an old encyclopedia published in 1890. It just happens to be the "D" volume. I looked up the term *democracy*, and right next to this word in brackets is "socialism." It explains that the term *democracy* is an old Greek form of government where the people choose their leaders by election, but the catch is that the rich are the only ones allowed to vote because the chattels don't know what is best for themselves, so they are represented by the rich. This is what the socialists or communists are trying to do today. They want this form of government, they want a king over the land, they want power and riches and control, and they want us the people to be their slaves and deliver us back over to the corporate system, even the Roman Empire ruled by the Catholic Church. The *Book of Mormon* talks about Gadianton robbers, and these are who the Democrats are. The sad part is that there are many Democrats in Republican clothes, such as George H. W. Bush. In the *Book of Mormon*, *4 Nephi 1:42* states, *"And it came to pass that the wicked part of the people began again to build up the **secret oaths and combinations of Gadianton.**"* *Alma 51:1–21* talks about the liberals of long ago and shows how they were just like the liberals today, but then there was a different outcome for them. They were either forced to uphold liberty, or they were hewn down with the sword.

So basically, America is split into two separate countries. Though we are citizens/sovereign of the American republic but are employed by a corporation, the IRS looks on this like we are receiving foreign-earned income, even though we are under the Constitution. They want to deceive you into believing that they have jurisdiction, even though they don't. If you assert your rights under the Constitution, then you are with God and under the republic, the country of America; you can work and receive remuneration from any lawful source, including corporations, at any amount. This includes capital gains. If, however, you have selfish desires and uphold lies and bad laws, like the IRS, its Sixteenth Amendment, and *Roe v. Wade*, then you are supporting socialism/democracy. I can't explain it any simpler than this.

The beauty of it all is that, as we learn, gain knowledge, and grow, we have the ability to change, hopefully for the good, before we die and prepare to meet God with our freedom intact, believing and accepting Christ as our Savior, not Satan. Our change must be sincere, with commitment. We cannot sit on the fence in a lukewarm state because God will spew us out of His mouth. *Revelation 3:15–16* states, *"I know thy works, that thou art neither cold nor hot: I would thou wert cold or hot. So then because thou art **lukewarm**, and neither cold nor hot, I will spue thee out of my mouth."* In other words, if you won't stand for the truth, then God won't have you. He will surrender you to the devil's jurisdiction. God wants you to choose.

The last year I had ever filed was 1992. Since then, it has been very educational. It was peaceful enough, until I allowed an alleged friend with his family to move a trailer house onto my land, with the intentions of giving him an opportunity to get ahead. The invitation was rent-free until he could get his finances together, allowing him to get his own land. He began taking liberties, which showed disrespect and inconsideration. There was a confrontation just before I asked him and his family to leave. For spite, Rory made an anonymous phone call to the mighty IRS, thus starting my educational journey contending with the scary octopus.

I battled the IRS from 1994 to 2001. I wrote an article to the *Idaho Observer*, and the editor Don Harkins ran it unedited in my own words, and I am including it here as I told it then in July of 2001. Don wrote an introduction to my article in his own words, referring to the IRS:

It cannot answer important questions. It simply goes from house to house; from business to business threatening to take peoples' property and put them in jail if they don't pay the protection money, they call income tax. Steve Sego and his wife of Rathdrum chose to stand up to the IRS and seem to have battled the federal monster to a standstill. What program did they use? What method do they employ? They confronted the IRS head on, asked the right questions and stood up in truth and faith. The following account should be an inspiration to us all.

One family's confrontation with the IRS

by Steven: Sego

In 1994 I quit filing Income tax returns and I notified the Tax Commissioner in Washington D.C. by mail, telling her I was ashamed of her, and that I would no longer be filing tax returns.

I started getting letters telling me of a tax-deficiency, and that I needed to file 1040s. I replied with letters, always in a timely manner, declaring my sovereignty and upholding my Constitutional Rights. Of course, the Internal Revenue Agents were deaf and still kept on a coming. Consequently, the correspondence between them and me has filled seven big notebooks full of documentation.

In my investigations about the income tax, I have learned that: (1) the Constitution was God's Law and; (2) The IRS was telling lies.

I made up my mind that I was going to obey God's Law. I bumbled and stumbled and made mistakes, but kept a steady prayer life to my Father in Heaven and observed to do all that I could, by learning the truth and then exercising what I knew to be true.

This has been a learning process and I have made mistakes. But I and my family are living testimonies that by going forward in truth and unafraid will lead to things working out for the best. I know that my knowledge and understanding of the IRS and what the truth really is has grown tremendously, and I am so grateful to my Heavenly Father for that.

In 1998 the IRS recorded In Kootenai County, a "Notice of Federal Tax Lien." I thought about what was going on and with a little more reading I ran across a document put out by the IRS that said anyone could visit any IRS office and the IRS would be happy to answer tax related questions.

So I did. I decided to go after the IRS and not wait for them to come after me. I called up my friend Herb Miles and asked him if he would like to go with me to visit the IRS because I had some questions I want to ask them. Herb agreed to meet me at their office. And so began my harassment of the IRS.

Our first meeting:

I had come upon some material where it appeared that something had been omitted from evidence, making an incomplete document and I wanted to ask the IRS about it. I wanted to put them on the spot. Herb and I met at the IRS office in Coeur d' Alene. We went up to the big steel door. We rang the doorbell, and after a minute a voice on the other side asked who we were and what we wanted. I told them that I was there to see John: Peterson (he is the supervisor for the Coeur d' Alene Office) the voice said just a minute. Pretty soon the door opened and a person opened the door and showed us to a room where we could wait for John: Peterson.

Shortly John: Peterson appeared and asked what this was concerning. I told him that I had some questions. He told me that I needed an appointment, because it was apparent that he didn't know what to do with me on such short notice. However, I pulled out my paper, it being the IRS's own literature, stating that is all I had to do if I had any questions was to come down to any office of the IRS, and they would be glad to answer them.

I asked him if the paper was true. He said okay what do you want to know. I started asking him questions about the omissions of paragraphs and words from IRS material which made the documents incomplete. He didn't want to answer these questions and so he tried to take control of the meeting.

I reminded him that I had called the meeting and that I had the questions and that he needed to provide the answers. He told me that he didn't have to answer any questions. I asked him if the IRS regards themselves as public servants or not. He said that they do. I said if you are the servant then I am the master and you will answer any question that I ask. I also reminded him that if he didn't answer my questions I would keep coming back until I got them answered.

Herb and I had taken recorders, but John: Peterson, would not let us record then, but we scheduled a meeting two weeks later telling him that we would be bringing recorders and witnesses.

John: Peterson, told IRS agent James Mason in Idaho Falls about the visit he received from us. James: Mason called me and said that I didn't need to bother John: Peterson and that If I had any questions concerning my account that I had to deal with him.

He also informed me that he could meet with me on January 7, 1999. I wrote back to James: Mason and told him that I accept the meeting gladly. I also reminded him that I called the meeting, and that he was the servant and that I will be asking the questions. I told him that when he came to be sure and bring some documents with him. I wanted him to produce the contractual agreement that I made with the IRS, if it is true that I do have an account with them. I also wanted him to provide the statute which accompanied the implementing regulations. I added, I will be bringing two tape recorders and three witnesses.

Our second meeting:

The meeting took place as planned, and James: Mason for the IRS had his own tape recorder. I piled into him demanding now to produce the documents I had requested that he bring with him prior to the meeting. The only thing that he pulled out was the statute on Individual taxes. I asked him where the contract that I had signed was. He said, it's like this Mr. Sego, if two people get into an accident by one running into another, even though one is clearly at fault, the other has to sue to get justice, there is no contract there. I told him that this is not any accident. When I asked him to provide the implementing regulations for the individual tax statute he told me that he was not going to show me anything more.

I pulled out a copy of 1.1-1 taken from IRC 26, and I asked him if this was the individual tax. He didn't want to answer (but remember the tape recorders were running and I had three witnesses). If he said no, I didn't owe anything, if he said yes, I still didn't owe him anything. He finally said, yes.

I told him that 1.1-1 is only referenced to Form 2555, Foreign earned Income. He couldn't say anything, he was had. I told him that the 1040 was an illegal form and asked him if he was trying to tell me to do something illegal. Just silence. He insisted that I needed to file 1040 forms. I asked him if it was mandatory to file the 1040s. James: Mason, said yes. I informed him about the head of Alcohol Tobacco and Firearms, under oath in front of Congress, testified that filing was 100 percent voluntary. I then asked James: Mason, who was lying—him or the Head of Alcohol Tobacco and Firearms. He said neither was lying. After this he got mad and terminated our meeting. I didn't want to leave, but he insisted.

Pretax court:

I started requesting my files from the IRS under the Freedom of Information Act. The IRS had created an account for me showing that all of the money I had earned, originated out of the Virgin Islands. My wife had received a letter before this, telling her that her account had been changed, and now she owed half of what I owed. They of course were trying to get to my family. The very next letter she received, was a notice of intent to levy. They obviously had failed to follow their own procedure, and knowing that the whole thing can be thrown out because of this violation, we were talked into filing an appeal to the tax court.

The Tax Court was held April 10, 2000, but about two days prior, we agreed to meet with the IRS to try and resolve the Tax Court issues as requested by the Tax Court Judge. So we did.

In attendance for the IRS was Senior Special Investigator Gerry: Morgan, and IRS Attorney Thomas: Tomashek. For our side was myself, and my wife.

My wife and I went in acting as though we were anxious to cooperate, and as though we wanted to get the issues settled. The way we were received was with great excitement and with relief that we were finally broken down enough to give in. We were actually on a fishing expedition. Gerry: Morgan admitted that the reason that we were targeted in the first place is that an anonymous caller had pointed us out. He also said that if we hadn't ever owned any land that we would not have been bothered. He showed me every business transaction that I had ever made, and explained how I had made it. He also admitted that I wasn't hiding anything, so therefore, wasn't subject to tax evasion. Thomas: Tomashek stated that if we were serious about wanting to get this situation resolved that we should file 1040 forms to show our intent, Gerry: Morgan, told me that my wife didn't need to, but that I should come down to the IRS office in Coeur d' Alene the following Monday and that I could file 1040s and that somebody would be glad to help me. He said to my wife, "You can stay home, all we need is Steven."

He told me to come to the office on Monday and bring my own envelope, my own stamps and that I was to address the envelope myself, put my own stamps on it, file, sign, drop the forms in the envelope, and seal it myself and then he would accompany me to the post office and watch me drop it in the mail.

He then asked me if I wanted to pay state taxes. I said of course not. He said, well if you do it the way I said, then you won't have to pay state taxes. My wife asked him how that worked. He said, by doing it the way he suggested I could avoid state taxes, and that I could trust him.

As we were getting ready to leave the meeting, I told the IRS that I knew how it justified proceeding against me. I say I am sovereign, but because I work for a corporation, the IRS treats my wages as Foreign Earned Income.

They both agreed, "that's right."

After we had gone out of the Federal building where the meeting was held, I asked my wife if she realized that Gerry: Morgan and Thomas: Tomashek had tried to set me up and send me to prison on two felonies. She was almost sick when she came to the realization.

Tax court:

At tax court on April 10, 2000, we appeared only to contest the deficiency notice to my wife, which she did not receive. The witness for the IRS was a mail lady who supposedly had delivered the notices of certified mail to our mail box. When it was our turn to question the witness, she said that she remembered delivering us the notices back in 1997, but she could not remember the names of the roads that she supposedly drives every day. There were two notices for two certified letters, the first notice was supposedly signed by her, but hadn't any signature or writing at all. The second, she testified, "this is my signature" and the letters were "RIS." Her name is Linda: V., which doesn't match the initials at all.

When we were done questioning the witness, the judge told us that if either of us wanted to say anything that we would have to be sworn in under oath and take the stand. We knew that if we wanted our story out that one of us would have to take the stand and one of us would have to ask the questions. My wife decided that she would rather take the stand, and so, was sworn in.

I asked her questions and, in the process, were able to show how the IRS had fabricated everything to do with the Notice of Deficiency that was supposedly sent. We used things that the IRS Attorney had said in our meeting, prior to the Tax Court, against him. I do not believe the IRS were ready for what they got. After the testifying, the Judge admitted that it was obvious that my wife didn't receive a deficiency notice, but that she would review the evidence and make a ruling later. The ruling later, however, was in favor of the IRS.

Before the Tax Court had started, I had requested a transcript of the proceedings. When the transcript had finally been sent to us, on review, I noticed that vital information had been omitted from the transcript. The part where Linda: Vezina, testified that her signature was on the attempted delivery notices, was missing. I immediately sent for a copy of the tape from the transcribers, located in Stockton, California. Their professional name or business is V/ARS, Inc. They notified me that the written word would serve me better and that they do not keep the tapes, but get rid of them. I have requested the tape another time. I just happened to have two witnesses in the court on that day, to prove the truth, plus I immediately made out affidavits and have sent them to the congressmen and women.

I heard nothing from the IRS until June 18, 2001, when James: Mason and John: Peterson showed up at my door. I saw them coming and went out to meet them. James: Mason asked, "are you Mr. Sego?"

I said, "yes."

He said, we are going to seize your property soon if you don't cooperate. I ordered him to leave, before he could say anything more. He stuttered and said, "Okay." They turned around and left. As they were turning, I said, "and don't come back, the only thing you are going to get is a law suit slapped against you so fast it won't quit."

They didn't say another word. I believe that the reason they came at that time is because, they thought my wife and family was home, alone, and they intended to intimidate her.

I know that we can prevail, by holding up God's Law and maintaining true principles.

You see, I knew the IRS is a fraud, and I knew that Form 1040 is fraudulent. And now if I was to file a demand or request for money on a form that I know is fraudulent and make the demand, like everyone does every year, by mail, then I would have just committed mail fraud. Moreover, the IRS agent would be the star witness because he would have watched me sign the form, which was affirmation to my intent, and then to top it all off would witness against me by watching me drop it in the mailbox. This would be a surefire conviction, which would send me up the creek without a paddle for ten years. On top of that, if I didn't file state taxes but filed only federal, then it would be construed as tax evasion, which is a felony with a penalty of another ten years in prison. The key to follow is that if you don't owe or file federal taxes, then you don't owe state taxes.

It is now 2020, and I have not filed for almost thirty years. I have not been bothered anymore by the IRS as I have kept out of their corporate jurisdiction. *John 15:19* states, *"If ye were of the world, the world would love his own: but because ye are not of the world, but I have chosen you out of the world, therefore the world hateth you."* The editor of the *Idaho Observer* Don Harkins, a great patriot, now deceased, put my story on the internet. Last I heard, my case was being used as a test case by attorneys, trying to figure out what I did. It talks about how Steven and his wife fought the IRS to a standstill. If the reader wants to know more about details concerning the IRS, the author of this book encourages the reader to seek out the author's book: **"Satan's Left Hand: The IRS! To the Kingdom of Hell Doth It Belong!".** This book will explain it very simply and clearly.

"My people are destroyed for lack of knowledge" (Hosea 4:6, KJV). God gives knowledge to those who are diligent, with the faith they exercise, in the knowledge they have, and then He gives more knowledge as it is used. When we tell God to take us and use us the way He sees fit, then be ready because faith can really hurt. I thank God every day for the knowledge He has given me so that I may inspire others to do His will and understand, and find their path back to Him. I feel that I have really lived. There is no middle ground.

CHAPTER 8

Fictional Foreign Jurisdiction

Since 1776 and since George Washington became the first president of the republic of America, the Constitution was adopted by the original thirteen states at the time as the "supreme law of the land". This Constitution signified common law and common-law jurisdiction. In this system, a person is presumed innocent until proven guilty. Only a person accused by two or more witnesses, along with the forensic evidence, is brought to trial for the injury of either person or property. This common law under the Constitution is guaranteed to every lawful citizen of America regardless of color, origin, gender, or age, including the unborn, and whether rich or poor. This system is a safeguard for our natural inalienable rights itemized within the Bill of Rights of the Constitution and made a part thereof.

The Constitution created government and set the procedures for electors in electing leaders through a democratic process. It allows for the election of presidents at the federal level and for representatives and senators, governors, state legislators, and other state officers as needed. The Constitution outlines responsibilities of both federal and state governments, setting the boundaries for them to operate in, without oppressing the people. The federal government was first formed in Washington, DC, or District of Columbia within ten square miles and told to stay there. Washington, DC, is the seat of the first corporation, and we know this corporation's name is the United States of America. Each state was then united in what we know as a "union of states", under the requirements of an "enabling act". An enabling act is a statute drafted by the United States Congress authorizing the people of a territory to frame a proposed state constitution as a step toward admission to the union. An enabling act details the procedure by which the territory will be admitted as a state after ratification of their constitutions and election of state officers.

Enabling acts can contain restrictions, such as that of Nevada, which was required to abolish slavery, and of course, Utah had to give up polygamy. Each state was to guarantee freedom of religious practices to all inhabitants and to agree that all public lands owned by the federal government at the time of statehood would be retained after admission. The applicant territory then was to submit its proposed constitution to Congress, which either accepted it or required changes. Each state was required to adopt the Federal Constitution into each of their respective state constitutions, recognizing the Federal Constitution as the supreme law of the land as well. This guaranteed the uniformity, peace, tranquility, and security of the union of states or the United States of America, a republic.

The Supreme Court was/is the court of original jurisdiction, giving all united states the system of "full faith and credit." Every state could not be a country unto itself, despite the states' rights clause. They could not secede now without the approval of a high majority of citizens in their respective states. They also needed the cooperation of the other states and federal government, since they were under contract and of one body. Each state adopted the same federal laws, the same money system, the same court system, the same education system, etc. All states were required to draft all state laws in harmony with the constitutions that were adopted by them.

The Republican Party was founded in March 20, 1854, in Ripon, Wisconsin, to combat the Kansas-Nebraska Act, combating the expansion of slavery. In 1860, Abraham Lincoln was the first president to run on the Republican platform. There was only one party before that due to the newness still of the country. Everyone emigrating from Europe came from countries who were all liberal as they were coming from systems of force under kings and dictators. Anytime there is a system of force prevalent, then that system only gives one choice for obedience; therefore, people mourn, and freedom is oppressed. The people came to America because they wanted freedom to choose who, when, where, and how they wanted to worship.

The Bill of Rights of the Constitution was formed and written by wise men and adopted to guarantee such rights to the people. There were countless good men who came, fleeing such oppressive countries, to America for the same reasons. Many were statesmen, scholars, lawyers, professors, inventors, among other hardworking and industrious people, such as farmers, ranchers, and miners. The Constitution was written by just, honest, and godly men who did not seek power over the people, riches, or grandeur but sought the welfare of the people. The Constitution was written and adopted "for the people, of the people and by the people."

The states, through the federal government and the Constitution, were given the power by the people in respective states to elect or choose their own officials such as senators and representatives, both federal and state levels. They also elected officials such as governors, judges, mayors in respective cities, and even down to the county and city councilmen. The federal judges were all appointed by the president of the United States and then ratified by the Senate, at least in most cases.

Under the Constitution, the state laws were written as public law. The judges were known as justices of the peace, and the police were called peace officers. These terms were used because a man or woman was not under investigation for a crime unless there was an accusation of injury to a person or someone's property. Therefore, only peace needed to be upheld.

This was a wonderful period, but nothing is left alone as the forces of good and evil are continually at opposition to each other, one insisting on peace and freedom and another wanting to cause chaos and slavery. God and Satan are mortal enemies, and all mankind is either on one side or on the other. The ones who will have Satan to be their god are had in all countries, states, and communities in all walks of life. Those anti-God people are a scourge to the freedom of men/women, and they were from the very beginning at the birth of this country of America, trying to bring about the destruction of our freedom. The people who scheme, manipulate, or collaborate have an agenda for a bigger goal for themselves; and that is control, riches, fame, and world domination. They are working to place a king, a dictator, a corporation, democracy, socialism, or communism in control over the people. In this case, these evil people are working for all of the above, and all are combined into one institution, and that is the pope of the Roman Catholic Church, attempting to bring about the return of the Roman Empire as discussed in the book of Daniel in the Old Testament. All the evidence points to this.

People known as liberals or Democrats in our government have ties to Catholic Jesuits and are schooled by secret societies. From among such men and women come assassins of presidents, such as Garfield, Lincoln, and Kennedy. They have assassinated congressmen and judges, among others, to bring about their dastardly plans. They are the source of wars, such as the revolution, the Civil War between the states, both world wars, and the Vietnam War. They are the ones who, through the house of Rothschild and the Federal Reserve bank, seek power and control over the world to bring about the downfall of America. The Rothschilds themselves are suspected in the murder of at least seven U.S. presidents. There were William Henry Harrison and Zachary Taylor, and they poisoned James Buchanan, but he survived. All three were obstructing Illuminati plans to begin the Civil War. The Rothschilds' Illuminati was also responsible, as stated earlier, for the killing of Abraham Lincoln by John Wilkes Booth. Sen. Huey Long and Presidents Garfield, McKinley, and Kennedy were all murdered by the Illuminati. There was an internet document called "The Mardi Gras Secrets" exposing these things. This document was created by Mimi L. Eustis, the daughter of Samuel Todd Churchill, a member of the New Orleans Mardi Gras Society called the Mystick Crewe of Comus. This society was a chapter of the Skull and Bones, the very same secret order that George W. H. Bush and his son George W. Bush belong to.

These evil people infiltrate every organization and institution as parasites and leeches to control every aspect of our lives to the extent that only God knows for sure their thoughts and nature and where these such people are hiding in our midst. They get a little control, and as they get this, they immediately begin to change small things to change the meaning of the whole picture to the point that what used to be white is now black and good is now evil. These such people are found in Congress and elsewhere in the land, where they obstruct and hinder the progress of good anywhere, they rear their ugly, evil heads, and they can be identified just by watching what they do. A man named Kevin Trudeau wrote a book titled *More Natural Cures Revealed*, where he talked about the societies, and I leave a quote out of his book to drive my point home. He left the secret society and began exposing their secrets: "*Never in history has someone left the society, and exposed its inside secrets. Think about, for a moment, that no one in history has exposed the secret writings kept at the Vatican, or Mormon headquarters. I am the first member of this society that is coming forward. Members of this society include politicians, captains of industry, news journalists, celebrities, musicians, writers, scientists, law enforcement officials, movie stars, and more."*

Our common law under the Constitution drastically changed in 1938. The Constitution still remained the supreme law of the land, but because of a case, *Erie Railroad Co. v. Harry J. Tompkins*, 304 U.S. 64, which was a landmark decision, the Supreme Court held that federal courts did not have the judicial power to create general federal common law when hearing state law claims under diversity jurisdiction. In reaching this holding, the court overturned almost a century of federal civil procedure case law and established the foundation of what remains the modern law of diversity jurisdiction as it applies to United States federal courts.

This diversity jurisdiction or commercial law is what went into place since 1938. Even though the Constitution is still the supreme law of the land, the federal jurisdiction accepts the Uniform Commercial Code as the law governing commerce in both state and federal jurisdictions.

The only way that common law exists now is if the person being injured asserts his or her constitutional rights by a statement or objection. Otherwise, the person is presumed to be guilty until proven innocent. Officers in commerce are now called policemen; the judiciary is called judges in tribunal courts, just like the courts of England. In this system of the world/commerce, it only takes one complaint issued against someone, without any evidence, for the police to arrest and drag the person in before the judge to prove his or her innocence.

The states each have taken and codified the Uniform Commercial Code into state codes. In Idaho, we know them as Idaho Code; in Wisconsin, they are called Wisconsin Code and so on. They are statutes of commerce and violate just about every constitutional right we have. We must know how to assert our constitutional rights so as not to be violated under commercial law. This system is used to abrogate or change the Constitution unless we stand against it. This kind of law, next to the supreme law of God, is what is called prima facie, meaning law until proven otherwise by assertion or objection. This inferior law, next to God's law, is a fictional foreign jurisdiction.

A previous chapter has outlined the IRS and what it stands for and explained the workings of how it is a big lie. It has shown how the IRS operates in an inferior capacity in this fictional foreign jurisdiction and the remedy we need so as not to become slaves to it. This is the prima facie law I am talking about. Each one of our rights in the Bill of Rights has been made hard to access due to deceit and smoke screen. However, our common law, with our constitutional rights, is still there; but we simply need to have knowledge and be willing to walk the walk, find them, and assert them. For instance, the right to travel falls under the Ninth Amendment. Every state requires anyone who wishes to operate a motor vehicle to have a valid driver's license. This requirement is reasonable because everyone should be qualified and know how to operate a motor vehicle safely and responsibly because it deals with the safety of person and property, which is under common law. The only problem is that, since 1938, the person will not be tried according to common law or the Constitution. The courts won't hear anything but commercial law or statutes.

Every state has to make it available somewhere in their statutes that the person can travel by right. They won't tell you about it, but you have to find it. The states won't tell you about the loopholes, no more than the IRS will tell you that you don't have to file. This all has to do with revenue and control. The statute telling you that the driver's license is required will also have a provision somewhere stating the conditions to meet to have the right to travel freely. This provision is that you need to be a farmer. Farmers make this country, feed the world, and have a closeness to the God of nature. If you are a farmer, then you don't need a driver's license when transporting farm equipment, produce, family, and anything to do with your farm within 100- to 150-mile radius of your farm. This is not considered commerce. You can operate any vehicle, even diesel semis, without a driver's license as long as you are on your own farm business.

Natural rights are those rights endowed by God. Another term for such rights is *inalienable rights*, such as life, liberty, and the pursuit of happiness; the right to freedom of religion, speech, education, self-defense, and travel; and many more. These rights are further guaranteed in the Bill of Rights of the Constitution. Most rights are protected by the state courts, but if you don't know them and how to assert them, you can possibly get the shaft.

Many people need to have an attorney to represent them in the court system now because of the complexity, the many hurdles put in the way, and the numerous loopholes of the system. Even though some criminals are guilty as can be, they may get away with their sins totally free because of some ridiculous technicality. Some people are very knowledgeable of the law, some more than others, mostly because of issues that have arisen that force them to have to defend themselves. Some know they are being violated by evil people, either attorneys or judges or both; and rather than give in and take it, they fight back the best way they know how, by fighting the system on their own. If they don't have the money to pay attorneys, which is no guarantee of success even then, they then need to educate themselves on the law and procedure and go into the court and represent themselves.

The courts will not hear constitutional arguments, so the argument has to be according to statute. The person needs to know the statutes not violated. The good thing about the statute is that it has to be uniform with the Constitution. The freedom of choice has to be in front of every person, as guaranteed by the Constitution, and made available to the people, even in the commercial system, in other words the fictional foreign jurisdiction. This type of jurisdiction makes it easier for the liberal-minded Democrats, once in power, to attempt to change the laws, rules, meanings, etc. by deceit and outright fraud, misrepresentations, and lies in everything they approach or touch or are involved in.

The Democrats have been successful in many areas of this prima facie catastrophe. Common examples are the Sixteenth Amendment, the IRS, Federal Reserve, Emergency War Powers Act, and *The Communist Manifesto*. I know I sound like a broken record when mentioning these things time and again, but they are important to know. Every plank of *The Communist Manifesto*, except one, has been instituted into our society and is in force as we speak, through statutes. The evil people are using these planks to tear at the very center and fiber of our people, especially the young. The people have let their guards down by not staying close to God with all their might, mind, and strength through worship and prayer. We worship God through obeying His commandments. The people have allowed their morals to be diminished and have let the system of commerce/the world lead them toward darkness.

The only right that the Democrats haven't destroyed is the right to bear arms, and they are working hard to destroy that. This year's presidential run by the Democrats and the school shootings are being orchestrated by the evil liberals/Jesuits who swear to take our guns, and legislation is already passed in the Democrat-majority-held House of Representatives to do just that if we let them. The people refuse to give this right up. If the people ever give this basic right up, they know that slavery is the result and might just as well lay everything on the line and have a civil war because there is nothing else left to do if they want to have a chance at keeping their freedom.

To destroy America, the communists needed to undermine our government and our laws, which they did in 1938 by instituting this fictional foreign government jurisdiction. They needed to stop the growth of our populace, and they accomplished this through *Roe v. Wade* by the killing of millions of our unborn, and they are currently waging war against the old and unproductive people through health care and drugs.

They needed to control the money system, and they accomplished this through the Federal Reserve central bank and forced the people into bondage by the muscleman of this bank, the IRS, instituting the graduated income tax. They needed to control the minds of our youth, pollute their minds, and cause depravity, and they have done this through the Department of Education and public schools and have unionized the teachers and controlled what the children are taught. They further have combined the education of our children with industry, teaching them what to think and the slavery mentality.

They needed to control transportation, which they did through limiting the right to travel, commerce, and regulation. They needed the people to be dependent on government, which they accomplished through the welfare programs. The Democrats promise the people free education, free health care, and free sex changes and even promise to pay those who won't work to not work. They promise to take more taxes from those who will work and give it to those who won't.

The communists needed the people to be unhealthy to more easily control them and keep them in a state of lethargy and sickness and not aggressive. They accomplished this through the American Medical Association and the Federal Drug Administration by the administering of harmful drugs to the people physically and in their food and by providing processed food where all nutrients have been removed. Because of these things, the people contract diseases, mainly cancer and heart disease, among many others, that are caused for the same reasons.

They had to do away with property ownership and have been very successful in every state, declaring the land tax by statute. Either way, the evil liberals get ownership of your property. They have managed to create a big government and agencies of the government, for the people themselves to police their own and report, make complaints, and oppress their fellow man.

They needed to make people unable to represent themselves in the courts by making it almost impossible. They needed to frustrate and cause them to be hopeless, and have done so by making fees only the rich can afford. The attorneys and judges collaborate to ensnare and make a man or woman offenders for a word. Also, in order to gain more revenue for themselves, and for the sake of their jobs, by fulfilling quotas to justify their jobs, or if they have something against that person, or don't like that person.

They needed to infiltrate the churches, which they have done through the 501(c)(3) charters, joining them to the system of commerce through incorporation. This caused the churches to be politically correct and polluted our most holy institutions, making the leaders afraid to preach the truth and instead, become charismatic.

The communists have put into place organizations consisting of evil people who hate God and the truth. These organizations are swarming with Jesuit Catholic secret orders. The Democratic Party is unequivocally the communist party in America. They consist of graduates from colleges like Harvard, Yale, Loyola, Sanford, and Fordham etc., These people learn to obstruct, organize, squelch, and diminish rights, and then hide among their secret orders where they have sworn oaths to protect their secrets. You look at the way these people operate and see for yourselves if these things are not true. You look at how some people will even kill to accomplish their goals and how their body count just gets bigger. They have no shame. The only language these Democrats/Jesuits/secret societies know how to speak, is the lies of the devil. The Democrats are the breeding ground for these secret orders that destroy our government.

The liberals do the same things they have done from the very beginning. They want nobility, they want power, and to do that, they want a king instead of a free government by the people. The book of Alma in the *Book of Mormon* tells us how these "king-men" were dealt with. This story is very synonymous with the way the Democrats tried to dethrone our duly elected president by the people, because he would not alter the Constitution or laws to suit their purposes. The division of the country made them very susceptible to invasion from foreign sources, which did come. When it came, the king-men refused to cooperate and support their country but would rather see it overrun before they would lift a finger in the cause of liberty. However, the military was called on to force these king-men to support the cause of liberty or be killed with the sword, and many of them were. The leaders were thrown in prison and later tried for treason. Liberals are a danger to our country and a scourge to every country in the world.

*And now it came to pass in the commencement of the twenty and fifth year of the reign of the judges over the people of Nephi, they having established peace between the people of Lehi and the people of Morianton concerning their lands, and having commenced the twenty and fifth year in peace; Nevertheless, they did not long maintain an entire peace in the land, for there began to be a contention among the people concerning the chief judge Pahoran; for behold, there were a part of the people who desired that a few particular points of the law should be altered. But behold, Pahoran would not alter nor suffer the law to be altered; therefore, he did not hearken to those who had sent in their voices with their petitions concerning the **altering of the law**. Therefore, those who were desirous that the **law should be altered** were angry with him, and desired that **he should no longer be their chief judge** over the land; therefore, there arose a warm dispute concerning the matter, but not unto bloodshed. And it came to pass that those who were desirous that Pahoran should be dethroned from the judgment seat were called **king-men**, for they were desirous that the **law should be altered in a manner to overthrow the free government to establish a king** over the land. And those who were desirous that Pahoran should remain chief judge over the land took upon them the name of **freemen**; and thus was the division among them, for the freemen had sworn or covenanted to maintain their rights and their privileges of their religion by a **free government**. And it came to pass that the matter of their contention was settled by the **voice of the people**. And it came to pass that the voice of the people came in favor of the freemen, and Pahoran retained the judgement-seat, which caused much rejoicing among the brethren of Pahoran and also many of the **people of liberty**, who also put the king-men to silence, that they durst not oppose but were obliged to **maintain the cause of freedom**. Now those who were in favor of kings were those of **high birth**, and they sought to be kings; and they were supported by those who sought power and authority over the people. But behold, this was a* *critical time for such contentions to be among the people of Nephi; for behold, Amalickiah had again stirred up the hearts of the people of the Lamanites against the people of the Nephites, and he was gathering together soldiers from all parts of his land, and arming them, and preparing for war with all diligence; for he had sworn to drink the blood of Moroni. But behold, we shall see that his promise which he made was rash; nevertheless, he did prepare himself and his armies to come to battle against the Nephites. Now his armies were not so great as they had hitherto been, because of the many thousands who had been slain by the hand of the Nephites; but notwithstanding their great loss, Amalickiah had gathered together a wonderfully great army, insomuch that he feared not to come down to the land of Zarahemla. Yea, even Amalickiah did himself come down, at the head of the Lamanites. And it was in the twenty and fifth year of the reign of the judges; and it was at the same time that they had begun to settle the affairs of their contentions concerning the chief judge, Pahoran. And it came to pass that when the men who were called **king-men** had heard that the Lamanites were coming down to battle against them, **they were glad in their hearts; and they refused to take up arms**, for they were wroth with the chief judge, and also with the **people of liberty**, that they would not take up arms **to defend their country**. And it came to pass that when Moroni saw this, and also saw that the Lamanites were coming into the borders of the land, he was exceedingly wroth because of the stubbornness of those people whom he had labored with so much diligence to preserve; yea, he was exceedingly wroth; his soul was filled with anger against them. And it came to pass that he sent a petition, with the voice of the people, unto the governor of the land, desiring that he should read it, and give him [Moroni] power to **compel those dissenters to defend their country or to put them to death**. For it was his first care to put an end to such contentions and dissensions among the people; for behold, this had been hitherto a cause of all their destruction. And it came to pass that it was **granted according to the voice of the people**. And it came to pass that Moroni commanded that his army should go against those **king-men, to pull down their pride and their nobility** and level them with the earth, or they should take up arms and **support the cause of liberty**. And it came to pass that the armies did march forth against them; and they did pull down their pride and their nobility, insomuch that as they did lift their weapons of war to fight against the men of Moroni they were hewn down and leveled to the earth. And it came to pass that there were four thousand of those dissenters who were hewn down by the sword; and those of their leaders who were not slain in battle **were*** *taken and cast into prison, for there was no time for their trials at this period. And the remainder of those dissenters, rather than be smitten down to the earth by the sword, yielded* **to the standard of liberty**, *and were compelled to hoist the title* **of liberty upon their towers, and in their cities, and to take up arms in defense of their country.** *And thus Moroni put an end to those king-men, that there were not any known by the appellation of king-men; and thus he put an end to the stubbornness and the pride of those people who professed* **the blood of nobility;** *but they were brought down to humble themselves like unto their brethren,* **and to fight valiantly for their freedom from bondage.** *(Alma 51:1–21, Book of Mormon)*

So you see, we have the two trees or systems of government in every aspect of our lives, in order to be given a choice. That is why I can say that I can see a communist coming from a mile away. I can also tell if the communist is ignorant or deliberate. An ignorant one doesn't know what he or she is doing or why and therefore can be taught. A deliberate one makes blatant, evil decisions that willingly hurts others.

This fictional foreign jurisdiction is the one whose fruits enticed our first parents to fall, figuratively speaking, and put us here to go through this miserable world. It was done deliberately by our first parents, enabling us all to have the opportunity at life and to prove to our Father in Heaven that we will serve Him, and if not Him, then Satan is our master. The world or kingdom of Satan is inferior and, therefore, is a fictional foreign jurisdiction and can only beat us if we don't have faith in Christ, and will not obey His commandments. Christ however, won't have lazy or ignorant people, so we must look up and believe. The Constitution is the "Supreme Law of the Land", which embodies the Ten Commandments.

The plan of God is to test us all in this probationary state or state of Hell/ telestial kingdom, which is an absolutely ingenious plan. Any reward or curse we receive is brought on ourselves by the decisions we make, therefore rendering the judgments of God on ourselves, and us having to admit that all the judgments of God are just. We won't be able to whine and say at the last that we don't deserve what we get. If we die in our sins, we will live in them forever. If we change, become clean, and have good habits, then when we die, we will be clean and have good habits forever.

We must forsake our weaknesses, traditions, sins, and vices and become the kind of person whom God wants to associate with if He comes into a room where we are. God is a glorified man. He once was where we are now, and we may become like Him and go to where He now is. There are only two churches, and everything and everyone is a member of one or the other. There is no middle ground.

CHAPTER 9

The Division of the Earth

We all know the story about Noah and how he built an ark to preserve his family and samples of animals of every kind and of every size, except those who lived in the water, from drowning in the great flood. Noah was considered by God as a perfect man or at least as perfect as one could be for his day. *Genesis 6:9* says, *"These are the generations of Noah: Noah was a just man and perfect in his generations, and Noah walked with God."* Noah was commanded by God to build an ark, and the measurements given by God to complete this task proved that this boat was going to be huge. This ark was going to be big enough to take two of each species of animals. Some people automatically picture in their minds the size of some of the species like the elephant, rhinoceros, hippopotamus, giraffe, and tigers. So they automatically imagine the size the boat would have to be. Suppose Noah only took babies of each species, male and female. The boat would still be huge because of the many, many species there were and are. Kent Hovind concurs that it probably was babies that were taken on the ark, which makes sense as Noah and his family were on the ark for about a year, long enough for the animals to be old enough by the time the boat settled on solid ground, ready and old enough to breed and multiply.

In a former chapter was discussed briefly the planet where the gods dwelled just above the earth, using a magnetic pull to stand massive amounts of water up toward the planet into a massive pillar as if Atlas was holding up the world. Kent Hovind also talked about a ring of ice around the earth that kept the sun's ultraviolet rays from aging man and beast. Up to Noah's day, people were living hundreds of years. Many of them were living past nine hundred years. This period was where lizards grew into dinosaurs. Up to the time of Noah, it had never rained on the earth; but to water it, God sent a mist up daily and solved this problem. Because of these ideal circumstances, you can picture how lush and green everything was and how thick the foliage grew. This was the period known as the golden age, where man only had to harvest what grew.

Despite the goodness of God in providing as He did for His family, it only takes one to abuse what is prepared or planned. This happened when Cain killed Abel. *"And Cain talked with Abel his brother: and it came to pass, when they were in the field, that Cain rose up against Abel his brother, and slew him. And the Lord said unto Cain, Where is Abel thy brother? And he said, I know not: Am I my brother's keeper?" (Genesis 4:8–9, KJV).*

Cain covenanted with Satan, and this was where the secret orders began. Cain had posterity of his own, one of which was Lamech, who killed a man and then entered into secret oaths with his wives. *"And Lamech said unto his wives, Adah and Zillah, hear my voice; ye wives of Lamech, hearken unto my speech: for I have slain a man to my wounding, and a young man to my hurt" (Genesis 4:23, KJV).*

It was from the time of Cain that men began to be evil and seek to gain honor, glory, riches, and power over one another. Cain was the first liberal. Most of the people became evil very quickly. They became violent and mean, except for a certain few, such as Seth, who was a good man. From Seth were born sons and daughters up to the time of Methuselah, who lived 969 years. He had a son also named Lamech, who was a good man. Lamech had Noah when he was 595 years old and then lived a total of 777 years before he died.

Lamech was the last good man who lived before Noah. All the rest were evil and violent and served Satan. *"And Noah begat three sons, **Shem**, **Ham**, and **Japheth**. The earth also was corrupt before God, and the whole earth was filled with violence. And God looked upon the earth, and, behold, it was corrupt; for all flesh had corrupted his way upon the earth. And God said unto Noah, the end of all flesh is come before me; for the earth is filled with violence through them; and behold, I will destroy them with the earth" (Genesis 6:10–13, KJV).*

So God commanded Noah to build an ark. It was really strange to the people around seeing a man and his family building such a weird huge contraption on dry land as the whole world was one landmass, and it had never rained before. So you can imagine the name-calling, the derogatory statements made, the disrespect by others, and of course the unbelief of the masses. To them, Noah was probably called mental and foolish, but he endured because he talked directly with God and observed His commandments.

Noah spent about 120 years preaching and building the ark when the day finally came to enter into it with all the animals. It probably took a lot of work caring and quartering all of them. Lastly, Noah went in with his wife and his three sons, Shem, Ham, and Japheth, each one having a wife. The total of people who entered the Ark was eight. *"In the selfsame day entered Noah, and Shem, and Ham, and Japheth, the sons of Noah, and Noah's wife, and the three wives of his sons with them, into the ark" (Genesis 7:13, KJV). "Which sometime were disobedient, when once the long suffering of God waited in the days of Noah, while the ark was a preparing, wherein few, that is, **eight souls** were saved by water" (1 Peter 3:20, KJV). "And spared not the old world, but saved **Noah the eighth person**, a preacher of righteousness, bringing in the flood **upon the world of the ungodly**" (2 Peter 2:5, KJV).*

From these verses, we know that only eight people got onto the ark, and all the rest were drowned in the flood, including people, animals of every kind, and fowls of the air.

*And the flood was forty days upon the earth; and the waters increased, and bare up the ark, and it was lift up above the earth. And the waters prevailed, and were increased greatly upon the earth; and the ark went upon the face of the waters. And the waters prevailed exceedingly upon the earth; and all the high hills, that were under the whole heaven, were covered. Fifteen cubits upward did the waters prevail; and the mountains were covered. And **all flesh died** that moved upon the earth, both fowl, and of cattle, and of beast, and of every creeping thing that creepeth upon the earth, and every man: All in whose nostrils was the breath of life, of all that was in the dry land, died. And every living substance was destroyed which was upon the face of the ground, both man, and cattle, and the creeping things, and the fowl of the heaven; and they were destroyed from the earth: and **Noah only remained alive**, and **they that were with him** in the ark. And the waters prevailed upon the earth an hundred and fifty days. (Genesis 7:17–24, KJV)*

Noah, with his family, stayed in that ark from the 17th day of the 2nd month of the year, which we call February, until the 2nd month of the next year before he was able to come out of the ark. It rained for 150 days straight before it quit or abated, which is about July 17, before the ark rested in the mountains of Ararat. It was about October 1 before Noah could even begin to see the tops of the mountains. Forty days after that, Noah was able to open a window and send forth the dove and the raven. The dove came back, but the raven didn't. It was 7 seven days later when he sent the dove out the second time, and the dove came back with the olive branch. Then on the 1st day of the 1st month, which we know as January, Noah removed the cover from the ark. Then on February 27, Noah was finally able to leave the ark. It was only Noah and his family who left the ark. They were the only living family on the face of the whole earth. There were no other people but them, which included Noah and his wife; Shem, Ham, and Japheth; and their three wives, making a total of eight people. Noah and his family were told to go forth and multiply on the face of the earth, the animals likewise. They were preserved to act as breeding stock.

Every man, woman, and child descended from Noah and his three sons. That means, today, no matter the nationality, color, or origin, we are one family and one race. *"And **the sons of Noah**, that **went forth of the ark**, were **Shem**, and **Ham**, and **Japheth**: and Ham is the father of Canaan. These are the three sons of Noah: and **of them was the whole earth overspread**"* (Genesis 9:18–19, KJV).

There are no different races; just colors, languages, and customs separate us. The whites came from the lineage of Shem, the orientals from the lineage of Japheth, and the blacks from the lineage of Ham. You wonder why Ham was black. The truth was that Ham did something foolish, even though he knew better, that caused him to be cursed with black skin.

*And Noah began to be a husbandman, and he planted a vineyard: And he drank of the wine, and was drunken; and he was uncovered within his tent. And **Ham, the father of Canaan**, saw the nakedness of his father, and told his two brethren without. And Shem and Japheth took a garment, and laid it upon both their shoulders, and went backward, and covered the nakedness of their father; and their faces were backward, and they saw not their father's nakedness. And Noah awoke from his wine, and knew what his younger son had done unto him. And he said, **Cursed be Canaan**; a servant of servants shall he be unto his brethren. (Genesis 9:20–25, KJV)*

And Noah awoke from his wine and knew what his youngest son had done unto him, and he said, cursed be Canaan; a servant of servants shall he be unto his brethren. And he said, Blessed be the Lord God of Shem; and Canaan shall be his servant, and **a veil of darkness shall cover him**, *that he shall be known among men. (Genesis 9:29–30, JST of the KJV)*

Noah lived a total of 950 years, and he died.

Ham or Canaan had a son named Cush, and Cush had a son named Nimrod. The beginning of the kingdom of Nimrod was Babel. There was also Erech, Accad, and Calneh, in the land of Shinar, the same land where Nimrod began the Tower of Babel. At this time, because they were all family, everyone spoke the same language; they were just different colors because of the curse of Ham. Because Ham was cursed, all of Ham's posterity carried the mark of the black skin. Ham's posterity is not responsible for Ham's sins, but it is because of Ham's sins that his posterity has to deal with what Ham did. The same happened when Adam and Eve transgressed in the Garden of Eden. It is not Adam's transgressions that we are responsible for, but it is because of Adam's transgressions that we have to deal with this devil's jurisdiction and choose what we will do, according to our situations. We all must still have the free agency to choose who we will serve.

Because we are all family, we are not different races, but we are just different colors. At the Tower of Babel, all mankind spoke the same language. At this time, the planet where the God's dwelled, or in mythical terms Mount Olympus, hovered just above the earth, and the earth was still one landmass. The magnetic pull of the planet of the gods on the water made a giant pillar of water stand up toward the planet, making it appear as if Atlas were holding up the world. This was where Nimrod got the wild idea that he and everyone in the land of his kingdom of Shinar were going to build a great tower that would reach up to Heaven.

And **the whole earth was of one language**, *and* **of one speech**. *And it came to pass, as they journeyed from the east, that they found a plain in the land of Shinar; and they dwelt there. And they said one to another, Go to, let us make brick, and burn them throughly, and they had brick for stone, and slime had they for morter. And they said, Go to, let us build us a city and* **a tower**, **whose top may reach unto heaven**; *and let us make us a name, lest we be scattered abroad upon the face of the whole earth. And the Lord came down to see the city* *and the tower that the children of men builded. And the Lord said, Behold, the people is one, and they have all one language; and this they begin to do: and now nothing will be restrained from them, which they have imagined to do. Go to, let us go down, and there confound their language, that they may not understand one another's speech. So **the Lord scattered them abroad** from thence **upon the face of all the earth**: and they left off to build the city. Therefore is the name of it called Babel; because the Lord did there confound the language of all the earth: and from thence did the Lord scatter them abroad upon the face of all the earth. (Genesis 11:1–9, KJV)*

It was in these days that Japheth's and Shem's posterity was also growing on the face of the earth. Shem had a son called Eber, who had a son named Peleg. And it was in Nimrod's Day when the language of the people, because of the Tower of Babel, was confounded, and the people were scattered to different parts of the earth. It wasn't until the days of Peleg that the earth was divided. *"And unto Eber were born two sons: the name of one was **Peleg**; for **in his days was the earth divided**; and his brother's name was Joktan"* (Genesis 10:25, KJV).

The timing of the confounding of the language of the people and the time when the heavens fled away were closely coordinated. Revelation mentioned the heavens fleeing away. *"Then I saw a great white throne, and him that sat on it, from whose face **the earth and the heaven fled away**; and there was found no place for them"* (Revelation 20:11, KJV).

So after the language of the people was confounded, the people gathered into groups and went to different parts of the world to be alone with the ones they could understand. Later, the planet where the Gods dwelled left, breaking the magnetic pull on the watery pillar and returned the water to the earth, making the water level higher, thus dividing the earth into continents and into islands. Remember, before, it was one solid landmass. God later led certain groups out of certain countries, and they were instructed to build ships or barges at various times, whatever the case might be, and flee persecution with the promise of prosperity and peace if they would obey the commandments of the Lord.

It is amazing to see just how wise and great God is. We all started out as one family, regardless of color, speaking the same language for generations up to the time of the Tower of Babel. God then confounded the languages, thus dividing the people into areas of the earth and then sending the earth away from before Him and dividing the landmass with water. Now in these latter days, we can see how the people are beginning to return to speaking the same language again.

The ability to get around the world and come together is so much faster, and the speed and ability to obtain knowledge through the internet and to communicate worldwide is so fantastic. Knowledge does flow over the earth like a flood. *"For **the earth shall be filled with the knowledge of the glory of the Lord**, as the waters cover the sea" (Habakkuk 2:14, KJV).* It is literally at our fingertips.

I can see how close our Father in Heaven is in getting set to return again. He has told us that in the days of Noah, so shall it be in the days of the coming of the Son of Man. We are there, but for the wicked, that is going to be a terrifying day. *"But as the days of Noah were, so shall also the coming of the Son of man be" (Matthew 24:37, KJV).* We don't know the day nor the hour, but we still know the time is close at hand.

CHAPTER 10

The Nature of God

This chapter's purpose is to further drive home the fact that God was/is also a man but now glorified and perfect and that we are created in His likeness. The Father and His Son, Jesus Christ, have appeared to many of the holy prophets down through the ages as seemeth them good. We will start from the Creation.

*And God said, let us make man after **our** likeness: and let them have dominion over the fish of the sea, and over the fowl of the air, and over the cattle, and over all the earth, and over every creeping thing that creepeth upon the earth. So God created man in his own image, in the image of God created he him; male and female created he them. (Genesis 1:26–27, KJV)*

*And the Lord God said, Behold, the man is become as one of **us**, to know good and evil: and now, lest he put forth his hand, and take also of the tree of life, and eat, and live forever. (Genesis 3:22, KJV)*

This is the book of the generations of Adam. In the day God created man in the likeness of God made he him; Male and female created he them; and blessed them, and called their name Adam, in the day when they were created. And Adam lived an hundred and thirty years, and begat a son in his own likeness, after his image; and called his name Seth. (Genesis 5:1–3, KJV)

So after God placed Adam here on the earth, Adam in turn created sons and daughters in His own likeness, as described here, and named them after Him because Adam is the surname by which all men are called. We are His children, the children of God. God has endowed all the same attributes that

He has on His children from generation to generation.

The children of Adam, including Adam, were living into or near the 900-year-old bracket. Adam personally lived 930 years, while Seth lived 912 years, Enos lived 905 years, Cainan lived 912 years, Mahalaleel lived 895 years, Jared lived 962 years, Enoch lived while on the earth 365 years before he and his people were taken up to God, Methuselah lived 969 years, and Lamech lived 777 years. Noah, after coming off the ark, lived to the ripe old age of 950 years. Since the days of Noah, the protection ring that encircled the earth was now broken and allowed the sun's ultraviolet rays to age man. Man, now began to age faster and not live nearly as long.

A point to remember, is if a lizard can get as big as a dinosaur in 900-plus years, then how big do you think a man can get in this same amount of time? After the flood men no longer lived over 900 years, but to live 120 years was a good long time. There were still huge men living at the same time, with the men who only were living 120 years. I would consider them as giants in the land.

*And it came to pass, when men began to multiply on the face of the earth, and daughters were born unto them, That the sons of God saw the daughters of men that they were fair: and they took them wives of all which they chose. And the Lord said, my spirit shall not always strive with man, for that he also is flesh: yet his days shall be 120 years. There were **giants** in the earth in those days; and also, after that, when the sons of God came in unto the daughters of men, and they bear children to them, the same became mighty men which were of old, men of renown. (Genesis 6:1–4, KJV)*

The sons of God were the ones who kept the commandments of God early on and, because of their size, were considered as giants and were men of renown. They, however, were all beginning to stray away from doing what God wanted them to do. They were becoming evil and violent and leaving God rather quickly from generation to generation. Just look at the size of their generations. Nine hundred years? The Lord was already contemplating reducing their life span down to 120 years because He had foreseen the wickedness, the violence, and the godlessness of the people. After the ring around the earth was broken, the shortening of the life span of man happened rather quickly. Noah lived the remainder of his life out to that of 950 years, and then after his sons on down, the life span was shortened dramatically.

Christ was and is greatly responsible for the creation and organization of all things.

Christ is described in John: *"In the beginning was the **Word**, and the Word was with God, and the Word was God. The same was in the beginning with God. All things were made by him; and without him was not anything made that was made. . ... And the Word was made flesh, and dwelt among us, (and we beheld his glory, the glory as of the only begotten of the Father,) full of grace and truth" (John 1:1–3, 14, KJV).* These scriptures testify of Christ being in the beginning with God/Adam and as having the office of God, and by Him and through Him were all things created. Christ was one of the "us" when the scriptures record that God said, "Let *us* make man in *our* own image."

Many people get hold of the scripture in John: *"No man hath seen God at any time; the only begotten Son, which is in the bosom of the Father, he hath declared him" (John 1:18, KJV).* The people use this scripture to argue that no man has seen God nor talked to him face-to-face. The explanation is later found in John: *"Not that any man hath seen the Father, save he which is of God, he hath seen the Father. Verily, verily, I say unto you, he that believeth in me hath everlasting life" (John 6:46–47, KJV).* This is Christ speaking to us as He has seen the Father and is telling us that we can too. I am here to tell you that God is real, kind, wise, and loving. We have His attributes, we know who He is, and we have the knowledge and ability to accomplish a close relationship with Him and His Son.

"And no man hath ascended up to Heaven, but he that came down from heaven, even the Son of man which is in heaven" (John 3:13, KJV). We all have come from Heaven, and if we will believe in Christ and follow Him, we all have the ability to go back into the presence of Christ and the Father. *"And that ye put on the new man, which after God is created in righteousness and true holiness" (Ephesians 4:24, KJV). "And have put on the new man, which is renewed in knowledge after the image of him that created him" (Colossians 3:10, KJV).* These scriptures touch on the fact that we are created after the likeness of God, our Father.

This next scripture drives home the fact that both Christ and we have the same Father, and this is what makes us joint heirs with Christ if we are obedient to God and believe in His Son. Christ is telling us that we have the same Father. *"Jesus saith unto her, touch me not; for I am not yet ascended* to my Father: but go to my brethren, and say unto them, I ascend unto **my Father, and your Father**; and to my God, and your God" (John 20:17, KJV). "Jesus answered them, Is it not written in your law, I said, **ye are gods**? If he called them gods, unto whom the word of God came, and the scripture cannot be broken; Say ye of him, whom the Father hath sanctified, and sent into the world, thou blasphemist; because I said, I am the **Son of God**?" (John 10:34–36, KJV).

Stephen, the apostle of Christ, saw God the Father and His Son, Jesus Christ, on the right hand of God as he was being stoned to death. He sealed his testimony of God and Christ with his life. *"But he, being full of the Holy Ghost, looked up stedfastly into heaven, and saw the glory of God, and Jesus standing on the right hand of God, And said, Behold, I see the heavens opened, and the Son of man standing on the right hand of God" (Acts 7:55–56, KJV).*

The apostle Paul explains the term *gods* because there are many, whether pagan or heavenly. To me however, there is one God, being a term with a plural meaning. There are three separate personages, God the Father, His Son, Jesus Christ, and the Holy Ghost. *"For though there be that are called gods, whether in heaven or in the earth, (as there be gods many, and lords many,) But to us there is but one God, the Father, of whom are all things, and we in him; and one Lord Jesus Christ, by whom are all things, and we by him" (1 Corinthians 8:5–6, KJV).*

Christ was resurrected and stood before His apostles and told them to feel His body so that they would know the reality that He was not a spirit but a body of flesh and bone. He wanted them to know that He was really alive.

And as they thus spake, Jesus himself stood in the midst of them, and saith unto them, Peace be unto you. But they were terrified and affrighted, and supposed that they had seen a spirit. And he said unto them, why are ye troubled? And why do thoughts arise in your hearts? Behold my hands and my feet, that it is I myself: handle me, and see; for a spirit hath not flesh and bones, as ye see me have. And when he had thus spoken, he shewed them his hands and feet. And while they yet believed not for joy, and wondered, he said unto them, Have ye here any meat? And they gave him a piece of broiled fish, and of an honeycomb. And he took it, and did eat before them. (Luke 24:36–43, KJV)

And being assembled together with them, commanded them that they should not depart from Jerusalem, but wait for the promise of the Father which, saith he, ye have heard of me. . . .. And when he had spoken these things, while they beheld, he was taken up; and a cloud received him out of their sight. And while they looked steadfastly toward heaven as he went up, behold, two men stood by them in white apparel; Which also said, ye men of Galilee, why stand ye gazing up into heaven? This same Jesus, which is taken up from you into heaven, shall so come in like manner as ye have seen him go into heaven. (Acts 1:4, 9–11, KJV)

While Moses was in the wilderness with the children of Israel after they had left Egypt, he was rehearsing unto them how God had written on two tables of stone with His finger. He saw the finger of God as a man's finger, that of flesh and blood. He also related how the tables of stone were then given to him by Christ the Lord. *"And the Lord delivered unto me two tables of stone written with the finger of God; and on them was written according to all the words, which the Lord spake with you in the mount out of the midst of the fire in the day of the assembly"* (Deuteronomy 9:10, KJV).

Abraham, on the plains of Mamre, was visited by the Lord.

*And the **Lord** appeared unto him in the plains of Mamre: and he sat in the tent door in the heat of the day; And he lift up his eyes and looked, and, lo, three men stood by him: and when he saw them, he ran to meet them from the tent door, and bowed himself toward the ground, And said, My **Lord**, if now I have found favour in thy sight, pass not away, I pray thee, from thy servant. . . . And he took butter, and milk, and the calf which he had dressed, and set it before them; and he stood by them under the tree, and they did eat. (Genesis 18:1–2, 8, KJV)*

These scriptures are talking about the Lord visiting Abraham. Abraham was known as the friend of God. If Christ was a spirit at the time He visited Abraham, He would not have eaten like He did. In Luke 24:36–43, Christ asked for something to eat to prove to His disciples that He wasn't a spirit but a body of flesh and bone.

Everything is possible with God. Christ the Lord had not yet been born in Bethlehem to redeem the people of this world, so this would really make a person think. Christ was born way later through the lineage of Judah, who was a son of Jacob, who was a son of Isaac, who was a son of Abraham. One explanation is that Jesus Christ had a body before visiting Abraham and appeared with two other angels who had bodies. This is a mystery that many people don't think about. Adam and Christ are a team, and they have and will continue to create worlds without end. Does that then mean that for Christ to help in the creation of worlds without end and to be a Savior for these worlds, it required him to lay down the body he had before to the next world, come down again in the spirit, be born again into the new world, and be slain again, worlds without end?

Remember that Christ held the office of God before He came down to this earth. This also would explain why Mary was handpicked to be the mother of Christ, not only because she was clean and an obedient virgin but also because her genes would guarantee Christ being in the express image of the Father. *"The angel answered and said unto her, The Holy Ghost shall come upon thee, and the power of the **Highest shall overshadow thee**: Therefore also, that holy thing which shall be born of thee shall be called the Son of God"* (Luke 1:35, KJV). It was Christ's Father and our Father, the Most High, who overshadowed Mary and not the Holy Ghost, as the Holy Ghost is spirit.

Men who love God will obey His commandments and, because of this, earn the right to be called the sons of God as the men back during the times of Noah who were also called the sons of God. *"Behold, what manner of love the Father hath bestowed upon us, that we should be called the **sons of God**: therefore the world knoweth us not, because it knew him not. Beloved, now are we the **sons of God**, and it doth not yet appear, we shall be like him; for we shall see him as he is. And every man that hath this hope in him purifieth himself, even as he is pure"* (1 John 3:1–3, KJV).

Paul explains further:

*Now I say, that the **heir**, as long as he is a child, differeth nothing from a servant, though he be lord of all; But is under tutors and governors until the time appointed of the Father. Even so we, when we were children, were in bondage under the elements of the world: But when the fulness of the time was come, God sent forth his Son, made of a woman, made under the law, To redeem them that were under the law, that we might receive the adoption of sons. And because ye are sons, God hath sent forth the Spirit of his Son into your hearts, crying, Abba, Father. Wherefore thou art no more a servant, but an **heir** of God through Christ. Howbeit then, when ye knew not God, ye did service unto them which by nature are no gods, But now, after that ye have known God, how turn ye again to the weak and beggarly elements, whereunto ye desire again to be in bondage?*

Ye observe days, and months, and times, and years. (Galatians 4:1–10, KJV)

To develop and have a close relationship with God and to know who He is, like you know your earthly father, is so fantastic. It gives us a glimpse of eternity and makes us grow and have something great to look forward to. *"And this is **life eternal**, that they might **know thee**, the only true God, and Jesus Christ, whom thou hast sent" (John 17:3, KJV).* These words were spoken by Jesus before He was delivered up by Judas. He was praying for His apostles and those of us who believe in Him.

Paul, to the Thessalonians, teaches and explains further about the return of Christ and His judgments on the wicked.

*Seeing it is a righteous thing with God to recompense tribulation to them that trouble you; And to you who are troubled rest with us, when the Lord Jesus shall be revealed from heaven with his mighty angels, In flaming fire taking vengeance on them that **know not God**, and that obey not the gospel of our Lord Jesus Christ: Who shall be punished with everlasting destruction from the presence of the Lord, and from the glory of his power; When he shall come to be glorified in his saints, and to be admired in all them that believe (because our testimony among you was believed) in that day. (2 Thessalonians 1:6–10, KJV)*

Jacob wrestled with God all night until he prevailed on God to give him a blessing. Jacob was very faithful to God; therefore, he was able to accomplish the task of getting this desired blessing from God.

*And Jacob was left alone; and there wrestled a man with him until the breaking of the day. And when he saw that he prevailed not against him, he touched the hollow of his thigh; and the hollow of Jacob's thigh was out of joint as he wrestled with him. And he said, let me go, for the day breaketh. And he said, I will not let thee go, except thou bless me. And he said unto him, what is thy name? And he said, Jacob. And he said, Thy name shall be called no more Jacob, but Israel: for as a prince hast thou power with **God** and with men, and hast prevailed. And Jacob asked him, and said, Tell me, I pray thee, thy name? And he said, wherefore is it that thou dost ask after my name? And he blessed him there. And Jacob called the name of the place Peniel: for **I have seen God face to face**, and my life is preserved. (Genesis 32:24–30, KJV)*

Just as Enoch, Abraham, and Jacob all saw God face-to-face, so did Moses, Aaron, Nadab, Abihu, and seventy of the elders of Israel. *"Then went up*

Moses, and Aaron, Nadab, and Abihu, and seventy of the elders of Israel: And **they saw the God of Israel**: *and there was under his feet as it were a paved work of a sapphire stone, and as it were the body of heaven in his clearness. And upon the nobles of the children of Israel he laid not his hand: also* **they saw God**, *and did eat and drink" (Exodus 24:9–11, KJV).* Now what they saw was absolutely fantastic. It would have to be like a dream, but in reality, it was so true.

Even though Moses was allowed to talk with God face-to-face, Moses wanted all the children of Israel to know for sure that God was with them as they went forward to cross the river Jordan and commence driving out the inhabitants of that land. Moses wanted God to show Himself to the people so that they would know that God was with them, giving them more courage in their undertaking.

And the **Lord spake unto Moses face to face, as a man speaketh unto his friend**. *And he turned again into the camp: but his servant Joshua, the son of Nun, a young man, departed not out of the tabernacle. And Moses said unto the Lord, see, thou sayest unto me, bring up this people: and thou hast not let me know whom thou wilt send with me. Yet thou hast said, I know thee by name, and thou hast also found grace in my sight . . . And he said, My presence shall go with thee, and I will give thee rest. And he said unto him, If thy presence go not with me, carry us not up hence . . . And the Lord said unto Moses, I will do this thing also that thou hast spoken: for thou has found grace in my sight, and I know thee by name. And he said, I beseech thee, shew me thy glory. And he said, I will make all my goodness pass before thee, and I will proclaim the name of the Lord before thee; and will be gracious to whom I will be gracious, and will shew mercy on whom I will shew mercy. And he said, thou canst not see my face: for there shall no man see me, and live. And the Lord said, Behold there is a place by me, and thou shalt stand upon a rock. And it shall come to pass, while my glory passeth by, that I will put thee in a clift of the rock, and will cover thee with my hand, and thou shalt see my* **back parts**: *but my face shall not be seen. (Exodus 33:11–12, 14–15, 17–23, KJV)*

The Lord came down in a cloud and called Aaron and Miriam out from the doorway of the tabernacle because Moses's brother and sister complained about Moses, the Lord's anointed, and the Lord had come to rebuke them.

And the Lord came down in the pillar of the cloud, and stood in the door of *the tabernacle, and called Aaron and Miriam: and they both came forth. And he said, Hear now my words: If there be a prophet among you, I the Lord will make myself known unto him in a vision, and will speak unto him in a dream. My servant Moses is not so, who is faithful in all mine house. **With him will I speak mouth to mouth**, even apparently. And not in dark speeches; and the similitude of the Lord shall he behold: wherefore then were ye not afraid to speak against my servant Moses? (Numbers 11:5–8, KJV)*

Just imagine an angry God coming down in a cloud and calling you out to give you a scolding you probably deserve and then leaving you with a disease of leprosy, like God did to Miriam. It could be quite terrifying, wouldn't you think? If you lived through it, you surely wouldn't do it twice. *"God, who at sundry times and in divers manners spake in times past unto the fathers by the prophets, Hath in these last days spoken unto us by his Son, whom he hath appointed **heir** of all things, by whom also he made the **worlds**; Who being the brightness of his glory, and the **express image** of his person, and upholding all things by the word of his power, when he had by himself purged our sins, sat down on the right hand of the Majesty on high"* (Hebrews 1:1–3, KJV).

The day is coming when the people of God will all see God's face, even Adam and Jesus Christ together.

And there shall be no more curse: but the throne of God and of the Lamb shall be in it; and his servants shall serve him; And they shall see his face; and his name shall be in their foreheads. And there shall be no night there; and they need no candle, neither light of the sun; for the Lord God giveth them light: and they shall reign forever and ever. And he said unto me, these sayings are faithful and true: and the Lord God of the holy prophets sent his angel to shew unto his servants the things which must shortly be done. (Revelation 22:3–6, KJV)

Christ, as spoken of in John 1:1–3, 14, is the Word. He was with God and is God and helped in the creation of all things. *"Let this mind be in you, which was also in Christ Jesus: Who, being in the form of god, thought it not robbery to be **equal with God**: But made himself of no reputation, and took upon him the form of a servant, and was made in the **likeness of men**: And being found in fashion as a man, he humbled himself, and became obedient unto death, even the death of the cross"* (Philippians 2:5–8, KJV). So God commanded men everywhere that they should repent and keep His commandments, and the first of these is *"Thou shalt have no other gods before me"* (Exodus 20:3, KJV).

"And the hour cometh, and now is, when the true worshipers shall worship the Father in Spirit and in truth; for the Father seeketh such to worship him. For unto such hath God **promised his Spirit**. And they who worship him, must worship in Spirit and in truth" (John 4:25–26, JST of KJV). Which makes more sense? Compare this: "But the hour is coming, and now here, when the true worshipers will worship the Father in spirit and truth, for the Father is seeking such people to worship him. God is spirit, and those who worship him must worship in spirit and truth" (John 4:23–24, KJV). You can see the contradiction of God, in the KJV, who is a glorified man in some places but now is called only a spirit in another place of the KJV.

God is our Father, we are just like Him, and we are His heirs, joint heirs with Christ. Not everyone of us can worship God face-to-face, but because He left us His Comforter, we can use the Spirit to worship the Father, and we must do so in faith.

The scriptures are teaming with evidence that Adam is our Father and the Father of Christ and that they both live today and are very much a part of our world. The plan of salvation is real, and it is an ingenious plan mainly because we decide for ourselves to whom we will give allegiance and where we will spend the rest of eternity. We can choose to spend it either with an all-wise, loving, intelligent, and heavenly Father or in bondage to the evil, despicable Satan. I choose my Father in Heaven, who is one and the same as Adam, the Father of all living.

What Christ did was what His Father did before Him. This is the true nature of God.

But Jesus answered them, My Father worketh hitherto, and I work. Therefore the Jews sought the more to kill him, because he not only had broken the sabbath, but said also that God was his Father, making himself equal with God. Then answered Jesus and said unto them, Verily, verily, I say unto you, the Son can do nothing of himself, but what he seeth the Father do: for what things so ever he doeth, these also doeth the Son likewise. For the Father loveth the Son, and sheweth him all things that himself doeth: and he will show him greater works than these, that ye may marvel. For as the Father raiseth up the dead, and quickeneth them; even so the Son quickeneth whom he will. For the Father judgeth no man, but hath committed all judgment unto the Son: That all men should honour the Son, even as they honour the Father which hath sent him.

*Verily, verily, I say unto you, He that heareth my word, and believeth on him that sent me, hath everlasting life, and shall not come into condemnation; but is passed from death unto life. Verily, verily, I say unto you, the hour is coming, and now is, when the dead shall hear the voice of the Son of God: and they that hear shall live. For as the **Father hath life in himself**; so hath he given to the **Son to have life in himself**; And hath given him authority to execute judgment also, because he is the Son of man. Marvel not at this: for the hour is coming, in the which all that are in the graves shall hear his voice, And shall come forth; they that have done good, unto the resurrection of life; and they that have done evil, unto the resurrection of damnation. I can of mine own self do nothing: as I hear, I judge: and my judgment is just; because I seek not mine own will, but the will of the Father which hath sent me. (John 5:17–30, KJV)*

I cannot explain it any better than this. I am going to believe in Christ and live my life to be as close to Him as I can get. Where Christ is, there will be the Father also. That is where I want to be. *"That Christ may dwell in your hearts by faith; that ye, being rooted and grounded in love, May be able to comprehend with all saints what is the breadth, and length, and depth, and height; And to **know the love of Christ, which passeth knowledge**, that ye might be filled with the fulness of God"* (Ephesians 3:17–19, KJV).

The true and full nature of God is that we are created in His image and are just like Him in form and ability. He is our literal Father and Christ's Father, but we are either going to learn and become like Him in every way or going to reject Him and go somewhere else other than back to His presence. To become like Him in every way is to accept and take upon ourselves His attributes, such as kindness, thoughtfulness, willingness to forgive others, and loving others like we love ourselves. Colossians chapter 3 talks about many of the good attributes of God that He wants us, as His children, to strive for to the end so that when we go back into His presence, we will be like Him spiritually and physically. I am only going to write just a few verses from this chapter but encourage everyone to read the whole chapter.

Lie not one to another, seeing that ye have put off the old man with his deeds; And have put on the new man, which is renewed in knowledge after the image of him that created him: Where there is neither Greek nor Jew, circumcision nor uncircumcision, Barbarian, Scythian, bond nor free: but Christ is all, and in all. Put on therefore, as the elect of God, holy and beloved, bowels of mercies, kindness, humbleness of mind, meekness, longsuffering; Forbearing one another, and forgiving one another, if any man have a quarrel against any: even as Christ forgave you, so also do ye. And above all these things put on charity, which is the bond of perfectness. And let the peace of God rule in your hearts, to the which also ye are called in one body; and be ye thankful. Let the word of Christ dwell in you richly in all wisdom; teaching and admonishing one another in psalms and hymns and spiritual songs, singing with grace in your hearts to the Lord. And whatsoever ye do in word or deed, do all in the name of the Lord Jesus, giving thanks to God and the Father by him. (Colossians 3:9–17, KJV)

CHAPTER 11

The Lord's Day

God revealed His Sabbath from the very beginning, after the creation of everything. He made the law even for Himself, though I am sure, as a kind, loving Father, He was setting an example for us all. *"Thus the heavens and the earth were finished, and all the host of them. And on the **seventh day** God ended his work which he had made; and he rested on the **seventh day** from all his work which he had made. And God blessed the **seventh day**, and sanctified it: because that in it he had rested from all his work which God created and made" (Genesis 2:1–3, KJV).*

After God had led Moses and the children of Israel out from Egypt after about four hundred years of bondage, God revealed to Moses the Ten Commandments. He revealed the keeping of the Sabbath day as one of them for the purpose of honoring God. *"Remember the sabbath day, to keep it holy. Six days shalt thou labour, and do all thy work: But on the **seventh day** is the sabbath of the LORD thy God: in it thou shalt not do any work, thou, nor thy son, nor thy daughter, nor thy man servant, nor thy maid servant, nor thy cattle, nor thy stranger that is within thy gates: For in six days the LORD made heaven and earth, the sea, and all that in them is, and **rested the seventh day**: wherefore the LORD blessed the sabbath day and hallowed it" (Exodus 20:8–11, KJV).*

From then on, the children of Israel kept the Sabbath. In fact, the Sabbath was included in their ordinances, feasts, celebrations, memorials, and so many others, so much so that I am sure they eventually got tired of them, besides all the sacrifices and burnt offerings. I know God didn't like it, but

He loved the people despite the enmity between Him and them. The main seventh-day Sabbath was strictly observed, and many times, other sabbaths or memorials were practiced in connection with the seventh-day Sabbath. The seventh-day Sabbath was practiced by the children of Israel all the way up to the time that Christ was killed and had been included into the Jewish laws. This made it a violation to do anything on the seventh day, which the ones in authority saw as breaking the Sabbath. *"And the Lord spake unto Moses, saying, speak unto the children of Israel, saying, In the seventh month, in the first day of the month, shall ye have a sabbath, a memorial of blowing of trumpets, an holy convocation. Ye shall do no servile work therein: but ye shall offer an offering made by fire unto the LORD . . . Ye shall do no manner of work: it shall be a **statute forever throughout your generations** in all your dwellings" (Leviticus 23:23–25, 31, KJV)*. If the people would not keep the Sabbath, they were cut off from among the people.

To this day, there are certain religions, including the Jewish people and the Seventh-day Adventists, that insist on a seventh-day Sabbath, each one for apparently different reasons. The Jewish people are still waiting for their savior to come, not willing to recognize Christ as their king, whereas the Seventh-day Adventists recognize Christ as their Savior but are misunderstanding the scriptures. They miss the point that times have changed concerning the Lord's Day, from the seventh day of the week to the first day of the week, and then are accusing the Catholic Church for making the change. They insist that the Catholic Church has changed the Sabbath from the seventh day to the first day of the week. They don't understand that only God can and will, as it pleases Him, change the times and the seasons.

*"Daniel answered and said, Blessed be the name of God for ever and ever: for wisdom and might are his: **And he changeth the times and the seasons**: he removeth kings, and setteth up kings: he giveth wisdom unto the wise, and knowledge to them that know understanding; He revealeth the days and secret things: he knoweth what is in the darkness, and the light dwelleth with him" (Daniel 2:20–22, KJV)*. This saying was given by Daniel when he was interpreting the dream for King Nebuchadnezzar. God writes His program, and only He determines the times and the seasons. In this interpretation, Daniel explained to King Nebuchadnezzar that he was the head of gold on this great image.

The Catholic Church comes as part of the fourth beast or kingdom with the legs of iron and the feet partly of iron and partly of clay. This beast has ten horns, resembling the ten kingdoms of the earth, and ten crowns. Daniel speaks about the Catholic Church as the one who thinks to change times and seasons but cannot because God has done it already.

After this I saw in the night visions, and behold a fourth beast, dreadful and terrible, and strong exceedingly; and it had great iron teeth: it devoured and brake in pieces, and stamped the residue with the feet of it: and it was diverse from all . . . the others, exceedingly dreadful, whose teeth were of iron, and his nails of brass; which devoured, brake in pieces, and stamped the residue with his feet; And of the ten horns that were in his head, and of the other which came up, and before whom three fell; even that horn that had eyes, and a mouth that spake very great things, whose look was more stout than his fellows. I beheld, and the same horn made war with the saints, and prevailed against them. (Daniel 7:7, 19–21, KJV)

The horn that came up and had eyes and that made war against the saints was the pope of the Roman Empire. The pope was also the one who unseated three kings, including the emperor, Constantine. He spoke and still speaks blasphemies against God in his effort to undermine the things of God. The pope was the one seeking to change times and seasons. *"And the ten horns out of this kingdom are ten kings that shall arise: and another shall rise after them; and he shall be diverse from the first, and he shall subdue three kings. And he shall speak great things against the Most High, and **think to change times and laws:** and they shall be given into his hand until a time and times and the dividing of time"* (Daniel 7:24–25, KJV).

The Catholic Church did think to change times and laws, but God has always been five steps ahead of the pagans at every turn. The Mormons, in their *Doctrine and Covenants* through Joseph Smith, touch on this subject. *"And also that **God hath set his hand** and seal to **change the times and seasons**, and to blind their minds, that they may not understand his marvelous workings; that he may prove them also and take them in their own craftiness; Also because their hearts are corrupted, and the things which they are willing to bring upon others, and love to have others suffer, may come upon themselves to the very uttermost; That they may be disappointed also, and their hopes may be cut off"* (Doctrine and Covenants, section 121:12–14).

God, not the Catholic Church, has changed the Sabbath and, in so doing, has made the pope appear foolish. Not only did Christ change the Sabbath but he also fulfilled the law of the prophets and now sits back and laughs at the futility of man.

Think not that I am come to destroy the law, or the prophets: I am not come to destroy, but to fulfill. For verily I say unto you, Till heaven and earth pass, one jot or one tittle shall in no wise pass from the law, till all be fulfilled. Whosoever therefore shall break one of these least commandments, and shall teach men so, he shall be called the least in the kingdom of heaven: but whosoever shall do and teach them the same shall be called great in the kingdom of heaven. For I say unto you, that except your righteousness shall exceed the righteousness of the scribes and pharisees, ye shall in no case enter into the kingdom of heaven. (Matthew 5:17–20, KJV)

The key to understanding when and how the Sabbath changed from the seventh day of the week (Saturday) to the first day of the week (Sunday) is after the resurrection of Jesus Christ. This was when it began to be called the Lord's Day. Up to the death of Jesus Christ, the seventh-day Sabbath was observed by Him, all the while teaching the people who He was. He was the Lord of the Sabbath, and He was literally the Son of God. Many didn't understand, and many hated Him for it and were jealous and attempted to cause Him problems but to no avail. Jesus Christ, as He was also God, had the right to determine what the Sabbath would be. He declared Himself as the Lord of the Sabbath to the Pharisees and the Saduccees, who wanted to kill Him for it because they were unwilling to comprehend the truth as it would take power from them, in their minds.

*At that time Jesus went on the sabbath day through the corn; and his disciples were a hungered, and began to pluck the ears of corn, and to eat, but when the pharisees saw it, they said unto him, Behold, thy disciples do that which is not lawful to do upon the sabbath day. But he said unto them, have ye not read what David did, when he was an hungered, and they that were with him; How he entered into the house of God, and did eat the shewbread, which was not lawful for him to eat, neither for them which were with him, but only for the priests? Or have ye not read in the law, how that on the sabbath days the priests in the temple profane the sabbath, and are blameless? But I say unto you, that in this place is one greater than the temple. But if ye had known what this meaneth, I will have mercy, and not sacrifice, ye would not have condemned the guiltless. For the **Son of man is Lord even of the sabbath**. (Matthew 12:1–8, KJV)*

---

*And he said unto them, the **sabbath was made for man**, and **not man for the sabbath**: Therefore the Son of man is Lord also of the sabbath. (Mark 2:27–28, KJV)*

And it came to pass also on another sabbath, that he entered into the synagogue and taught: and there was a man whose right hand was withered. And the scribes and Pharisees watched him, whether he would heal on the sabbath day; that they might find an accusation against him, But he knew their thoughts, and said unto the man, which had the withered hand, Rise up, and stand forth in the midst. And he arose and stood forth. Then said Jesus unto them, I will ask you one thing; Is it lawful on the sabbath days to do good, or to do evil? To save life, or to destroy it? And looking round about upon them all, he said unto the man, stretch forth thy hand, and he did so; and his hand was restored whole as the other. And they were filled with madness; and communed one with another what they might do to Jesus. (Luke 6:6–11, KJV)

Saying, The Son of man must suffer many things, and be rejected of the elders and chief priests and scribes, and be slain, and be raised on the third day. (Luke 9:22, KJV)

And he spake also a parable unto them; no man putteth a piece of a new garment upon an old; if otherwise, then both the new maketh a rent, and the piece that was taken out of the new agreeth not with the old. And no man putteth new wine into old bottles; else the new wine will burst the bottles and both be spilled, and the bottles shall perish. But new wine must be put into new bottles; and both are preserved. No man also having drunk old wine straightway desireth new: for he saith, the old is better. (Luke 5:36–39, KJV)

This parable was given to the scribes and Pharisees before He was killed, but they could not understand what He was talking about because they were unbelievers and the cause of the problems.

Jesus was crucified on a Thursday and hung on the cross through Friday. He was taken down from the cross before the Sabbath, on Saturday, but was laid in the sepulchre through Saturday. This was the three days He told His disciples about, that on the third day the Son of Man would arise. He was resurrected on the first day of the week, which was now the Lord's Day. Everything was finished, and newness started.

After this, Jesus knowing that all things were now accomplished, that the scripture *might be fulfilled, saith, I thirst. Now there was set a vessel full of vinegar: and they filled a spunge with vinegar, and put it upon hyssop, and put it to his mouth. When Jesus therefore had received the vinegar, he said, **it is finished**: and he bowed his head, and gave up the ghost. The Jews therefore, because it was the preparation, that the bodies should not remain upon the cross on the sabbath day, (for that sabbath day was an high day,) besought Pilate that their legs might be broken, and that they might be taken away. (John 19:28–31, KJV)*

No one understood, not even the disciples, until He arose. Our Lord and Savior was betrayed and tried by evil men, exactly like the Democrats did to Donald J. Trump, forty-fifth president of the United States in their sham impeachment process. They trumped up charges, they conspired with witnesses, they changed transcripts to read the way they wanted, and they forged ahead quickly with lies to get the job done. In President Trump's case, it is backfiring big-time; but in Christ's case, they pulled it off because Christ let them.

The liberal Pharisees and Sadducees made false accusations, gathered false witnesses through bribery, and appealed to Pontius Pilate for support. It was these people who were responsible, the evil liberal-minded obstructionists, for what happened to Jesus. He was hung on the cross, made to suffer and be humiliated for doing nothing wrong, and then taken down and placed in a tomb, thinking that was the end of it. Liberals have got to be stupid to think they can lie, cheat, steal, or even kill to accomplish their end. What they fail to acknowledge is that God is still always in control and very far ahead of them.

*In the end of the sabbath, as it began to dawn [early Sunday morning] toward the first day of the week, came Mary Magdalene and the other Mary to see the sepulcher. And, behold, there was a great earthquake: for the angel of the Lord descended from heaven, and came and rolled back the stone from the door, and sat upon it. His countenance was like lightning, and his raiment white as snow: And for fear of him the keepers did shake, and became as dead men. And the angel answered and said unto the women, fear not ye: for I know that ye seek Jesus, which was crucified. He is not here: for **he is risen**, as he said, Come, see the place where the Lord lay. And go quickly, and tell his disciples that he is risen from the dead; and, behold, he goeth before you into Galilee; there shall ye see him: lo, I have told you. And they departed quickly from the sepulcher with fear and great joy; and did run to bring his disciples word. And as they went* *to tell his disciples, behold, Jesus met them saying, all hail. And they came and held him by the feet, and worshipped him. Then said Jesus unto them, be not afraid: go tell my brethren that they go into Galilee, and there shall they see me. Now when they were going, behold, some of the watch came into the city, and shewed unto the chief priests all the things that were done. And when they were assembled with the elders, and had taken counsel, they gave large money unto the soldiers, Saying, say ye, His disciples came by night, and stole him away while we slept. And if this come to the governor's ears, we will persuade him, and secure you. So they took the money, and did as they were taught: and this saying is commonly reported among the Jews until this day. Then the eleven disciples went away into Galilee, into a mountain where Jesus had appointed them. And when they saw him; they worshiped him: but some doubted. And Jesus came and spake unto them, saying, All power is given unto me in heaven and in earth. (Matthew 28:1–18, KJV)*

John also made an account of all that happened. *"The **first day of the week** cometh Mary Magdalene early, when it was yet dark, unto the sepulcher, and seeth the stone taken away from the sepulcher"* (John 20:1, KJV). Seeing that Jesus was not there, Mary dashed away to tell the disciples that He was gone. They all came back with her to see for themselves if it was true or not. They still couldn't comprehend what was happening. *John 20:9* stated, *"For as yet they knew not the scripture, that he must rise again from the dead."* Mary, however, stayed behind after the others saw and were satisfied that Jesus was gone. She was crying and showing much remorse for Jesus. She stooped, looked in the tomb one more time, and there saw two angels sitting where Jesus had lain. One was at the head, and the other was at the feet. As she turned back around, she saw Jesus, and He spoke to her, saying to not touch Him, for He first needed to ascend unto His Father, but He told her to go and tell the others that He is alive. *"Then the same day at evening, being the **first day of the week**, when the doors were shut where the disciples were assembled for fear of the Jews, came Jesus and stood in the midst, and saith unto them, peace be unto you"* (John 20:19, KJV).

Thomas was the only disciple not present with the others when Christ appeared the first time, but he was there the second time. It was Christ who probably instructed them to meet again the next first day of the week, which we know as Sunday. The days then did not carry the pagan titles as they do today.

*And **after eight days** again his disciples were within, and Thomas with them; then came Jesus, the doors being shut, and stood in the midst, and said, Peace be unto you. Then saith he to Thomas, Reach hither thy finger, and behold my hands; and reach hither thy hand and thrust it into my side: and be not faithless, but believing. And Thomas answered and said unto him, My Lord and my God. Jesus saith unto him, Thomas, because thou hast seen me, thou hast believed: blessed are they that have not seen, and yet have believed. And many other signs truly did Jesus in the presence of his disciples, which are not written in this book: But these are written, that ye might believe that Jesus is the Christ, the Son of God; and that believing ye might have life through his name. (John 20:26–31, KJV)*

From then on, the disciples continued to meet together often on the first day of the week, along with the other followers and new converts to the truth. However, the disciples would also visit the synagogues on the Jewish Sabbath, the seventh day of the week, to preach to them that Christ was risen and that the law of the Sabbath had been fulfilled and to invite them to observe now the Lord's Day.

Be it known unto you therefore, men and brethren, that through this man is preached unto you the forgiveness of sins: And by him all that believe are justified from all things, from which ye could not be justified by the law of Moses. Beware therefore, lest that come upon you, which is spoken of in the prophets; Behold, ye despisers, and wonder, and perish: for I work a work in your days, a work which ye shall in no wise believe, though a man declare it unto you. And when the Jews were gone out of the synagogue, the Gentiles besought that these works might be preached unto them the next sabbath. Now when the congregation was broken up, many of the Jews and religious proselytes followed Paul and Barnabas; who, speaking to them, persuaded them to continue in the grace of God. And the next sabbath day came almost the whole city together to hear the word of God. But when the Jews saw the multitudes, they were filled with envy, and spake against those things which were spoken by Paul, contradicting and blaspheming. (Acts 13:38–45, KJV)

What those leaders in Jerusalem, both religious and political, remind me very strongly of is the way the Democrats in the House of Representatives and the Senate are obstructing, contradicting, and working against President Trump in all the good that he is doing. The Democrats also use the lying media to help them deceive the people, if the people are dumb enough to listen.

Paul was traveling around, now teaching the Gentiles, because the Jews were so unbelieving. He came to Corinth, even though early on he met resistance because of the bad-mouthing from certain Jews. He resolved to quit attempting to teach the Jews and began striving to deal only with the Gentiles. The Lord spoke to Paul in a night vision and told him to not be afraid there because there were many good people where he was at. So Paul stayed for over a year preaching Christ to them and all about the Lord's Day. Eventually, there is always conflict, but it is really comforting when sweet justice is handed out to those who deserve it.

*And when Gallio was the deputy of Achaia, the Jews made insurrection with one accord against Paul, and brought him to the judgment seat, Saying, this fellow persuadeth men to **worship God contrary to the law**. And when Paul was now about to open his mouth, Gallio said unto the Jews, if it were a matter of wrong or wicked lewdness, O ye Jews, reason would that I should bear with you: But if it be a question of words and names, **and of your law**, look ye to it; for I will be no judge of such matters. And he drave them from the judgment seat. Then all the Greeks took Sosthenes, the chief ruler of the synagogue, and beat him before the judgment seat. And Gallio care for none of those things. . . . And upon the **first day of the week**, when the disciples came together to break bread, Paul preached unto them, ready to depart on the morrow; and continued his speech until midnight. (Acts 18:12–17, 20:7, KJV)*

There are just so many examples of the Lord's people meeting on the first day of the week that it is so amazing to me how people can be so blind. Many are not blind at all but insist in believing a lie as long as it serves their selfish purpose. *"Now concerning the collection for the saints, as I have given order to the churches of Galatia, even so do ye. **Upon the first day of the week** let every one of you lay by him in store, as God hath prospered him, that there be no gatherings when I come"* (1 Corinthians 16:1–2, KJV).

Paul traveled back to Jerusalem for the feast of Pentecost, and there confronted the Jews pertaining to the law of Moses concerning the Sabbath, and preached faith in Jesus Christ. Christ came to fulfill the law, and now everyone must live by faith in Jesus Christ. *"We who are Jews by nature, and not sinners of the Gentiles, Knowing that a man is **not justified by the works of the law, but by the faith of Jesus Christ**, even we have believed in Jesus*

Christ, that we might be justified by the faith of Christ, and not by the works of the law: for by the works of the law shall no flesh be justified" (Galatians 2:15–16, KJV).

The children of Israel coming out of Egypt were used to being told every move to make, what to think, and how to think; and if they didn't perform accordingly to the slave master's wishes, they were killed, severely beaten, starved, or subjected to other forms of punishment. So they needed a schoolmaster to get their attention, and through Moses, they were given the law—the law of Moses. The precursor to the law of Moses was the Ten Commandments, and the Law of Moses showed them how to keep the Ten Commandments in a roundabout way.

The first four commandments are about loving and respecting God, while the other six are directly related to how we treat and respect our fellow man. The Ten Commandments are like the short version of a decree by the king, while the law acts as its implementing regulations that enforce the decree. For instance, if a man stole from his neighbor, he was required to pay back sevenfold to his neighbor. If a man killed another, he was required to give up his life. I am sure everyone has heard "An eye for an eye, and a tooth for a tooth." This was what it took to bring true justice and make the children of Israel understand the wishes of God.

To worship God took discipline, all of forty years to sink in while they were kept in the wilderness, traveling in circles, until it did. When they finally began to exercise faith in God, they were allowed to cross over the river Jordan. They were still living the law of Moses up to the time that Christ was crucified on the cross. Many had become so settled into their way of life that many didn't want the change and were stagnating.

Many like the scribes, Pharisees, and Sadducees had it pretty good, having authority over the people and making a pretty good living off the misery of the people as long as they could be in control. It reminds me of the liberals today. They lie, steal, embezzle, commit fraud, and even kill to accomplish their selfish goals at even their own expense, much less their families or their fellow man. They look at themselves as being the elite, and they are afraid of losing their power and prestige. Yes, they are very comparable to the liberals today.

The sacrifice of animals was a substitute for the last blood sacrifice to be offered by Jesus Christ when He was crucified. The Sabbaths were also included in their observation of ordinances, which taught the people to reverence and respect God. Many of the Jews had become so set in their ways that change was hard, except for those who were more in tune with the Spirit of Christ and those who were given to understand more readily when the truth was declared to them.

The Pharisees and Sadducees rebelled, because they thought they were about to lose their power, and so they banded together regardless of right or wrong; they didn't want to lose their money flow, and they wanted to retain control of the people. They were truly of a socialist mindset. *"Even so we, when we were children, were in bondage under the elements of the world; But when the fulness of the times was come, God sent forth his Son, made of a woman, made under the law, To redeem them that were under the law, that we might receive the adoption of sons. And because ye are sons, God hath sent forth the Spirit of his Son into your hearts, crying Abba, Father"* (Galatians 4:3–6, KJV).

The plan of God to redeem His people is so ingenious, even during the times the children of Israel were wandering around in the wilderness for forty years while they worked on their faith and obedience. That whole generation was allowed to die off except for Joshua and Caleb, who were examples of great faith and allowed to cross over with the children of Israel, Joshua as their prophet and Caleb leading the armies of Israel. I am sure, though, that among that generation, even though they died in the wilderness, there were many saved in the kingdom of God. They were saved by just adhering to the commands of Moses, like following Moses through the Red Sea, not worshipping the golden calf or other idols, observing the Sabbath, preparing for the Sabbath by following strict instructions on collecting the manna, and looking up to the serpent on the pole to be healed from their snakebites.

I am sure that there were many during that time who were very sorry for their lack of faith, but their change of heart was shown in their posterity, taught by their parents that one good lesson. All these things took a certain amount of faith. As the people gained experience and knowledge, more was expected of them. So it was in the day that Christ was born in Bethlehem. The people had been looking forward to this day and automatically believed when they saw and heard. These were the ones who were in tune with the Spirit and whom Jesus talked about to Thomas, how blessed they are who have not seen yet believed wholeheartedly.

*That at that time ye were without Christ; being aliens from the commonwealth of Israel, and strangers from the covenants of promise, having no hope, and without God in the world: But now in Christ Jesus ye who sometimes were far off are made nigh by the blood of Christ, For he is our peace, who hath made both one, and hath broken down the middle wall of partition between us; Having **abolished in his flesh the enmity, even the law of commandments contained in ordinances**; for to make in himself of twain one new man, so making peace; And that he might reconcile unto God in one body by the cross, **having slain the enmity** thereby. (Ephesians 2:12–16, KJV)*

Verse 15 talks about the enmity the people were experiencing from God and vice versa. God was not happy with their stubbornness, their stiff-neckedness, their ignorance, and their willingness to rebel. For these reasons, He was very strict with what we know as the law of Moses. Many thousands of them were killed when they were disobedient as God tried to get their attention. Finally, He did, and then they were ready to cross the river Jordan and claim the land; but even then, they didn't always do what they were commanded to do and were severely punished for it. Their punishments came because of their own actions. Because of their stubbornness, there was an enmity or hostility between them and God. It was because of the promises and covenants God made with their fathers, Abraham, Isaac, and Jacob, that God preserved the people. He loved the children of Israel, and even though He wasn't always happy with the things that they did, He was tolerant, patient, and always teaching, even if He had to use a two-by-four to get His point across.

All the way up to the time that Christ was killed, in other words when Christ allowed Himself to be crucified, this enmity was present, especially with the unbelievers and the Pharisees and Sadducees. The irony of that was that Christ didn't come to redeem everyone but only those who would believe and follow Him. When Christ, while hanging on the cross, said, "It is finished," and then gave up the ghost, the law of Moses was fulfilled. Every jot and tittle had been joined in victory over Satan, and the people of God were free to choose their own master. Everything had now become new—new wine into new bottles and out with the old.

After Christ was resurrected, there was now a newness of life, and now we are to believe and act in faith. Knowing the scriptures and what Christ had done and who He is, we can have an understanding of what this all means to us. As it states in verse 15 of Ephesians chapter 2, Christ—being the Lord of the Sabbath—has the right and the power to change even the commandment contained in ordinances, which He did by changing the Sabbath day of worship. The only commandment contained in ordinances was the seventh-day sabbath, which He changed to the first day of the week, therefore reconciling man with God, which was a great undertaking and a great mercy from God to us.

Now that we are reconciled with God and no longer have this enmity between us, Paul cautions us to beware of liars who will try to separate us from God, like the lying Democrats. The liberals prey on our young people today in the universities and colleges, such as Berkeley, Yale, and Harvard, through their philosophy programs that outright lie to our youth, thus turning them from God.

*As ye have therefore received Christ Jesus the Lord, so walk ye in him; Rooted and built up in him, and **stablished in the faith**, as ye have been taught, abounding therein with thanksgiving. Beware lest any man spoil you through **philosophy and vain deceit**, after the tradition of men, after the rudiments of the world, and not after Christ . . . Buried with him in baptism, wherein also ye are risen with him through the faith of the operation of God, who hath raised him from the dead . . . Let no man therefore judge you in meat, or in drink, or in respect of an holy day, or of the new moon, or of the sabbath days . . . Wherefore if ye be dead with Christ from the rudiments of the world, why, as through living in the world, are ye subject to ordinances. (Touch not; taste not; handle not; Which all are to perish with the using;) after the commandments and doctrines of men? (Colossians 2:6–8, 12, 16, 20–22, KJV)*

Paul, in speaking to the Hebrews, mentioned another day for the saints of God.

For he spake in a certain place of the seventh day from all his works. And in this place again, if they shall enter into my rest. Seeing therefore it remaineth that some must enter therein, and they to whom it was first preached entered not in because of unbelief: Again, he limiteth a certain day, saying in David, To day, after so long a time; as it is said, To day if ye will hear his voice, harden not your hearts. For if Jesus had given them rest, then would he not afterward have spoken *of **another day**. There remaineth therefore a rest to the people of God. For he that is entered into his rest, he also hath ceased from his own works, as God did from his. Let us labour therefore to enter into that rest, lest any man fall after the same example of unbelief. (Hebrews 4:4–11, KJV)*

Chapter 7 of Hebrews talks about a Melchizedek, to whom Abraham paid tithes and who also held a higher priesthood other than what the children of Israel held. The children of Israel were given only a lesser priesthood and named after the tribe of Levi as the Levitical priesthood. This priesthood only functioned for the purpose of administering ordinances contained in the law of Moses. The time of Melchizedek preceded that of the Exodus of the children of Israel out of Egypt by almost one thousand years. The scriptures had all along testified of another higher priest to come after the order of Melchizedek. That other was Jesus Christ through Judah and not through Levi.

*If therefore perfection were by the **Levitical Priesthood, (For under it the people received the law,)** what further need was there that another priest should rise after the order of Melchizedek, and not be called after the order of Aaron? For the **priesthood being changed**, there is made a necessity a **change also of the law**. For he of whom these things are spoken pertaineth to another tribe, of which no man gave attendance at the altar. For it is evident that our Lord sprang out of Judah; of which tribe Moses spoke nothing concerning priesthood. And it is yet far more evident; for after the similitude of Melchizedek there ariseth another priest, Who is made, not after the law of carnal commandment, but after the power of endless life. For he testifieth, Thou art a priest forever after the order of Melchizedek. For there is verily a disannulling of the commandments going before, for the weakness and unprofitableness thereof. For the law made nothing perfect, but the bringing in of a better hope did; by the which we draw nigh unto God. (Hebrews 7:11–19, KJV)*

Now of the things which we have spoken this is the sum: We have such an high priest, who is set on the right hand of the throne of the Majesty in the heavens; A minister of the sanctuary, and of the true tabernacle, which the Lord pitched, and not man, For every high priest is ordained to offer gifts and sacrifices: wherefore it is of necessity that this man have somewhat also to offer. For if he were on earth, he should not be a priest, seeing that there are priests that offer gifts according to the law: Who serve unto the examples and shadow of heavenly things, as Moses was admonished of God when he was about to *make the tabernacle: for, see, saith he, that thou make all things according to the pattern shewed to thee in the mount. But now hath he obtained a more excellent ministry, by how much also he is the mediator of a better covenant, which was established upon better promises. For if that first covenant had been faultless, then should no place have been sought for the second. For finding fault with them, he saith, Behold, the days come, saith the Lord, when I will make a new covenant with the house of Israel and with the house of Judah; Not according to the covenant that I made with their fathers in the day when I took them by the hand to lead them out of the land of Egypt; because they continued not in my covenant, and I regarded them not, saith the Lord. For this is the covenant that I will make with the house of Israel after those days, saith the Lord; I will put my laws into their mind, and write them in their hearts: and I will be to them a God, and they shall be to me a people: And they shall not teach every man his neighbour, and every man his brother, saying, know the Lord: for all shall know me, from the least to the greatest. For I will be merciful to their unrighteousness, and their sins and their iniquities will I remember no more. In that he saith, **A new covenant**, he hath made **the first old**. Now that which decayeth and waxeth old is ready to vanish away. (Hebrews 8:1–13, KJV)*

*Above when he said, Sacrifice and offering and burnt offerings and offering for sin thou wouldest not, neither hadst pleasure therein; which are offered by the law; Then said he, Lo, I come to do thy will, O God. He **taketh away the first**, that he may **establish the second**. (Hebrews 10:8–9, KJV)*

John, in Revelation, mentions the Lord's Day. *"I was in the Spirit on the **Lord's day**, and heard behind me a great voice, as of a trumpet" (Revelation 1:10, KJV)*. Joseph Smith, the Mormon prophet, in accordance with the change of the Sabbath by the Lord from the seventh day of the week to the first day of the week, has further revealed that this is true.

*And that thou mayest more fully keep thyself unspotted from the world, thou shalt go to the house of prayer and offer up thy sacraments upon my holy day. For verily this is a day appointed unto you to rest from your labors, and to pay thy devotions unto the Most High; Nevertheless thy vows shall be offered up in righteousness on all days and at all times. But remember that on this, the **Lord's day**, thou shalt offer thine oblations and thy sacraments unto the Most High, confessing thy sins unto thy brethren, and before the Lord. And on this day, thou shalt do none other thing, only let thy food be prepared with singleness of heart that thy fasting may be perfect, or, in other words, that thy joy may be full.*

(*Doctrine and Covenants, section 59:9–13*)

The bottom line is that the Sabbath day had been changed since the resurrection of Jesus Christ by Christ Himself and not by the Catholic Church, thinking to change times and seasons. The Sabbath day was changed to the Lord's Day long before the idea of a Catholic church was ever conceived. Compared with the wisdom, power, and majesty of God, any king, emperor, president, or dictator doesn't stand a hope if they are against the will of God. To God, they are considered as very inferior and laughable. "*And also that **God hath set his hand and seal, to change the times and seasons**, and to blind their minds, that they may not understand his marvelous workings; that he may prove them also and take them in their own craftiness; Also because their hearts are corrupted, and the things which they are willing to bring upon others, and love to have others suffer, may come upon themselves to the very uttermost; That they may be disappointed also, and their hopes may be cut off*" (*Doctrine and Covenants, section 121:12–14*).

CHAPTER 12

The Abomination of Desolation

For many years now, I have given much thought and consideration about what God means with the "abomination of desolation". I have to ask the question, what is the purpose of life? Knowing that we are the children of God, and His work and glory is to bring to pass the immortality and eternal life of man, then we must be up and doing, to help God fulfill His work and glory. We must love our fellow man; have families ourselves, as God intended; and allow others to have their free agency to grow. If we refuse to do these things and only pursue our own selfish lusts and desires, then we are fighting against God and His plan. We are against our brother if we are supporting bad laws that suppress our brother or are in contradiction to the teachings of God. If we ignore what is morally right, then we are in open rebellion against God.

There are many ways that we can become the "natural man" and at the same time an enemy to God. We are told that the first greatest commandment is to love God. We show love of God by the way we listen to Him, pray to Him, show respect in observance of His day of rest, obey His commandments, and treat His offspring. By loving God first, we will automatically love our neighbor. We love our neighbor by the way we treat him physically and vocally, the party we support, the people we elect into office and place in our government, and the laws we uphold, and it doesn't end here. We love God by obeying all His commandments, and by doing this, we are showing love for our neighbor.

If we are obeying the commandments, then we will be virtuous as well because being virtuous is one very important commandment. It is almost impossible to break one commandment and not break several others. For instance, if we steal something from our neighbor, then we end up feeling the necessity to lie about it, and then maybe we will fight about it. This is the same thing with immorality of the sexual kind. If we commit adultery, then this can open up many cans of worms. Your brother or sister is violated. Then you feel it necessary to cover it up and lie about it. Such a thing can destroy many trusts and confidences and wrecks families. By having children outside the bounds of marriage, automatically the children are wards of the state; and it hurts the children now because they are put unnecessarily in positions of abuse, neglect, mistreatment, and unloved, fighting over custody rights, parental rights, and many others. Because of such conflict, a judge automatically becomes the ward of that child. To have children is a great honor and privilege and lets us become like God and create our own worlds but within the bounds of marriage as God has ordained.

Many people who don't care about God probably won't care about their brother or neighbor. They then will disregard any commandment or a sense of right in order to fulfill their own selfish desires, no matter who else they hurt. These such people are the "natural man" and are enemies to God because they are working to destroy the work of God.

There is one very serious thing that works harder than any other to destroy God's work, and that is the homosexual and lesbian agenda. The bringing of children into the world or God's family is God's work. When that stops, God's work is hindered, and He calls that an "abomination." For the question: If everyone in a country, or the world for that matter, were homosexual or lesbian, how many children would there be? The answer is *none,* because the civilization would die out.

All past civilizations had struggled with this problem of immorality. Many civilizations had lost their might and were conquered by other empires because of immorality problems. The Macedonians' Alexander the Great, a homosexual himself, showed a very poor example to the people of his realm and very quickly went downhill because the blessings of God will not always strive with those who won't obey His commandments. Some civilizations had completely died out. When God sees that kingdoms of the people will not do His will, He simply removes them by bringing another nation in to conquer them or destroys them entirely as He did with the flood.

We can recall Sodom and Gomorrah, but the insolence of man never ceases to amaze me, thinking they are more clever than God. They are stubborn and selfish, having necks of iron and brows of brass. The people had every opportunity to change from their godlessness but chose death instead. From the very beginning, God has given the law of chastity, that homosexuality of any kind should not be allowed to prosper. Men and women are breeding stock to accomplish God's purposes and to bring men and women real joy.

It gives me great joy and glory to see my children grown, doing well, and observing God's commandments as perfectly as they can, but no one in this world is completely perfect. The very first commandment in the Garden of Eden to Adam and Eve was to multiply and replenish the earth. So if everyone in the world were either homosexual or lesbian, there would be no children and no future generations. The bottom line is this: God created some people with penises; to others he gave vaginas and told them to multiply. If you have a penis, you are a male; and if you have a vagina, then you are a girl. God makes no mistakes about it. Once you can figure out what sex you are, then it is your responsibility to match up with the opposite sex and raise a family within the bounds of marriage, contributing to God's work.

Let's look at this point on a practical level. If Noah and his three sons were homosexual, how many people would there be? The answer again is none, and there were not many, only four, and Noah had none to spare. If a farmer had a herd of cows and his living depended on him producing a calf crop but his bulls went around chasing one another instead of paying attention to the cows/females, then the farmer wouldn't have any calf crop. What do you think the farmer would have to do to rectify his problem? He would, in some way, destroy his bulls and get others to replace his unprofitable bulls. This is the same with any such crop, whether cows, pigs, horses, chickens, or rabbits. The farmer would cull those unproductive animals, wicked abominations, and would immediately and absolutely get rid of them. If the females were chasing females instead of standing for the bull, then the cows would have to go. God's purpose is essentially the same. Those people who continue to commit these sexual depravities and abominations are not any good to themselves or to God. He receives no glory there. Unless they speedily change and get a different theory on life, they will assuredly be destroyed just as God has declared.

Most people involved in homosexual or lesbian acts know what they are doing isn't right but have let their consciences be seared, as it were, by a hot iron. They choose to discredit God because of their lustful desire or depravity of mind. They don't want to hear about God or believe in Him because they know He teaches completely opposite to what they are doing or want to accept. They learn to hate God because they don't want to be told they are wrong, and they hate the people of God because they remind them of their own wickedness.

There are several schools—including high schools, middle schools, and grade schools—that have closed their doors in western Oregon because there are simply not enough children there to justify them staying open. The reason for this is that the majority of the people in these areas don't have any children. Even though the areas are quite highly populated, the lack of children is because most young couples in these areas are either homosexual or lesbian. We have already had a homosexual couple in the White House as president and first lady. The Obamas paved the way for the LGBT movement to come out of their closets unashamedly. Barack not only fueled the LGBT movement but he also tried to destroy America financially, militarily, and morally. Some people even go so far as to think he is the Antichrist. One thing for sure, though, is that he is an Antichrist, but he is not *Thee*, Antichrist. He and his other half are definitely abominations in the sight of God, and they must speedily change because, as they stand right now, they belong to the "whore of all the earth."

The children of Israel in the wilderness, after leaving Egypt, were given strict instructions to not commit such abominations as homosexual acts. *"If a **man lie with mankind**, as he lieth with a woman, both of them have committed an **abomination:** they shall **surely be put to death**; their blood shall be upon them" (Leviticus 20:13, KJV).* As the children of Israel went across the river Jordan and began conquering the land, God further admonished them.

*When thou art come into the land which the Lord thy God giveth thee, thou shalt not learn to do **after the abominations of those nations**. There shall not be found among you any one that maketh his **son or daughter to pass through the fire**, or that useth **divination**, or an **observer of times**, or an **enchanter**, or a **witch**, Or a **charmer**, or a **consulter with familiar spirits**, or a **wizard**, or a **necromancer**. For all that do these things are an **abomination unto the LORD**: and because of these abominations the LORD thy God doth drive them* *out from thee. (Deuteronomy 18:9–12, KJV)*

How many instances can you name where Democrats are involved in homosexual acts, lesbianism, sex trafficking of little children, Satan worship, witchcraft, child sacrificing, pedophilia, or even eating of sacrificed children? This is going on even in America in record numbers. America has that great statue of the great whore Ishtar, called the Statue of Liberty, standing in the harbor at New York City. These are all abominations in the sight of God, and they contradict His work and His glory. The book of Daniel talks more about the abomination of desolation. *"And he shall confirm the **covenant** with many for one week: and in the midst of the week he shall cause the sacrifice and the oblation to cease, and for the overspreading of **abominations he shall make desolate**, even until the consummation, and that determined shall be poured upon the desolate" (Daniel 9:27, KJV).*

Daniel 8 describes how the Medes and the Persians (ram) were defeated by the Macedonians/Greeks under Alexander the Great (goat). Alexander was a homosexual, and after he was killed, his four generals divided his kingdom, later to lose it to the Romans. However, I believe that one of these generals headed the growth of the Roman Empire. Daniel mentions the transgression of desolation concerning the Macedonians.

*And an host was given him against the daily sacrifice by reason of transgression, and it cast down the **truth** to the ground; and it practiced and prospered. Then I heard one saint speaking, and another saint said unto that certain saint which spake, How long shall be the vision concerning the daily sacrifice, and **the transgression of desolation**, to give both the sanctuary and the host to be trodden under foot? . . . And in the **latter time** of their kingdom, when the **transgressors** are come to the full, **a king of fierce countenance**, and understanding dark sentences, **shall stand up**. And **his power shall be mighty**, but **not by his own power**; and he shall destroy wonderfully, and shall prosper, and practice, and shall destroy the mighty and the holy people. And through his policy also **he shall cause craft to prosper** in his hand: and he shall magnify himself in his heart, and by **peace shall destroy many**: he shall also stand up against the **Prince of princes**; but he shall be broken without hand. (Daniel 8:12–13, 23–25, KJV)*

This latter kingdom was the Roman Empire, under the pope of the Catholic Church. Because of the transgressions of desolation by Alexander the Great, the empire was given to the Romans, and the pope carried on in these evil practices, even more so, encouraging witchcraft and Satanism. He reviles and blasphemes against God, and Satan gives him his power. He has set about to destroy the people of God. He calls himself the vicar of Christ, but we know the Prince of princes will destroy the alleged vicar when He comes again, and He will. He will come quietly and catch the Antichrist in his acts of evil.

Wherefore if they shall say unto you, Behold, he is in the desert; go not forth: behold, he is in the secret chambers; believe it not. For as the lightning cometh out of the east, and shineth even unto the west; so shall also the coming of the Son of man be. (Matthew 24:26–27, KJV)

Compare:

*Behold, I have told you before, Wherefore, if they shall say unto you, Behold, he is in the desert; go not forth. Behold, he is in the secret chamber; believe it not. For as the **light of the morning cometh out of the east, and shineth even unto the west, and covereth the whole earth; so shall also the coming of the Son of man be.** (Matthew 24:26–27, JST of KJV)*

When Christ comes again, He will come out of the east on His planet that used to hover over the whole earth before and during the days of Noah. *"But **as the days of Noah were, so shall also the coming of the Son of man be"** (Matthew 24:37, KJV)*. It will be subtle and will cover the whole earth, and everyone will see Him when He comes.

The saints, who are the people of God—where else could they be swept up to meet Him in the air and be able to rest while He destroys the wicked and burns the earth? *"For whosoever the carcass is, there will the eagles be gathered together" (Matthew 24:28, KJV)*. Compare: *"And now I show unto you a parable. Behold, **whosoever the carcass is, there will the eagles be gathered together; so likewise shall mine elect be gathered from the four quarters of the earth"** (Matthew 24:28, JST)*. This is fantastic, and God is so good.

All people, regardless of which Christian church they belong to, if they have received the "Gospel of Jesus Christ" and are living it sincerely, will be caught up into the Kingdom of God. This is the least that Christ will do for those who love Him. This the **"Grace"** spoken of in the scriptures, that when we put our faith and trust in Christ, and receive His gospel, then we are the ones that He has come to redeem. They are the "sons and daughters" of God, and are the ones who are "saved by grace." *"And John answered him, saying, Master, we saw one casting out devils in thy name, and he followeth not us: and we forbad him, because he followeth not us. But Jesus said, Forbid him not: for there is no man which shall do a miracle in my name, that can lightly speak evil of me. For he that is not against us is on our part. For whosoever shall give you a cup of water to drink in my name, because ye belong to Christ, verily I say unto you, **he shall not lose his reward.**"(Mark 9:38-41, KJV)* These are the "good people of the earth".

The pope has begun the World Council of Churches and has gained much advantage and power over all the churches in the world because of it. Today he is planning a globalist meeting with all the churches in the world and is calling it "reinventing the global educational alliance," scheduled on May 14, 2020, for the purpose of nurturing the "dream of humanism." This meeting will take place in a specially built building resembling the form of a serpent called Reptile Hall. This is another all-out attempt to create a global, one world church, with the pope being the head of it. Imagine that, a one world church located in Rome with the alleged vicar of Christ as the head of it, officiating from a beautiful building in the image of a serpent, resembling the jurisdiction of Satan. That will be *enough* to make God pour out His overflowing scourge, don't you think?

Looking up the definition of *humanism* in the dictionary, I found three meanings, and all three are related to the same thing: (1) human character or quality; (2) the study of the humanities; the study of Greek and Roman classics; (3) thought or action centered on distinctively human interests, specifically a recent cult substituting faith in man for faith in God. I know that Pope Francis has no interest in the God in Heaven but is trying to conquer all religions peaceably through flattery and deceit. He is going to substitute his faith in man for a time to make it appear he puts his faith in God to fool the masses. The scriptures in Daniel have already warned us of who the pope is, what he is trying to do, and how he is trying to do it. Pope Francis is inviting world leaders and young people to come together at the Vatican in Rome on May 14, 2020, in the hopes of deceiving the people into believing he is God while wearing his fish-head hat. The truth is, Popes are not men of God now, nor ever will be. He gets his power from Satan as the scriptures testify about him.

*And arms shall stand on his part, and they shall pollute **the sanctuary of** strength [churches], and shall take away the daily sacrifice, and they shall place **the abomination that maketh desolate**. And such as **do wickedly against the covenant** [marriage] shall he corrupt by flatteries: but the people that do know their God shall be strong, and do exploits. . . . And the king shall do according to his will; and he shall exalt himself, and magnify himself above every god, and shall speak marvelous things against the **God of gods**, and shall prosper till the indignation be accomplished: for that that is determined shall be done. Neither shall he regard the God of his fathers, **nor the desire of women,** nor regard any god: for he shall **magnify himself above all**. (Daniel 11:31–32, 36–37, KJV)*

Daniel is still talking about the Catholic Church, and in verse 31, it mentions the abomination of desolation by polluting the sanctuary of strength, which is the churches. Verse 32 goes on to explain that the churches are polluted by all who do wickedly against the covenant, which is the holy covenant of marriage. In verse 37, speaking about the pope, he shall not regard God or the desire of women, meaning he desires men or boys and is a homosexual as the head of his church. When we begin to see transgender or gay couples officiating in any of the churches, then we will know that the time is near for the overflowing scourge. *"And from the time that the daily sacrifice shall be taken away, and the **abomination that maketh desolate** set up, there shall be a **thousand two hundred and ninety days"** (Daniel 12:11, KJV).*

What is really interesting is that 1,290 days is the equivalent of 3½ years. The May 14, 2020, seminar with the theme "Reinventing the Global Educational Alliance" is coming at about the same time as Israel is about to sign a very significant peace treaty with its neighboring countries. This makes a person very wary toward the pope, knowing how he is a liar, and he blasphemes against God. It is prophesied that Israel will have 3½ years of peace and then immediately after will have 3½ years of extreme tribulation.

*When ye therefore shall see the **abomination of desolation**, spoken of by Daniel the prophet, **stand in the holy place** (whoso readeth, let him understand:) Then let them which be in Judaea flee into the mountains: Let him which is on the housetop not come down to take anything out of his house: Neither let him which is in the field return back to take his clothes. And woe unto them that give suck in those days! But pray ye that your flight be not in the winter, neither on* *the sabbath day: For then shall be great **tribulation**, such as was not since the beginning of the world to this time, no, nor ever will be. And except those days should be shortened, there should no flesh be saved: but for the elect's sake those days shall be shortened. (Matthew 24:15–22, KJV)*

When we as a people of God live to see homosexuals stand in authority in our churches, we had better head for the hills as Lot, with his family, fled Sodom and Gomorrah. As already spoken earlier, an abomination has already filled our seat of government as the president of the United States, and the pope is just as guilty. Almost every church now is pandering to the gay agenda, especially the Methodists; and most recently, the Mormons have announced that they welcome the gays. When we begin allowing them to run our churches or have any position of authority there, may God have mercy on us because this is a form of abomination of desolation, and God is going to destroy the land through wars and famine, with 3½ years of intense tribulation. It is understood that we cannot turn them from our churches if they are seeking to repent of their sins as we all are sinners, and fall short of the kingdom of God. We go to church because we are sinners, but to exalt this abomination before the people, especially the young, as if they are doing right, and not rebuke them with the truth of Christ, then we are in open rebellion against God and fighting against His work and His glory.

We are to keep our eyes on Israel in these latter days. God has given us a signal to watch for so that we will know when the desolation is near. *"And when ye shall see Jerusalem compassed with armies, then know that the desolation thereof is nigh. Then let them which are in Judaea flee to the mountains; and let them which are in the midst of it depart not out; and let not them that are in the countries enter. For these be the days of vengeance, that all things which are written be fulfilled"* (Luke 21:20–22, KJV).

It is very close to the time when all these things will begin to happen. The timing will be almost perfect between the time Israel signs their peace treaty and whoever it is, will sign that peace treaty with Israel, will more likely be that Anti-Christ spoken of by the prophets, who will sit in the temple declaring he is God. These two factors will begin the first 3½ years of peace as talked about in the scriptures. After this period will begin 3½ years of severe tribulation for the wicked. This is the time when the last Antichrist will sit in the Holy of Holies, of the temple. This is also the "Abomination of Desolation", adding to the already numerous other abominations put amongst us by previous Antichrists. When we see these things, then know that Christ is set to come immediately, because He has had enough.

Make no mistake, the capitol building in Washington D.C. is regarded by the liberals; Obama, Pelosi, Biden, to name a few, as their temple. This is the same place where many tunnels are located, under the building, where all the sacrificial children have been found. This is also where a huge pedophile ring has been uncovered.

Washington D.C. is set up in the image of a five cornered star, resembling the "Goat's Head of Mendez". This is the seat of Satan in America. Many of the people there worship Satan, and perform their satanic rituals, and many of them involving children. You will find the liberals/democrats at the core of this abomination, and their left leaning GOP allies.

Another factor adding to this period of peace is the fact that Great Britain has been able to withdraw from the European Union. Other countries worldwide are pushing for freedom. France is attempting to unseat Macron, and Hong Kong is insisting on rights of freedom there. The whore of all the earth must be destroyed at the end of these years of tribulation and their secret works of darkness and secret orders. The whore of all the earth includes the organization of the Catholic Church, which is the source of all abominable things because Satan gives the pope his power. Democrats, liberals, secret orders, Jesuits, witchcraft, Satanism, evolution, atheism, and immorality all must be destroyed by Christ when he comes again.

*And the great and abominable church, which is **the whore of all the earth,** shall be cast down by the devouring fire, according as it is spoken by the mouth of Ezekiel the prophet, who spoke of these things, which have not come to pass but surely must, as I live, for **abominations** shall not reign. (Doctrine and Covenants, section 29:21)*

*And there shall be standing in that generation, that shall not pass until they shall see an **overflowing scourge; for a desolating sickness shall cover the land**. But **my disciples shall stand in holy places**, and shall not be moved; but **among the wicked**, men shall lift up their voices and curse God and die, And there shall be earthquakes also in divers places, and many **desolations;** yet men will harden their hearts against me, and they will take up the sword, one against another, and they will kill one another. (Doctrine and Covenants,*

In a previous chapter was discussed the destruction of Babylon, identified as New York City, New York, that same city that sits on many waters where the kings of the world fulfill their many pleasures and get rich. This same city has standing, overlooking its harbor, that great statue of Ishtar/Isis/Semiramis, which is a pagan goddess who was a whore when she lived on the earth. The statue was delivered to America by the Catholic Church out of France. The city of New York will be destroyed because of their many depravities and great wickedness.

Nevertheless, let the bishop go unto the city of New York, also to the city of Albany, and also to the city of Boston. And warn the people of those cities with the sound of the gospel, with a loud voice, of the **desolation and utter abolishment** *which await them if they do reject these things. For if they do reject these things the hour of their judgment is nigh, and their house shall be left unto them* **desolate** *. . . . And verily I say unto you, the rest of my servants, go ye forth as your circumstances shall permit, in your several callings, unto the great and notable cities and villages, reproving the world in righteousness of all their unrighteous and ungodly deeds, setting forth clearly and understandingly* **the desolation of abomination** *in the last days. (Doctrine and Covenants, section 84:114–115, 117)*

Therefore, tarry ye, and labor diligently, that you may be perfected in your ministry to go forth among the Gentiles for the last time, as many as the mouth of the Lord shall name, to bind up the law and seal the testimony, and to prepare the saints for the hour of judgment which is to come; That their souls may escape the wrath of God, **the desolation of abomination which awaits the wicked,** *both in this world and in the world to come. Verily, I say unto you, let those who are not the first elders continue in the vineyard until the mouth of the Lord shall call them, for their time is not yet come; their garments are not clean from the blood of this generation. Abide ye in the* **liberty** *wherewith ye are made free; entangle not yourselves in sin, but let your hands be clean, until the Lord comes. (Doctrine and Covenants, section 88:84–86)*

Because of the wicked abominations committed by the whore of all the earth and her minions, unless they speedily repent, a scourging sickness will cover the land. The wicked will die in great numbers. When you see this happening, get out of the area. It appears to be as it was in the days of the

Passover in Egypt, when the firstborns were killed all throughout the land of Egypt, from the Egyptians to the children of Israel. If the children of Israel didn't have the blood of the lamb on their doorposts, then the angels of God entered and struck their firstborn. If they did what they were told to do, they were prepared, and the angel of the Lord passed them by. Here it is with the wicked. If the children of God unite with the whore of all the earth in these latter times, then they will be struck also. God's laws are what counts, not man's.

We must put away our sins and be clean before God to survive these days of tribulation. These judgments are only prescribed for the wicked, and the people of God need not fear. The true believers of God must wait and watch for these things to begin to happen.

*And the blood of that **great and abominable church** which **is the whore of all the earth**, shall turn upon their own heads; for **they shall war among themselves**, and the sword of their own hands shall fall upon their own heads, and they shall be drunken with their own blood . . . For behold, saith the prophet, the time cometh speedily that Satan shall have no more power over the hearts of the children of men; for the day soon cometh that all **they who do wickedly** shall be as stubble; and the **day cometh that they must be burned**. For the time soon cometh that the fulness of the wrath of God shall be poured out upon all the children of men; for he will not suffer that **the wicked shall destroy the righteous**. Wherefore, **he will preserve the righteous** by his power, even if it so be that the fulness of his wrath must come, and the righteous be preserved, even unto the destruction of their enemies by fire. Wherefore, the **righteous need not fear**; for thus saith the prophet, they shall be saved, even if it so be as by fire. (1 Nephi 22:13, 15–17, Book of Mormon)*

*When thou, therefore, shall see the **abomination of desolation**, spoken of by Daniel the prophet, concerning the destruction of Jerusalem, then you shall stand in the holy place; whoso readeth let him understand. (Matthew 1:12, JST of KJV)*

The scriptures are very clear that the abomination of desolation is because of the many abominable sins committed by the whore of all the earth and those joined to and entangled with her. These sins include what has been mentioned earlier in this chapter, and because of these depravities committed and being committed—including homosexuality, lesbianism, pedophilia, any form of Satanism, child sacrifices, witchcraft, the lies and pollution in and out of the churches, and many others—there will be judgment.

We might ask ourselves, "Isn't there supposed to be an Antichrist standing in some place that he shouldn't be standing or somewhere he shouldn't be sitting?" The answer to that is there have already been and are now those who shouldn't be sitting or standing where they are at. There are many Antichrists who shouldn't be in the positions they are in, but *Thee,* Antichrist has not yet revealed himself/herself.

"THEE" Antichrist is made up of many antichrists. THEE Antichrist is the "BEAST", and is simply the "Corporate System". It is the "World", and the mouth of this Antichrist at this time is Joe Biden, along with all of his liberal and GOP allies, who are helping him to pull off their despicable lies through fraud. These people are enemies to God.

The day is coming soon, when, the corporate system, run by liberal-minded people, will rise up and think to fight against, even Christ, to prevent His return. *"And I saw heaven opened, and behold a white horse; and He [Jesus] that sat upon him was called Faithful and True, and in righteousness He doth judge and make war...And I saw the **beast** [corporate system/Antichrist], and the kings of the earth, and their armies, gathered together to make war against Him that sat on the horse, and against His army. And the **beast** was taken, and the false prophet [Pope] that wrought miracles before him, with which he deceived them that had received the **mark of the beast** [corporate system/Antichrist], and them that worshipped his **image** [the money], these both were cast into a lake of fire and brimstone."(Revelation 19:11, 19-20, KJV)*

"Here is wisdom. Let him that hath understanding count the number of the beast: for it is the number of a man; and his number is Six hundred threescore and six."(Revelation 13:18, KJV)

"The pope wears upon his pontifical crown in jeweled letters, this title: **'Vicarius Filii Dei', 'Vice-regent of the Son of God'** the numerical value of which is just six hundred and sixty-six." (See review and Herald 28:196, November 20, 1866, by Marcocapelle).

The point of all of this is, that the Pope of the Catholic Church is behind everything that goes on, and it is his number that is associated with the corporate system. His number comes up very often, especially to do with the IRS. His voices he uses are the very liberals in our government, including presidents, senators, congress men and women, both federal and state. He uses judges and county officials, and others at all levels of government. He also uses businesses in commerce to do his bidding. Look at Bill Gates and his microsoft, Soros, Zuckerberg and his facebook, and Dorsi and his Twitter. He also uses government agencies and the media, CNN, MSNBC, the Washington Post, New York Times, just to name a few. These are all part of the corporate system, and God calls them the "Whore of all the earth".

Make no mistake, the Democrats are the Gadianton robbers that are talked about in the *Book of Mormon*. These such Antichrists infiltrate representatives, senators, FBI agents, teachers, mayors, governors, police, city councilmen, judges, businesses, and White House presidents, and even our churches. Whenever we see any of these people in positions of authority, we must work to have them thrown out of office. Any alleged Christian who turns and says they are Democrats are revolting. On one hand, they vote or support a candidate who supports open borders, which implies drug trafficking, child trafficking, criminals coming in unchecked, voter fraud, etc., or they support high taxes that they intend to take from you and your children to give to illegals.

Other things they support are the women having the right to kill their own babies. They don't believe in God, they are involved themselves in different crimes, they are Satanists or into witchcraft and child sacrifice and very immoral, they violate their oath of office to uphold the Constitution, they want to take your guns, they are pushing socialism. The list just goes on and on. Then on the other hand, they say they are Christian.

They may not do the things listed here personally, but they vote for someone who will do it for them. These kinds of people want a foot in both camps. They say, "If I want this benefit, I will vote for him, even though it is not the right thing to do, but I am not doing it personally, so it can't be my fault if he gets caught," or "I am going to go to church and do all the things a Christian is supposed to do, but just in case I get found out, I can still be saved in the kingdom of God." Sorry, folks, it doesn't work that way. Ignorance of the law is no excuse. If you want to be lukewarm, you better think twice. *"So then because thou art **lukewarm**, and neither cold nor hot, I **will spue thee out of my mouth**" (Revelation 3:16, KJV).*

I believe the world is building to the moment when the worst of these Antichrists are about to surface into a position of power. The scriptures talk about the whore of all the earth and about the great and abominable church. These are one and the same. The scriptures tell us that it is the one who blasphemes God's name and also describes the riches he holds and the colors he wears—scarlet, purple, and gold. The scriptures cannot be talking about any other than the pope of the Catholic Church. The one living today is just one of many popes who have died in the past. The pope acts like God and blasphemes the name of God. He has Christ hung on the cross in perpetual death. He has organized a World Council of Churches, with himself as the head of it. Now he is trying to organize a one world church, with himself as the head of it.

If these other churches or the people of the world for that matter allow the pope to pull this off, then there are a lot of churches that will be cleaned out when Christ comes again. When He comes, He will burn the wicked. *Thee* Antichrist sitting where he shouldn't be doesn't necessarily mean the world will break out in instant war or violence, but it does mean that God has had enough, and for His true believers and worshippers, He will come and cut His time short. So when we see this person or persons where he or they shouldn't be, we need to understand and then leave quickly because the overflowing sickness is on its way. We need to be sure we are separate from the wicked so that the destroying angel will pass us by. God knows who we are and the thoughts of our hearts. We need to seek God early because He will not always strive with man.

*"Let no man deceive you by any means: for that day shall not come, except there be a falling away first, **and that man of sin be revealed, the son of perdition**;" "Who opposeth and exalteth himself above all that is called God, or that is worshipped; so that he **as God sitteth in the temple pf God**, shewing himself that **he is God.**" "Remember ye not, that, when I was yet with you, I told you these things?" And now ye know what withholdeth that **he might be revealed in his time.**" "For the **mystery** of iniquity doth already work: only he who now letteth will let, until he be taken out of the way." "And then shall that **Wicked be revealed**, whom the Lord shall consume with the spirit of his mouth, and shall **destroy with the brightness of his coming:**" "Even him, whose coming is after the **working of Satan** with all power and **signs and lying wonders,**" "And with all **deceivableness** or unrighteousness in them that*

perish; because they received not the love of the truth, that they might be saved." "And for this cause God shall send them strong delusion, that they should believe a lie:" "That they all might be damned who believed not the truth, but had pleasure in unrighteousness."(2 Thessalonians 2:3-12, KJV)

When we see THEE Anti-Christ in the temple, then know Christ is not far off, and if you have received the gospel of Jesus Christ, then you will be taken out of the way. Does not the scriptures say that when that day comes: *"Then shall two be in the field; the one shall be taken, and the other left." "Two women shall be grinding at the mill; the one shall be taken, and the other left." (Matthew 24:40-41, KJV)* This is also why, when that day comes, that there is no need to go back to your house to get anything, because if you are a good person, God is coming to get you, and you will not have a need of any worldly thing.

We must be separate from the world, but we must continue to preach the gospel to every creature, for we know not at what point he or she will turn and repent of their sins, even to the last hour. It is my prayer that people everywhere will change and serve the only true God by obeying His commandments. *Wherefore come out from among them, and be ye separate, saith the Lord, and touch not the unclean thing; and I will receive you" (2 Corinthians 6:17, KJV).* This, my friends, is a mighty strong promise.

Christ so often told the people to repent and be baptized because the kingdom of God is at hand. What He is saying is that those who receive His gospel are in a completely different kingdom from the world. Christ so often told His people to be in the world but not joined to it. He is telling us that the world is this Hell, Satan's jurisdiction in the telestial kingdom.

If the world hates you, know that it has hated me before it hated you. If you were of the world, the world would love you as its own; but because you are not of the world, but I chose you out of the world, therefore the world hates you. (John 15:18–19, KJV)

Do not be conformed to this world, but be transformed by the renewal of your mind, that by testing you may discern what is the will of God, what is good and acceptable and perfect. (Romans 12:2, KJV)

Jesus answered, "My kingdom is not of this world. If my kingdom were of this world, my servants would have been fighting, that I might not be delivered over *to the Jews. But my kingdom is not from the **world**." (John 18:36, KJV)*

*Do not love the **world** or the things in the **world**. If anyone loves the **world**, the love of the Father is not in him. For all that is in the world—the desires of the flesh and the desires of the eyes and pride and possessions—is not from the Father but is from the **world**. And the **world** is passing away along with its desires, but whoever does the will of God abides forever. (1 John 2:15–17, KJV)*

*I have given them your word, and the **world** hateth them because they are not of the **world**, just as I am not of the **world**. (John 17:14, KJV)*

For we do not wrestle against flesh and blood, but against rulers, against authorities, against the cosmic powers over this present darkness, against the spiritual forces of evil in the heavenly places. (Ephesians 6:12, KJV)

*You adulterous people! Do you not know that friendship with the **world** is enmity with God? Therefore whoever wishes to be a friend of the **world** makes himself an enemy to God. (James 4:4. KJV)*

*For God so loved the **world**, that he gave his only begotten Son, that whosoever believes in him should not perish but have eternal life. (John 3:16, KJV)*

Receiving the gospel of Jesus Christ and swearing allegiance to the kingdom of God through baptism puts us into the terrestrial kingdom, in Christ's jurisdiction, under the Constitution. Both the telestial and the terrestrial kingdoms are here on this earth right now at the same time and are always at war with each other. Christ has told His people to occupy and endure until He comes again.

Satan cannot try Christ's people unless he receives permission from God, just as it was with Job. We know that trials and temptations are necessary to refine God's people as fire is necessary to refine gold. When you are to the point that nothing can turn you away from God, then you know for certain that you are a son or daughter of God, and you are worthy of redemption. Christ only came to redeem the sons and daughters of God. There are countless people who will not receive the gospel of Jesus Christ, and they will not be redeemed when He comes, and of this I am sure.

In those days came John the Baptist, preaching in the wilderness of Judaea, And saying, Repent ye: for the kingdom of heaven is at hand. (Matthew 3:1–2, KJV)

The people which sat in darkness saw great light, and to them which sat in the region and shadow of death light sprung up. From that time Jesus began to preach, and to say, Repent: for the kingdom of heaven is at hand. (Matthew 4:16–17, KJV)

CHAPTER 13

The Millennium

When God placed Adam and Eve here on earth, He also loosed on earth Satan and Hell with him. The Bible records that Satan was cast down, and also with him was one third of the hosts of heaven, and they fell like lightning. *"And he said unto them,I beheld Satan as lightning fall from heaven."(Luke 10:18, KJV)*

"And there appeared another wonder in heaven; and a great red dragon, having seven heads and ten horns, and seven crowns upon his heads"."And his tail drew the third part of the stars of heaven, and did cast them to the earth: and the dragon stood before the woman which was ready to be delivered, for to devour her child as soon as it was born."(Hebrews 12:3-4, KJV)

Here, the devil's kingdom was already on earth, and Satan also knew that Christ's kingdom was to be established here on earth, as well. Satan also knew that Christ was still to be born, and who would be his mother, and stood poised to destroy the Christ child at birth, with the idea that, if he could kill the child, it would also destroy the kingdom of God. Satan was very wroth with God for throwing him out of heaven, and binding him from time to time, worlds without end, so he was raging.

And there was war in heaven: Michael and his angels fought against the dragon; and the dragon fought and his angels,""And prevailed not; neither was their place found anymore in heaven.""And the great dragon was cast out,, that old serpent, called the Devil, and Satan, which deceiveth the whole world: he was cast out into the earth, and his angels were cast out with him."; "Therefore, rejoice, ye heavens, and ye that dwell in them. Woe to the inhabitants of the earth and of the sea! For the devil is come down unto you, having great wrath, because he knoweth that he hath but a short time.""And the dragon was wroth with the woman, and went to make war with the remnant of her seed, which keep the commandments of God, and have the testimony of Jesus Christ. (Revelation 12:7-9, 12,17, KJV)

Satan was unsuccessful at destroying Christ when he was a baby, in fact Jesus Christ went on to live to adulthood, and establish his church on earth in Jerusalem. The "mother" refers to the church that was established, and Satan is waging war against those who have received the "gospel of Jesus Christ", and who keep the commandments of God. So, you can see that both, the kingdom of Satan/telestial, and the Kingdom of Jesus Christ/ terrestrial are here on earth at the same time. There is opposition in all things, and Christ tells his people to be in the world, but be separate and not joined to it. *"Do not love the world or the things in the world. If anyone loves the world, the love of the Father is not in him.""For all that is in the world—the desires of the flesh and the desires of the eyes and pride and possessions—is not from the Father but is from the world.""And the world is passing away along with its desires, but whoever does the will of God abides forever."(1 John 2:15-17, KJV).*

Even though Satan and his demons are all around us, be not partakers of what the people who delight in Satan, do. There are many people today that are believing that Satan is more powerful than God. You see them from all classes showing the devils' symbol with their hands. They delight in the occult, witchcraft, magic, and "spirit cooking", satanic worship. There are the pedophiles, and the sex trafficking, the prostitution, and rapes. They are even going as far as to participate in satanic worship, and the sacrificing of children to Satan. Some have made sports their god, and there are many more. Most are seeking riches even if it is at the expense of their fellowman. Some seek power as the Democrats do. The depravity of the world is too gruesome and horrible to mention all, and too numerous to list.

*"You adulterous people! Do you not know that friendship with the world is enmity with God? Therefore whoever wishes to be a **friend** of the **world** makes himself an **enemy of God**."(James 4:4, KJV) "Do not be **conformed** to this world, but be transformed by the renewal of your mind, that by testing you may discern what is the will of God, what is good and acceptable and perfect."(Romans 12:2, KJV)*

Satan and his Hell, was cast into the earth, and he used the Catholic Church as his seat, as it mentions in Hebrews 12:3-4. The Catholic Church in Rome sits on seven hills, and controlled ten kings, with ten crowns. Rome, Italy is the center of the Roman Empire. Constantine, the Roman Emperor, set up a seat of government also in Turkey, in the city of **Pergamos**, or Istanbul. Istanbul is the Middle East's way of saying Constantinople.

"And to the angel of the church in Pergamos write; These things sayeth he which hath the sharp sword with two edges;"" I know thy works and where thou dwellest, even where Satan's seat is.""And thou holdest fast my name, and hast not denied thy faith, even in those days wherein Antipas was my faithful martyr, who was slain among you, **where Satan dwelleth.** *".(Revelation 2:12-13, KJV)*

In Pergamos/Istanbul, Turkey is the seat of the military arm of the Catholic Church, or the black pope/Jesuits. At the time of Christ's birth, the Roman empire had Israel in subjection. Israel was full of selfish Jewish rulers, both religious and political, who were yes men for the Romans, who sought power and control over their own countrymen. King Herod was among those who sought to kill Christ soon after his birth, by ordering his soldiers to Bethlehem for the purpose of killing all of the baby boys in the age bracket the wisemen told him about. The wisemen mentioned Christ as being the newborn king, which worried Herod that someone was here to challenge his right to the throne of Israel. Christ sure wasn't interested in that, because he was on a higher plane, and king of a higher and greater kingdom, but someone from Hell cannot understand the things of God until they come down to the depths of humility, and turn to God in faith.

"Jesus answered, My kingdom is not of this world: If my kingdom were of this world, then would my servants fight, that I should not be delivered to the Jews: but now is my kingdom not from thence."(John 18:36, KJV) And he said to them, **Ye are from beneath; I am from above:** *ye are of this world; I am not of this world.*

Christ, upon reaching a mature age, began to be about his Father's business, being an example and teaching the people about his Father, about himself and his mission and who he was. He established his church/ his kingdom here on earth with apostles, and himself in the position of prophet. After his death, Peter then filled that office. He taught the people in all the land roundabout concerning faith, repentance and baptism, and that they needed to receive his gospel if they had any hope of leaving this kingdom of the devil/Hell, and going back into the presence of the Father.

The Romans did not have an organized church at this time, but they carried with them many pagan beliefs, or devilish ideas and theories. of which Satan and his demons abounded. The cruelty, the fear, the depravity, and the despotism, was prevalent. It truly was the epitome of Hell. It is identical to that system of socialism, or communism. There is no difference. It wasn't until approximately 200 years after Christ established his church, or kingdom, when the Roman Empire succeeded in killing off all of Christ's apostles, and drove his church into the wilderness, which began the "Dark Age" period.

The Catholic Church was then organized and established by Constantine, because he realized how effective it was to have a common bond in beliefs that would bind people together, and strengthen his kingdom. So, both the telestial kingdom and the terrestrial kingdom exists here on earth, right now. You can literally see the scriptures from the Bible unfold before our very eyes. By having these two kingdoms together, is such an ingenious plan, for the purpose of either convincing non-Christians into believing in Jesus Christ, or on the other hand, tempt the believers in Christ into straying from Christ and the truth.

This is what is meant when the scriptures say that Christ overcame the world. He didn't give in to any temptation from Satan, because he remembered who he was, why he is here on earth, and that his kingdom is greater. He had the power given to him by the Father to destroy the devil and his kingdom if he wanted to, but he allowed himself willingly, to be tortured, ridiculed, insulted, and was even born in a barn. He even went so far as to let Satan kill him, when he had the power to destroy Satan. Christ tolerated the world because of those few people who appreciate his sacrifices, and showing gratitude by them exercising faith in him. Christ knows what his people are going through as they go through this dreary world. He knows our trials, and what our thoughts and hopes are, and he knows that Satan is raging in the hearts of the wicked. He has told his people to keep the faith and endure for a time, and he will come.

I know the time is near when Christ will come again, this time to judge the earth, and destroy the wicked. He has told his people that they need not fear. *"When the Son of man shall* **come** *in his glory, and all the holy angels with him, then shall he sit upon the throne of his glory: ""And before him shall be gathered all nations: and he shall separate them one from another, as a shepherd divideth his* **sheep from the goats:** *""And he shall set the* **sheep on his right hand,** *but the* **goats on the left.** *""Then shall the king say unto them on his right hand, Come, ye blessed of my Father,* **inherit the kingdom** *prepared for you from the foundation of the world:"(Matthew 25:31-34, KJV)*

"For the time speedily cometh that the Lord God shall cause a great division among the people, and the **wicked will he destroy;** *and he will spare his people, yea, even if it so be that he must* **destroy the wicked by fire.***"(2 Nephi 30:10, Book of Mormon)*

"And these shall go away into everlasting punishment: but the righteous into life eternal."(Matthew 25:46, KJV)

In Chapter 6, it is mentioned how the Latter-day Saints, as they go through their temples, they pass through three different rooms, each resembling a stage or period in eternal progression. The first one is the telestial room, symbolizing this dreary world of Satan. This is the point where we are all at right now. It is called a "probationary state". This is where we prepare to meet our Savior, Jesus Christ, by receiving his gospel and living it. If we don't receive the gospel of Christ, then we are rejecting him and driving ourselves further into the devil's jurisdiction, and ultimately away from the truth and into "outer darkness."

When Christ comes to destroy the wicked, this will be the "**first judgment**". This will also usher in the morning of the "**first resurrection**" of the ones who are justified and right before God. *"For the hour is nigh and the day soon at hand when the earth is ripe; and all the proud and they that do wickedly shall be as stubble; and* **I will burn them up** *, saith the Lord of Hosts, that wickedness shall not be upon the earth;""For the hour is nigh, and that which was spoken by mine apostles must be fulfilled; for as they spoke so shall it come to pass;""For I will reveal myself from heaven with power and great glory, with all the hosts thereof, and* **dwell in righteousness with men on earth a thousand years, and the wicked shall not stand.***"(Doctrine and Covenants 29:9-11)*

While Christ is dwelling with the sons and daughters of God, Satan will be bound for these same thousand years, with those who did wickedly while here on earth, and gave ear to Satan, and worshipped him, or didn't obey the commandments of Jesus Christ. These will be countless numbers who, because of their sins will not be resurrected until Christ has put all enemies under his feet, and must endure the buffetings of Satan. This is the Hell that they must endure. Sure sounds like a long time doesn't it?

*And again we saw the glory of the telestial, which glory is that of the lesser, even as the glory of the stars differs from that of the glory of the moon in the firmament.""These are they who received not the gospel of Christ, neither the testimony of Jesus.""These are they who deny not the Holy Spirit.""These are they who are thrust down to hell.""These are they who shall **not be redeemed from the devil until the last resurrection, until the Lord, even Christ the Lamb, shall have finished his work**.""These are they who receive not of his fulness in the eternal world, but of the Holy Spirit through the ministration of the terrestrial;"(Doctrine and Covenants section 76:81-86)*

*"And the time cometh speedily that the righteous must be led up as calves of the stall, and the Holy One of Israel must reign in dominion, and might, and power, and great glory.""And he gathereth his children from the **four quarters of the earth;** and he numbereth his sheep, and they know him; and there shall be one fold and one shepherd; and he shall feed his sheep, and in him they shall find pasture.""And because of the **righteousness of his people, Satan has no power**; wherefore, he cannot be loosed for the space of **many years**; for he hath no power over the hearts of the people, for they dwell in righteousness, and the Holy One of Israel reigneth."(1 Nephi 22:24-26, Book of Mormon)*

*"And I saw an angel come down from heaven, having the key of the **bottomless pit** and a great chain in his hand.""And he laid hold on the dragon, that old serpent, which is the Devil, and Satan, and **bound him a thousand years**,""And cast him into the bottomless pit, and shut him up, and set a seal upon him, that he should deceive the nations no more, till the **thousand years should be fulfilled**: and after that he must be loosed a little season.""And I saw thrones, and they sat upon them, and judgment was given them: and I saw the souls of them that were beheaded for the witness of Jesus, and for the word of God, and which had not **worshipped the beast**, neither his image, neither had received **his mark upon their foreheads, or in their hands**; and they lived and reigned with Christ **a thousand years**.""But the rest of the*

*dead lived not again until the **thousand years** were finished. **This is the first resurrection.**""Blessed and holy is he that hath part in the first resurrection: on such the **second death** hath no power, but they shall be priests of God and of Christ, and shall reign with him **a thousand years**.""And when the thousand years are expired, Satan shall be loosed out of his prison."(Revelation 20:1-7, KJV).*

There were many people who were resurrected at the resurrection of Jesus Christ, also construed as a first resurrection. The righteous up to that time, all came forth from their graves, and appeared to many. What it all boils down to, is that Jesus Christ is in charge, and the good people and the wicked, will be dealt with in Christ's time, as seemeth Him good. Whether, the resurrection of the just is an ongoing thing, and not making them wait past a designated time, is completely up to my Father in Heaven and Christ, and it makes me happy that they are so merciful and good. Also that, if the wicked die and have to wait a thousand years, or seven thousand years, before they are redeemed and resurrected, and possibly that is an ongoing thing, does not concern me, as to Christ's designated time for them also. Even as Alma, in the Book of Mormon, has written, he admits to not knowing all of these things, but these things he does know because an angel of the Lord has told him personally:

*"Now concerning the state of the soul between death and the resurrection— Behold, it has been made known unto me by an angel, that the spirits of all men, as soon as they are departed from this mortal body, yea, the spirits of all men, whether they be good or evil, are taken home to that God who gave them life.""And then shall it come to pass, that the spirits of those who are righteous are received into a state of happiness, which is called **paradise**, a state of rest from all their troubles and from all care, and sorrow""And then shall it come to pass, that the spirits of the wicked, yea, who are evil—for behold, they have no part nor portion of the Spirit of the Lord; for behold, they chose evil works rather than good; therefore the spirit of the devil did enter into them, and take possession of their house—and these shall be **cast out into outer darkness**; there shall be weeping and wailing, and gnashing of teeth, and this because of their own iniquity, being led captive by the will of the devil."(Alma 40:11-13, Book of Mormon)*

*"For the great **Millennium**, of which I have spoken by the mouth of my servants, shall come.""For Satan shall be bound, and when he is loosed again he*

shall only reign for a little season, and then cometh the end of the earth.""And he that liveth in righteousness shall **be changed in the twinkling of an eye**, *and the earth shall pass away so as by fire.""And the wicked shall go away into unquenchable fire, and their end no man knoweth on earth, nor ever shall know, until they come before me in judgment."(Doctrine and Covenants 43:30-33)*

When Christ comes to burn the wicked, this will be the beginning of the Millennium. It will be the first judgment for this group of wicked, and the first resurrection for this group of the righteous. Satan will be bound for one thousand years, because it is only the righteous who are still alive and in the presence of Jesus Christ. The righteousness of the people is what binds Satan for the thousand years, and he has no power. The righteous still have their bodies of flesh and bone, when they are caught up into the air to be with Christ while he destroys the wicked. It is at the end of this thousand years that Satan is loosed for a little season, because the people have begun again to become evil, even while in the presence of Christ. Fire from heaven is then sent to burn up the wicked and evil forces. This is a second death for those wicked, who never knew death, before Christ came to begin the Millennium, and this is also the "**second judgment**" for the righteous.

The secret orders, and the wicked/evil people must be destroyed from off of the earth, both in the first and second judgments, in order to prepare the earth for it's **"celestial glory"**. The second room the Latter-day Saints go through in the temple, is symbolic of the terrestrial kingdom, which is a "preparatory state". This is exactly what begins for the righteous, because it is they who are taken up to Christ in the air. This begins the Millennium, and the preparing of the saints of God for the Celestial Kingdom. There are also those who won't want to live the laws of this kingdom, just like those who reject the laws of the terrestrial kingdom, and of course there is a place prepared for them as well. The earth however, was created specifically to gain it's own celestial glory, and to be the abode of those who attain this glory.

"And again, verily I say unto you, the earth abideth the law of a **celestial kingdom,** *for it filleth the measure of its creation, and transgresseth not the law--""Wherefore, it shall be sanctified; yea, notwithstanding it shall die, it shall be quickened, and the* **righteous** *shall inherit it.""For notwithstanding they die, they also shall rise again, a spiritual body.""They who are of a celestial spirit shall receive the same body; even ye shall receive your bodies, and your glory shall be that glory by which your bodies are quickened.""Ye who are quickened by a*

portion of the celestial glory shall then receive the same, even a fulness."(Doctrine and Covenants 88:25-27)

"And the kingdom and dominion, and the greatness of the kingdom under the whole heaven, shall be given to the people of the saints of the most High, whose kingdom is an everlasting kingdom, and all dominions shall serve and obey him."(Daniel 7:27, KJV)

When Christ was preaching his Sermon on the Mount, he mentioned the inheritance of the *"meek"*. *"Blessed are the meek: for they shall inherit the earth."(Matthew 5:5, KJV)*

During this time when Christ comes, he will have overcome the world and Satan will be bound. The terrestrial kingdom is in the presence of Jesus Christ, not the Father, and Christ will reign with power. *"And the Lord shall be king over all the earth: in that day shall there be one Lord, and his name one.""And it shall be, that whoso will not come up of all the families of the earth unto Jerusalem to worship the King, the Lord of hosts, even upon them shall be no rain."(Zechariah 14:9,17, KJV)*

The heathen, those who never had a chance to receive the gospel of Jesus Christ will have it at this time. Those who have been bowed down by oppressive leaders, such as Moab. Moab is the descendants of Lot, the nephew of Abraham, and Christ is calling after them. *"And in mercy shall the throne be established: and he shall sit upon it in truth in the tabernacle of David, judging, and seeking judgment, and hasting righteousness."(Isaiah 16:5, KJV)*

"And he will swallow up death in victory; and the Lord God will wipe away tears from off all faces; and the rebuke of his people shall he take away from off all the earth: for the Lord hath spoken it."(Isaiah 25:8, KJV)

"Then the moon shall be confounded, and the sun ashamed, when the Lord of hosts shall reign in mount Zion, and in Jerusalem, and before his ancients gloriously."(Isaiah 24:23, KJV)

"The sun and the moon shall be darkened, and the stars shall withdraw their shining.""The Lord shall roar out of Zion, and utter his voice from Jerusalem; and the heavens and the earth shall shake: but the Lord will be the hope of his people, and the strength of the children of Israel.""So shall ye know that I am

*the Lord your God **dwelling in Zion**, my holy mountain: and there shall no strangers pass through her any more."(Joel 3:15-16, KJV)*

During this thousand years of peace, only the good people of the earth will be there. It will be more glorious than we can imagine. The burned cities will be rebuilt, and the waste land, like the deserts will become as the Garden of Eden. *"And the desolate land shall be tilled, whereas it lay desolate in the sight of all that passed by.""And they shall say, This land that was desolate is become like the **Garden of Eden**; and the waste and desolate and ruined cities are become fenced, and are inhabited.""Then the heathen that are left round about you shall know that I the Lord build the ruined places, and plant that that was desolate: I the Lord have spoken it, and I will do it."(Ezekiel 36:34-36, KJV)*

During this Millennium will the wolf and the lamb lay down together in peace, and not be afraid. *"And there shall come forth a rod out of the stem of Jesse, and a Branch shall grow out of his roots:""And the spirit of the Lord shall rest upon him, the spirit of wisdom and understanding, the spirit of counsel and might, the spirit of knowledge and of the fear of the Lord;""And shall make him of quick understanding in the fear of the Lord: and he shall not judge after the sight of his eyes, neither reprove after the hearing of his ears:""But with righteousness shall he judge the poor, and reprove with equity for the **meek of the earth:** and he shall smite the earth with the rod of his mouth, and with the breath of his lips shall **he slay the wicked**.""and righteousness shall be the girdle of his loins, and faithfulness the girdle of his reins.""The **wolf shall dwell with the lamb,** and the leopard shall lie down with the kid; and the calf and the young lion and the fatling together; and a **little child shall lead them**.""And the cow and the bear shall feed; their young ones shall lie down together: and the lion shall eat straw like the ox.""And the sucking child shall play on the hole of the asp, and the weaned child shall put his hand on the cockatrice den.""They shall not hurt nor destroy in all my holy mountain: for the earth shall be full of the **Knowledge of the Lord, as the waters cover the sea**."(Isaiah 11:1-10, KJV)*

All the children who died as infants and before accountability, and those who would have received the gospel of Jesus Christ, had they lived, will have the privilege of growing up, experiencing life, being able to choose and have opportunity. When they become old, they shall not die for long, because there will be the resurrection made possible because of Jesus Christ, for they will be changed in the twinkling of an eye. *"Wherefore, children shall grow up until they become old; old men shall die; but they shall not sleep in the dust, but they shall be changed in the twinkling of an eye.""Wherefore for this cause preached the apostles unto the world the resurrection of the dead.""These things are the things that ye must look for; and, speaking after the manner of the Lord, they are now nigh at hand, and in a time to come, even in the day of the coming of the Son of Man."(Doctrine and Covenants 63:51-53)*

Compare Isaiah: *"For, behold, I create new heavens and a new earth: and the former shall not be remembered, nor come into mind.""But be glad and rejoice forever in that which I create: for, behold, I create Jerusalem a rejoicing, and her people a joy""And I will rejoice in Jerusalem, and joy in my people: and the voice of weeping shall be no more heard in her, nor the voice of crying.""There shall be no more thence an infant of days, nor an old man that hath not filled his days: for the child shall die an hundred years old; but the sinner being an hundred years old shall be accursed.""And they shall build houses, and inhabit them; and they shall plant vineyards, and eat the fruit of them".(Isaiah 65:17-21, KJV)*

Other than this new Jerusalem to be built, the city of Enoch will also be restored to the earth, and all of the good people who lived will also be here, past, present , and future, according to the judgment of Jesus Christ. We will all live together for a thousand years, while the goodness of the people bind Satan, and his minions of Hell. People who lived here that rejected the gospel of Christ while on earth, and chose to do wickedly, will be controlled by Satan, for they are his. There are those like the thief on the cross, who recognized Christ and realized and repented, and acknowledged that he is Lord and Savior. Even at the last minute, that thief will have an opportunity, after the designated time in the spirit world, to be redeemed. My opinion is that he will be taught for a while in the spirit world before this happens.

*"And one of the malefactors which were hanged railed on him, saying, If thou be Christ, save thyself and us.""But the other answering rebuked him, saying, Dost not thou fear God, seeing thou art in the same condemnation?""And we indeed justly; for we receive the due reward of our deeds: but this man hath done nothing amiss.""And he said unto Jesus, Lord, remember me when thou comest into thy kingdom.""And Jesus said unto him, Verily I say unto thee, To day shalt **thou be with me in paradise.**"(Luke 23:39-43, KJV).*

Only Christ is the keeper of the gate, and he employs no servant there, as it describes in the Book of Mormon: *O then, my beloved brethren, come unto the Lord, the Holy One. Remember that his paths are righteous. Behold, the way for man is narrow, but it lieth in a straight course before him,* **and the keeper of the gate is the Holy One of Israel; and he employeth no servant there; and there is none other way save it be by the gate; for he cannot be deceived, for the Lord God is his name.** *"*

To be saved in the Kingdom of God one must exercise faith in Christ, and live his gospel. First by faith, then repentance, and then by baptism by immersion. There are many people who have attributes of good people, but they must go through this gate of Christ. If they die in their tradition, or false beliefs, being too stubborn to look up, and live, they will be sadly disappointed. I believe this spirit prison is made for them, where they will still be taught, but because they have on the wrong wedding garment, they have sold themselves short. The Catholic people are a very good example of this. Many have come to Christ, but there are many who believe they are Christian in word only, but have not taken their eyes off of the pope, and they look to him as their salvation. They are going to be sadly disappointed. They must put their complete trust in Jesus Christ, and do the things that they have seen and heard of Him doing.

"For for this cause was the **gospel preached also to them that are dead,** *that they might be judged according to men in the flesh, but live according to God in the spirit."(1Peter 4:6, KJV)*

The truth of the matter is, that those who do not receive the gospel of Jesus Christ, is the same as not receiving Christ. Christ has told us in the Bible that if we are not for Him, then we are against Him. *"He that is not with me is against me; and he that gathereth not with me scattereth abroad."* *(Matthew 12:30, KJV)* He describes such people as the "natural man", and therefore an enemy to God. These also will be destroyed at His coming, because He must put all enemies under His feet, before He delivers the kingdom over to the Father, even the Ancient of Days.

"And it came to pass that Enoch cried unto the Lord, saying: When the Son of Man cometh in the flesh, shall the earth rest? I pray thee, show me these things.""And the Lord said unto Enoch: Look, and he looked, and he looked and beheld the Son of Man lifted up on the cross, after the manner of men;""And

he heard a loud voice; and the heavens were veiled; and all the creations of God mourned; and the earth groaned; and the rocks were rent; and the saints arose, and were crowned at the right hand of the Son of Man, with crowns of glory;""And as many of the **spirits as were in prison** came forth, and stood on the right hand of God; and the remainder were reserved in **chains of darkness** until the judgment of the great day."(Moses 7:54-57, Pearl of Great Price)

King Benjamin in the book of Mosiah talks about the state of the wicked: "And now , I say unto you, my brethren, that after ye have known and have been taught all these things, if ye should transgress and go contrary to that which has been spoken, that ye do withdraw yourselves from the Spirit of the Lord, that it may have no place in you to guide you in wisdom's paths that ye may be blessed, prospered, and preserved--""I say unto you , that the man that doeth this, the same cometh out in open rebellion against God; therefore he listeth to obey the evil spirit, and becometh an enemy to all righteousness; therefore, the Lord **has no place in him**, for he dwelleth not in unholy temples.""Therefore if that man repenteth not, and remaineth and dieth an enemy to God, the demands of divine justice do awaken his immortal soul to a lively sense of his own guilt, which doth cause him to shrink from the presence of the Lord, and doth fill his breast with guilt, and pain, and anguish, which is like an unquenchable fire, whose flame ascendeth up forever and ever."And now I say unto you, that **mercy hath no claim on that man;** therefore his final doom is to endure a never-ending torment."(Mosiah 2:36-39,Book of Mormon)

Alma in the Book of Mormon, can testify to how a person will feel when confronted with all of his guilt. He gives us a little indication of how it consumes our whole being when we know that we have violated any of the commandments of God. He states: "And the angel spake more things unto me, which were heard by my brethren, but I did not hear them; for when I heard the words—**If thou wilt be destroyed of thyself, seek no more to destroy the church of God**—I was struck with such great fear and amazement lest perhaps I should be destroyed, that I fell to the earth and I did hear no more.""But I was racked with eternal torment, for my soul was harrowed up to the greatest degree and racked with all my sins.""Yea, I did remember all my sins and iniquities, for which I was tormented with the pains of hell; yea, I saw that I had rebelled against my God, and that I had not kept his holy commandments,""Yea, and I had murdered many of his children, or rather led them away unto destruction; yea, and in fine so great had been my iniquities,that the very thought of coming into the presence of my God did rack my soul with inexpressible horror." "Oh thought I, that I could be banished and become extinct both soul and body, that I might not be brought to stand in the presence of my God, to be judged of my deeds," "And now, for three days and for three nights was I racked, even with the pains of a damned soul." "And it came to pass that as I was thus racked with torment, while I was harrowed up by the memory of my many sins, behold, I remembered also to have heard my father prophesy unto the people concerning the coming of one Jesus Christ, a Son of God, to atone for the sins of the world." "Now as my mind caught hold upon this thought, I cried within my heart; O Jesus, thou Son of God, have mercy on me, who am in the gall of bitterness, and am encircled about by the chains of death." "And now, behold, when I thought this, I could remember my pains no more; yea, I was harrowed up by the memory of my sins no more." (Alma 36:11-19, Book of Mormon)*

Also in Alma, he has this to say about procrastinating the day of repentance: *"For behold, **this life is the time to prepare to meet God**; yea, behold the day of this life is the day for men to perform their labors." "And now, as I said unto you before, as ye have had so many witnesses, therefore, I beseech of you that ye do not **procrastinate the day of your repentance** until the end; for after this day of life, which is given us to **prepare for eternity**, behold, if we do not improve our time while in this life, then cometh the night of **darkness** wherein there can be no labor performed." "Ye cannot say, when ye are brought to that awful crisis, that I will **repent**, that I will return to my God. Nay, ye cannot say this; **for that same spirit which doth possess your bodies** at the time that ye go out of this life, **that same spirit will have power to possess your body in that eternal world.**" "For behold, if ye have **procrastinated** the day of your repentance **even unto death**, behold, ye have become subjected to the spirit of the devil, **and he doth seal you his**; therefore, the Spirit of the Lord hath withdrawn from you, and hath no place in you, and the devil hath all power over you; and this is the **final state of the wicked.**" "And this I know, because the Lord hath said he dwelleth not in unholy temples, but in the hearts of the righteous doth he dwell; yea, and he has also said that the righteous shall sit down in his kingdom, to go no more out; but their garments should be made white through the **blood of the Lamb.**" (Alma 34:32-36, Book of Mormon)*

My belief, is that God has a system of progress for all men continually. I believe that it is very busy in heaven at all times, the coming and going of the wicked, the resurrections of the righteous, the judgments being made and determined, and the eternal rewards, or punishments being handed out.

Like many of the holy prophets, they are able to tell us what they know for sure, but in many instances have to rely on their own opinions formed according to what they know for sure. We are all striving to know the mysteries of God, and we all base our knowledge on our own experiences, sayings, and quotes from prophets who have talked directly to God, and mainly from God himself, including the source of all truth, Jesus Christ. When he says it, then that is where I hang my hat. One thing I do know is that Christ's people need not fear. It is the wicked who need to do that, because God is not just love, he is also justice, and there certainly will be a reckoning. We must have the nature of God in our hearts, and seek to obey His commandments.

Towards the end of *The* Millennium, there will be a time when the devil will be loosed again on the earth, because once again the people begin to invite him into their lives. Satan and his forces, coupled with the wicked, who have lived to invite the devil into their hearts and lives, will amass one last time to attempt to destroy the people of God. This is called the "battle of Gog and Magog". This will prompt another destruction from God, which calls for another judgment on the wicked in the world, by burning. There has been no one dying for long during a thousand years, as all people are living to a hundred years, and then changed in the twinkling of an eye.

*"And when the thousand years are expired, Satan shall be loosed out of his prison.""And shall go out to deceive the nations which are in the four quarters of the earth, **God and Magog**, to gather them together to battle: the number of whom is as the sand of the sea.""And they went up on the earth, and compassed the camp of the saints about, and the beloved city: and fire came down from God out of heaven, and devoured them.""And the devil that deceived them was cast into the lake of fire and brimstone, where the beast and the false prophet are, and shall be tormented day and night for ever and ever."(Revelation 20:7-10, KJV)*

Compare Doctrine and Covenants 88:110-114: *"...that there shall be time no longer; and Satan shall be bound, that old serpent, who is called the devil, and shall not be loosed for the space of a thousand years.""And then he shall be loosed for a little season, that he may gather together his armies.""and Michael, the seventh angel, even the archangel, shall gather together his armies, even the hosts of heaven.""And the devil shall gather together his armies; even the* *hosts of **hell**, and shall come up to battle against Michael and his armies.""And then cometh the battle of the **great God**; and the devil and his armies shall be cast away into their own place, that they shall not have power over the saints any more at all."(Doctrine and Covenants 88:110-114)*

After the battle of the great God, Gog and Magog, and when Christ has subdued all things under his feet, and the second judgment is passed on the wicked, then the earth will be transformed again. This is the end of the preparatory state of the earth, and now it will receive it's celestial glory, and the righteous along with it. *And I saw a new heaven and a new earth: for the first heaven and the first earth were passed away; and there was no more sea..""And I John saw the holy city, new Jerusalem, coming down from God out of heaven, prepared as a bride adorned for her husband.""And I heard a great voice out of heaven saying, Behold, the tabernacle of God is with men, and he will **dwell with them**, and they shall be his people, and **God himself shall be with them,** and be their God.""And God shall wipe away their tears from their eyes; and there shall be no more death, neither sorrow, nor crying, neither shall there be any more pain: for the former things are passed away.""And **he that sat upon the throne** said, Behold, I make all things new. And he said unto me, Write: for **these words are true and faithful.**""And he said, It is done. **I am Alpha and Omega, the beginning and the end.** I will give unto him that is athirst of the fountain of the water freely.""He that **overcometh shall inherit all things**; and I will be his God, and he shall be my son.""But the fearful, and unbelieving, and the abominable, and murderers, and whoremongers, and sorcerers, and idolaters, and **all liars**, shall have their part in the lake which burneth with fire and brimstone: which **is the second death**."(Revelation 21:1-8, KJV)*

Christ will then come to the Father and deliver up the kingdom to God: *"Then cometh the end, when he shall have delivered up the kingdom to **God, even the Father**; when he shall have put down all rule and all authority and power.""For he must reign, till he hath put all enemies under his feet,""The last enemy that shall be destroyed is death."(1 Corinthians 15:24-26, KJV)*

*"And I beheld till the thrones were cast down, and **the Ancient of Days did sit**, whose garment was white as snow, and the hair of his head like pure wool: his throne was like the fiery flame, and his wheels as burning fire.""I saw in the night visions, and, behold, **one like the Son of man came** with the clouds of heaven, and came to **the Ancient of Days**, and they brought him near*

*before him." ""And there was given him **dominion**, and glory, and a kingdom, that all people, nations, and languages, should serve him: which shall not be destroyed."(Daniel 7:9,13-14, KJV)*

Now this is the beginning of the Celestial Kingdom, where God, even Almighty God, Ancient of Days, our Alpha and Omega, Archangel, and Adam, our beginning and our end, will be with his people. I am so proud and thankful for him and his great plan. He has promised great things to those who stay the course and overcome:

*"All thrones and dominions, principalities and powers, shall be revealed and set forth **upon all who have endured valiantly for the gospel of Jesus Christ.** ""According to that which was **ordained in the midst of the Council of the Eternal God** of all other gods **before this world was**, that should be reserved unto the **finishing and the end thereof,** when every man shall enter into his **eternal presence and into his immortal rest.**"(Doctrine and Covenants 121:29, 32)*

CHAPTER 14

The Celestial Kingdom

I am going to finish this book by giving the reader a look, hopefully, into eternity. We have talked in earlier chapters about the two trees placed in the Garden of Eden, which are representations of the telestial kingdom (Satan's world/probationary state) and the terrestrial kingdom (Christ's preparatory state). These two kingdoms must be dealt with before we have any hope of going back into the presence of our Father. First Corinthians of the Bible mentions another, third kingdom, and that is the celestial kingdom or celestial glory. *"There are also **celestial bodies**, and bodies terrestrial: but the glory of the **celestial** is one, and the glory of the terrestrial is another. There is the glory of the **sun**, and another glory of the moon, and another glory of the stars[telestial]: for one star differeth from another star in glory" (1 Corinthians 15:40–41, KJV)*

The telestial glory is compared to the stars. This is Satan's jurisdiction, where we are all born into, as a probationary state. As we learn and turn to Christ, and believe in Him, and obey His commandments, we move into the terrestrial kingdom and are able to abide in the terrestrial glory. This is a preparatory state. *"So also is the resurrection of the dead. It is sown in corruption; it is raised in corruption: It is sown in dishonour; it is raised in glory: It is sown in weakness; it is raised in power: It is sown a natural body; it is raised a spiritual body. There is a natural body, and there is a spiritual body. And so it is written, the first man Adam was made a living soul; the last Adam was made a quickening spirit" (1 Corinthians 15:42–45, KJV).*

We are all born into this world as mortals in this probationary state or condition, where we are the "natural man" at first. We are all continuously confronted by temptations, causing us to steadily have to choose. As we go through this dreary, dog-eat-dog world, we hopefully have learned that we don't want to serve Satan anymore; but instead, we want to serve the good Shepherd, Christ, and follow His examples and teachings. Christ came into this world to personally show us our way back into the presence of our Father in Heaven. Christ is the Way, the Truth, and the Life that will lead us back to the celestial kingdom if we will do what He tells us to do. *"Jesus saith unto him, **I am the way, the truth, and the life: no man cometh unto the Father, but by me**" (John 14:6, KJV).*

Even though the world rages on around us, the kingdom of Christ is right here among us and within our hearts, and our laws. It is the things we do, how we respect God, and how we treat each other that determine what mansion we will enter into when we die. Some people don't want to attain to something better than their understanding, like how much money they can make before they die. Money, they feel, gives them power. Many love immorality and make it a way of life. On the other hand, there are many good people who are content to follow Christ, to have peace, and to be able to make a living and enjoy their families on this earth. They love their fellow man, and they love God and just want to make it to the kingdom of God. These included, represent all of those who are the **"good people of the earth"**. *"Behold, these are they who died without law;""And also they who are the spirits of men kept in prison, whom the Son visited, and preached the gospel unto them, that they might be judged according to men in the flesh;""Who received not the testimony of Jesus in the flesh, but afterwards received it.""These are they who are **honorable men of the earth**, who were blinded by the craftiness of men."" these are they who receive of His glory, but not **of his fulness**.""These are they who receive of the **presence of the Son**, but not of the fulness of the Father.""Wherefore, they are bodies **terrestrial**, and not bodies celestial, and differ in glory as the moon differs from the sun.""These are they who are not valiant in the testimony of Jesus; wherefore, they obtain not the crown over the kingdom of God." (section 76:72-79, Doctrine and Covenants)*

There are those few who, because of the knowledge they have obtained on this earth, know there is something greater than settling for being the "good people of the earth" when they can have something much greater. They want to be back in the presence of their Father in Heaven; receive the promises that He made to Abraham, Isaac, and Jacob; and be united to the "Church of the Firstborn." Christ's job is to show us the way, but it is up to us to choose the path put before us. This ability comes from knowledge and understanding of what Christ is trying to tell us.

This third kingdom is the Celestial Kingdom, controlled through the "Law of the Priesthood". *"For thou wilt not **leave my soul in hell**; neither wilt thou suffer this Holy one to see corruption" (Psalm 16:10, KJV).* King David had a place prepared for him by God when he lived and obeyed God's commandments while here on the earth. He was called "the man after God's own heart." It probably broke God's heart to have to take it from him. David was well aware of the covenants he made before God, including the covenant of the *"everlasting priesthood"* and the *"new and everlasting covenant of marriage"*, both of which were performed by sealing in the temple of God. These two covenants are what sets the Church of Jesus Christ of latter-day Saints apart from other churches today, and are what determines how far a person can go in eternity. All Christian churches accept the "gospel of Jesus Christ", but they have not accepted His fullness. These two additional covenants were, and are mentioned, discussed, and implied through all ages of the Bible, beginning with Adam, when he was first commanded to multiply and replenish the earth from the Garden of Eden. This same commandment was then later given to Noah and his posterity, to the "sons of God".

Later God covenanted with Abraham with an "everlasting covenant". The covenant or law of the priesthood is directly linked with the "everlasting covenant of marriage". The outward showing expected of Abraham, was to have every male within his household, including sons, servants, slaves etc. within his jurisdiction or control. *"And when Abram was ninety years old and nine, the Lord appeared to Abram, and said unto him, I am the Almighty God; walk before me, and **be thou perfect**.""And I will make my **covenant** between me and thee, and will multiply thee exceedingly.""And Abram fell on his face: and God talked with him, saying,""As for me, behold, my **covenant** is with thee, and thou shalt be a father of many nations.""Neither shall thy name anymore be called Abram, but thy name shall be Abraham; for a father of many nations have I made thee.""And I will make thee exceedingly fruitful, and I will make nations of thee, and kings shall come out of thee.""And I will establish **my covenant** between me and thee and thy seed after thee in their generations for* *an **everlasting covenant**, to be a God unto thee, and to thy seed after thee."* (Genesis 17:1-7, KJV)

To the children of Israel, the Lord made great promises if they would keep their covenants. *"Incline thine ear and come unto me: hear, and your soul shall live; and I will make an **everlasting covenant** with you, even the sure mercies of David."(Isaiah 55:3, KJV)* In another place in Jeremiah talks about covenants. *"And I will make an **everlasting covenant** with them, that I will not turn away from them, to do them good; but I will put my fear in their hearts, that they shall not depart from me."(Jeremiah 32:40, KJV)*

Christ talks ahead to the time when he will come into the world at his birth and then dies for the sins of the world. He talks about **finishing the old covenant** under the law of Moses and the Levitical priesthood, or Aaronic priesthood. He is promising to bring a **perfect covenant** to replace the old when these things happen. *"Behold, the days come, saith the Lord, that I will make a **new covenant** with the house of Israel, and with the house of Judah."* (Jeremiah 31:31, KJV)

Christ also talks to the children of Israel through the prophet Ezekiel about a **covenant of peace**, which is the covenant of the everlasting priesthood. The law of the celestial kingdom is the **law of the priesthood**, and the covenant of marriage goes hand in hand with the law of the priesthood. *"Moreover I will make a **covenant of peace**[Melchizedek Priesthood] with them; it shall be an **everlasting covenant** with them: and I will place them and multiply them, and will set my sanctuary[temple] in the midst of them **forevermore**."(Ezekiel 37:26, KJV)*

Christ is still talking to the Children of Israel today through the prophet Joseph Smith, and is still making and renewing his **everlasting covenants** with them, me, us. Christ loves us as much as he loved them of old, of this I am sure. *"Behold, I say unto you that all **old covenants** have I caused to be done away in this thing; and this is a **new and everlasting covenant**, even that which was from the **beginning**."* (section 22:1, Doctrine and Covenants) *"And even so I have sent mine **everlasting covenant** into the world, to **be a light** to the world, and to be a standard for my people, and for the Gentiles to **seek to it**, and to be a messenger before my face to prepare the way before me."(section 45:9, Doctrine and Covenants)* *"Wherefore, I say unto you that I have sent unto you that I have sent unto you mine **everlasting covenant**, even* *that which was from the beginning." (section 49:9, Doctrine and Covenants)* Entering into these two covenants besides the "gospel covenant", are the "new and everlasting covenant of marriage", and the "everlasting priesthood covenant". They are essential in order to go on to the Celestial Kingdom, in the presence of God the Father/Adam. Of these things I am sure.

"They are they who received the testimony of Jesus, and believed on his name and were baptized after the manner of his burial, being buried in the water in his name, and according to the commandment which he has given--""That by keeping the commandments they might be washed and cleansed from all their sins and receive the Holy Spirit by the **laying on of the hands of him who is ordained** *and sealed unto this power;""And who overcome by faith, and are sealed by the Holy Spirit of promise, which the Father sheds forth upon all those who are just and true.""They are they who are the* **church of the Firstborn**.*""They are they into whose hands the Father has given all things--""They are they who are priests and kings, who have* **received of his Fulness**, *and of his glory;""And are priests of the Most High, after the order of* **Melchizedek,** *which was after the order of Enoch, which was after the order of the Only Begotten Son.""Wherefore, as it is written, they are gods, even the sons of God--""Wherefore all things are theirs, whether life or death, or things present, or things to come, all are theirs and they are Christ's, and Christ is God's.""And they shall overcome all things.""Wherefore, let no man glory in man, but rather let him glory in God, who shall subdue all enemies under his feet.""These shall dwell in the presence of God and his Christ forever and ever.""These are they whom he shall bring with him, when he shall come in the clouds of heaven to reign on the earth over his people.""These are they who shall have part in the* **first resurrection**.*""These are they who shall come forth in the resurrection of the just.""These are they who are come unto Mount Zion, and unto the city of* **the living God**, *the heavenly place, the holiest of all.""These are they who have come to an innumerable company of angels, to the general assembly and* **church of Enoch, and of the Firstborn.** *""These are they whose names are written in heaven, where God and Christ are the judge of all.""These are they who are* **just men made perfect** *through Jesus the mediator of the* **new covenant**, *who wrought out this perfect atonement through the shedding of his own blood.""These are they whose bodies are* **celestial**, *whose glory is that of the sun, even the glory of God, the highest of all, whose glory the sun of the firmament is written of as being typical.""And again, we saw the* **terrestrial world**, *and behold and lo, these are they who are of the terrestrial, whose glory differs from that of the* **church of the Firstborn**

*who have **received the Fulness of the Father**, even as that of the moon differs from the sun in the firmament." (section 76:51-71, Doctrine and Covenants)*

David sinned by sleeping with Uriah's wife and then trying to cover up his selfish act by conspiring to have his captain killed on the field of battle to make it look like an accident. However, it is recorded that David wasn't to be left in Hell, which is the telestial kingdom. So if he wasn't left in Hell, but lost his place in the celestial kingdom, then that would leave a place for him in the terrestrial kingdom, among the good people of the earth, which is a very great place to be. David never once sinned after that, but his one selfish act became the cause of the destruction of many souls through his bad example. Everyone had their eyes on the king. "If the king does it, then it must be all right," they say. "What is good for the goose is good for the gander." I pray that we all will be wiser than King David, but like him, we all have weaknesses that can bring us down also. The beauty of it all, is that God does not tempt us beyond what we can bear.

The celestial kingdom, as mentioned earlier, is governed by a different law, which is also based on passing through Christ's kingdom, the preparatory state of common law, and loving our fellow man. This higher law is hinted at all throughout the Bible. It is called the law of the priesthood. The children of Israel, starting out from Egypt, out of bondage, were instructed to build a temple out of animal skins, which they carried with them. This temple was erected here and there while they were wandering in the wilderness for at least forty years. The tribe of Levi was consecrated and set aside as the ones authorized to officiate in the temple ordinances, which constituted the adherence of the Sabbaths, offerings, blessings, baptisms, etc. The priesthood that the sons of Levi held was considered a lesser priesthood, named after Moses's brother, Aaron, also known as the Aaronic priesthood. The Levites' biggest responsibility was to carry and care for the "Ark of the Covenant". The Ark of the Covenant was an outward showing that Christ was with them and that He was going on before them. The officiating of the Ark of the Covenant in the temple at all times, was a similitude of having Christ as their High Priest with the authority of the higher priesthood, or the Melchizedek priesthood. The Levites, with the lesser priesthood, only had offices of deacon, teacher, and priest. To officiate in sealing ordinances, baptisms for the dead, etc., required the authority of the Holy Melchizedek Priesthood.

Again, the Levitical priesthood was a preparatory priesthood, preparing the children of Israel under the law of Moses, and teaching the people obedience and about covenants, leading up to the time when Christ was to come into the world. It also taught how He was to die, of His last final sacrifice, and of His resurrection. The children of Israel were still living the law of Moses even after Christ was born and living among them. Christ taught them all the way up to His time of death. He spoke to them about things to be made new and about a new covenant. He spoke to them about His death in parables and about putting new wine into new bottles. It was after Christ was resurrected when all things changed, and the law of Moses was fulfilled. Christ said it was fulfilled while He was hanging in agony on the cross when he said, "It is finished," and willingly gave up His life.

Christ was dead for three days as He said He would be. He hung on the cross from Thursday evening and all through Friday. He was taken down because of the Sabbath and placed in the tomb all Saturday. On Sunday or, as it is recorded, the first day of the week, Christ was resurrected, which was the key to when all things were to be made new. And the law of Moses was finished. The Sabbath was changed from the seventh day to the first day of the week; there was no longer a need for blood sacrifice by killing animals, because Christ acted as the final sacrifice by offering up Himself.

This unselfish act of Christ also changed the priesthood from the priesthood of ordinances on the earth to the new and everlasting covenant of the Melchizedek priesthood. This priesthood came into effect, having the power to bind on the earth and in Heaven. This priesthood has the sealing power to seal families together for time and all eternity within the new and everlasting covenant of marriage. Both of these new and everlasting covenants, of the priesthood and of marriage, are only possible through the Melchizedek priesthood. This is why the Ark of the Covenant was carried throughout the wilderness by the children of Israel; without Christ with them, they had no high priest to officiate in sealing ordinances.

In the Old Testament, it is recorded how men, before Christ, came into the world and held this Melchizedek priesthood, namely, Melchizedek, the king of Salem. He was the one to whom Abraham paid his tithes. The Melchizedek priesthood is what ties everything together in the universe with power. This is the power that God has, to create worlds without end, and He gives some of His authority to act in His name to mortals as they obey

His commandments.

*"Phinehas, the son of Eleazar, the son of Aaron the priest, hath turned my wrath away from the children of Israel, while he was zealous for my sake among them, that I consumed not the children of Israel in my jealousy. Wherefore, say, Behold I give unto him my covenant of peace: And he shall have it, and his seed after him, **even the covenant of an everlasting** priesthood; because he was zealous for his God, and made an atonement for the children of Israel"* (Numbers 25:11–13, KJV). The priesthood promised to Phinehas was the Melchizedek priesthood, an everlasting priesthood covenant, a priesthood of peace. Hebrews chapter 7 talks about a higher law under the Melchizedek priesthood, than that which was had under the Levitical priesthood.

*If therefore perfection were by the Levitical priesthood, (for under it the people received the law,) what further need was there that another priest should rise after the order of Melchizedec, and not be called after the order of Aaron? For the priesthood being changed, there is made of a necessity a **change also of the law**. For he of whom these things are spoken pertaineth to **another tribe**, of which no man gave attendance **at the altar**. For it is evident that our **Lord sprang out of Juda**; of which tribe Moses spake nothing concerning **priesthood**. And it is yet far more evident: for that after the **similitude of Melchizedec there ariseth another priest**, Who is made, not after the law of carnal commandments, but after the **power of an endless life**. For he testifieth, Thou art a **priest forever** after the **order of Melchizedec**. For there is verily a disannulling of the commandment going before the weakness and unprofitableness thereof. For the law made nothing perfect, but the bringing in of a **better hope did**; by the which **we draw nigh unto God**. (Hebrews 20:11–19, KJV)*

*For if he were on earth, he should not be a priest, seeing that there are priests that offer gifts according to the law . . . But now hath he obtained a **more excellent ministry**, by how much also he is the mediator of a **better covenant**, which was established on **better promises**. For if that first covenant had been faultless, then should **no place have been sought for the second**. For finding fault with them, he saith, Behold the days come, saith the Lord, when I will make a **new covenant** with the **house of Israel** and with the house of **Judah**: Not according to the covenant that I made with their fathers in the day when I took them by the hand to lead them out of the land of Egypt; because they continued not in my **covenant**, and I regarded them not, saith the Lord. For this is the **covenant** that I will make with the house of Israel after those days, saith the Lord; I will* *put **my laws into their minds and write them in their hearts: and I will be to them a God, and they shall be to me a people**: And they shall teach every man his neighbor, and every man his brother, saying, know the Lord: for all shall know me, from the least to the greatest. For I shall be merciful to their unrighteousness, and their sins and their **iniquities will I remember no more**. In that he saith, a **new covenant**, he hath made **the first old**. Now that which decayeth and waxeth old is ready to vanish away. (Hebrews 5:4, 6–13, KJV)*

This is what Christ was saying when He was talking about new wine into new bottles, for Christ, having new life after the resurrection in a new body, also changed the old covenant of ordinances to the new covenant of the Melchizedek priesthood. This priesthood is the key to the eternities. The Melchizedek priesthood is the key to a better hope.

I am certain that there is a life after this earthly life. I very much pray for all my loved ones, friends, and family and hope that I will see them again with immortal eyes. I know that we can't take any worldly thing with us when we leave this life, so one must ask themselves, "What will I do for eternity? Does everyone just die, and God throws us in a pretty room, and that is the end of it?" My answer is that we make eternity what we will have it to be, what we are willing to settle for. If we have obeyed God while here on the earth and fought for and gained our freedom by following Christ, then eternity is literally the limit, and it is accomplished through the power of the priesthood.

*When Jesus came into the coasts of Caesarea Philippi, he asked his disciples, saying, **whom do men say that I the Son of man am?** And they said, some say that thou art John the Baptist: some, Elias; and others, Jeremias, or one of the prophets. He saith unto them, But whom say ye that I am? And Simon Peter answered and said, **Thou art the Christ, the Son of the living God**. And Jesus answered and said unto him, Blessed art thou, Simon Barjona: **for flesh and blood hath not revealed it unto thee, but my Father which is in heaven**. And I say also unto thee, That thou art Peter, and upon this rock I will build my church; and the gates of hell shall not prevail against it. And I will give unto thee the **keys of the kingdom of heaven**: and whatsoever thou **shalt bind on earth shall be bound in heaven: and whatsoever thou shalt loose on earth shall be loosed in heaven**. (Matthew 16:13–19, KJV)*

The priesthood carries with it the powers of Heaven, and nothing is impossible, except when the one who claims to have it exercises unjust principles, such as force, and anything but a righteous life and attitude. *Righteous* means to be right with God or the way that God will do it, the right way.

"For many are called, but few are chosen" *(Matthew 22:14, KJV)*. Moses received the holy Melchizedek priesthood from his father-in-law, Jethro.

*And the sons of Moses, according to the Holy Priesthood which he received under the hand of his father-in-law, Jethro; And Jethro received it under the hand of Caleb; And Caleb received it under the hand of Elihu; And Elihu under the hand of Jeremy; And Jeremy under the hand of Gad; And Gad under the hand of Esias; And Esias received it under the hand of God. Esias also lived in the days of Abraham, and was blessed of him—Which Abraham received the priesthood from Melchizedek, who received it through the lineage of his fathers, even till Noah; And from Noah till Enoch, through the lineage of their fathers; And from Enoch to Abel, who was slain by the conspiracy of his brother, who received the priesthood by the commandment of God, by the hand of his father Adam, who was the first man—Which priesthood continueth in the Church of God in all generations, and is without beginning of days or end of years. And the Lord confirmed a priesthood also upon Aaron and his seed, throughout all their generations, which priesthood also continueth and abideth forever with the priesthood which is after the **holiest order of God**. And this **greater priesthood** administereth the **gospel** and holdeth the **Key of the mysteries of the kingdom**, even the **key of the knowledge of God**. Therefore, in the ordinances thereof, the power of godliness is manifest. And **without the ordinances thereof, and the authority of the priesthood, the power of godliness is not manifest unto men in the flesh**; For without this **no man can see the face of God, even the Father, and live**. Now this Moses plainly taught to the children of Israel in the wilderness, and sought diligently to sanctify his people that they might behold the face of God; But they hardened their hearts and could not endure his presence; therefore, the Lord in his wrath, for his anger was kindled against them, swore that they should not enter into his rest while in the wilderness, which rest is the **fulness of his glory**. And the lesser priesthood continued, which priesthood holdeth the key of the ministering of angels and the preparatory gospel. (Doctrine and Covenants, section 84:6–25)*

These scriptures plainly explain, through Joseph Smith, the importance of the Melchizedek priesthood, the same priesthood that Christ Himself holds; it is necessary for the flow of knowledge, the power of godliness, and the ability to be in the presence of Almighty God and see His face. This priesthood should be a very fundamental thing that all men want to seek and attain, in order to get close to God. This priesthood is necessary to be able to call your families up and have the sealing ordinances performed, thus blessing your families for eternity. *"For whoso is faithful unto the **obtaining these two priesthoods** of which I have spoken, and the magnifying their calling, are sanctified by the Spirit unto the **renewing of their bodies**" (Doctrine and Covenants, section 84:33)*

This is the "promise of the priesthood". I have been so blessed by having these priesthoods. God is so fantastic, for He has blessed me with knowledge, and He has blessed my family. We need to pay attention to what God is telling us. He has told us how we can know when His Spirit is speaking to us, and this is how:

*And now I give unto you a commandment to beware concerning yourselves, to **give diligent heed to the words of eternal life**. For you shall live by every word that proceedeth forth from the mouth of God. For the **word of the Lord is truth, and whatsoever is truth is light, and whatsoever is light is Spirit, even the Spirit of Jesus Christ**. And the Spirit giveth light to every man that cometh into the world; and the Spirit enlighteneth every man through the world, that **hearkeneth to the voice of the Spirit**. And everyone that hearkeneth **to the voice of the Spirit cometh unto God, even the Father**. (Doctrine and Covenants, section 84:43–47)*

Those people who hate God because they want to live in their sins or the way of life that makes them feel good, such as immorality of any kind, can't be drawn to God. They actually are repelling themselves away from God until they are in outer darkness. Perhaps you have noticed that people who are into bad habits, immorality, are evolutionists, are atheists, dishonest, and always trying to discredit God with their vain philosophies, in order to justify their actions. These people are not allowing the truth to be in them.

All Christian churches preach the gospel of Jesus Christ. They also teach that Christ is Lord, that He was born, and that we all need to repent, be baptized, and be born again of the Spirit. They also teach that Christ died for our sins, that He was resurrected, that we need to endure to the end, and that we will receive an honest judgment. These things are all 100 percent true, but these churches don't have any idea of what happens after this life or even if there is an earthly afterlife. These churches perform marriages, saying, "Till death do us part," as if that will be the end of it when we die, as if we all just go to sleep or find a comfortable rocking chair and sit by a peaceful river under an old shade tree for eternity. Imagine everyone sitting around just looking at one another forever or playing on a harp.

To die with having received the gospel of Jesus Christ, is receiving the "gospel covenant". It enables the individual to become a "son", or "daughter" of God, and be taken up to meet Christ in the air when He comes. However, there are two more covenants that most Christians do not enter into, because they do not understand them, nor do they have the true authority to attain to them. These covenants are the, "New and Everlasting Covenant of Marriage", for one. The Everlasting Covenant of Marriage was instituted at the time of Adam and Eve, in the Garden of Eden, along with the power of the priesthood, which Adam already had, and conferred it upon his righteous sons, namely: Able and Seth in the beginning, who in turn, conferred it upon their righteous sons, even down to Noah, and so on. This is why reference is made in the days of Noah to "Sons of God". They had the priesthood and were able to enter into the Everlasting Covenant of Marriage. *"Therefore shall a man leave his father and his mother, and shall cleave unto his wife: and they shall be one flesh." (Genesis 2:24, KJV)*

*"Yet ye say, Wherefore? Because the Lord hath been witness between thee and the wife of thy youth, against whom thou hast dealt treacherously: yet is she thy companion, and the wife of thy **covenant**," (Malachi 2:14, KJV)*

*"Till we all come in the unity of the faith, and of the knowledge of the Son of God, unto a perfect man, unto the measure of the stature of the **fullness of Christ**."(Ephesians 4:13, KJV)*

*"And to know the love of Christ, which passeth knowledge, that ye might be filled with all the **fullness of God**. Now unto him that is able to do exceeding abundantly above all that we ask or think, according to the power that worketh in us, unto him be glory in the church by Christ Jesus throughout all ages, **world without end**. Amen."(Ephesians 3:19-21, KJV)*

By receiving the gospel of Jesus Christ allows us to obtain that world spoken of here, because of the grace of God, but without receiving the fullness of the gospel through receiving the priesthood covenant, and the everlasting covenant of marriage while in this life, can only attain to that of angels. *"And Jesus answering said unto them, the children of this **world** marry, and are given in marriage,""" But they which shall be accounted **worthy to obtain that world,** and the resurrection from the dead, neither marry, nor are they given in marriage :" "Neither can they die any more: for they are equal unto the angels; and are the children of God, being the children of the resurrection."(Luke 20:34-36, KJV)*

*"Verily I say unto you, blessed are you for receiving mine **everlasting covenant,** even the **fullness of my gospel** sent forth unto the children of men, that they might have life, and be made partakers of the glories which are to be revealed in the last days, as it was written by the prophets and apostles of old."(Section 66:2 Doctrine & Covenants)*

*"In the **celestial glory** there are three **heavens or glories;**" "And in order to obtain the highest, a man **must** enter into this **order of the priesthood** [meaning the **new and everlasting covenant of marriage**];" "And if he does not, he cannot obtain it. He may enter, into the other, but that is the **end of his kingdom**; he cannot have an increase."(Section 131: 1-4, Doctrine & Covenants)*

*"For the unbelieving husband is **sanctified** by the wife, and the unbelieving wife is **sanctified** by the husband; else were your children unclean; but now are they holy." "For what knowest thou, O wife, whether thou shalt save thy husband? Or how knowest thou, O man, whether thou shalt save thy wife?(1 Corinthians 7: 14, 16, KJV)*

The other is the "Everlasting Covenant of the Priesthood". *"Wherefore say, Behold, I give unto him my **covenant of peace**:" "And he shall have it, and his seed after him, even the **covenant of an everlasting priesthood**; because he was zealous for his God, and made an atonement for the children of Israel."(Numbers 25:12-13, KJV)* This verse is talking about Phineas.

*"My **covenant** with him was one of **peace**, and I gave them to him as an object of reverence; so he revered Me and stood in awe of My name. True instruction was in his mouth and unrighteousness was not found on his lips; he walked with Me in **peace** and uprightness, and he turned many back from iniquity." (Malachi 2:5-6, KJV)* This verse is talking about Moses.

---

*"Remember them, O my God, because they have defiled the **priesthood** and the **covenant of the priesthood** and the Levites." (Nehemiah 13: 29, KJV)*

Every covenant we make before God, falls under one of these three. To seek and attain to the other two, will put the individual further ahead in eternity, if he or she abides by living what they have promised before God. These two covenants **are** the "**Fullness of the Gospel**" and require being performed by one who already has the proper priesthood and authority to act in the name of God. As you can see, the covenant of the priesthood supersedes the new and everlasting covenant of marriage. This is the power that God uses to create worlds without end.

Christ has told us about the many mansions in his Father's house and about different degrees of glory. He has explained to us that we have the freedom in this life to determine what advancement we can have in the life to come. I, for one, don't want to just sit around looking at everyone else, but I want to grow, have the knowledge, know what my Father in Heaven knows, and do what He does. Why would a person who has it within his power to do something better, settle for anything less? You can imagine how you would feel later in the afterlife, wishing you had been more adhering to the commandments; but because you didn't pay attention early on, you have come to the end of your kingdom. I guarantee that all of God's judgments will be just, because we will have done it to ourselves. What I am discussing in this chapter are things so fantastic that they are hard to fathom but are very true.

*"The power and authority of the higher, or Melchizedek Priesthood, is to hold the **keys of all spiritual blessings** of the church—To have the privilege of receiving **the mysteries of the Kingdom of Heaven**, to have the heavens opened unto them, to commune with the general assembly and **church of the Firstborn**, and to enjoy the communion and presence of **God the Father, and Jesus** the mediator of the **new covenant**" (Doctrine and Covenants, section 107:18–19).* Such things and such a promise is hard to conceive, and it takes one's breath away when contemplating it or pondering over it. The knowledge is limitless.

*For there is a time appointed for every man, according as his works shall be. God shall **give unto you knowledge by his Holy Spirit**, yea by the unspeakable gift of the Holy Ghost that has not been revealed since the world was until now;*

*Which our forefathers have awaited with envious expectation to be revealed in the last times, which their minds were pointed to by the angels, as held in reserve for the fulness of their glory; A time to come in the which **nothing shall be withheld**, whether there be **one God or many gods, they shall be manifest. All thrones and dominions, principalities and powers, shall be revealed** and set forth upon all those who have **endured valiantly for the gospel of Jesus Christ**. (Doctrine and Covenants, section 121:25–29)*

The people of God, if valiant and true, will inherit all heights and all depths; they will see all things and will know all things. This is the promise of God, for everything will be revealed.

We are also cautioned to use only righteousness and free agency in our exercise of the priesthood or authority to act in the name of God as Christ did.

*Behold there are many called, but few are chosen. And why are they not chosen? Because their hearts are set so much upon the things of this world, and aspire to the honors of men, that they do not learn this one lesson—**That the rights of the priesthood are inseparably connected with the powers of heaven, and that the powers of heaven cannot be controlled nor handled only upon the principles of righteousness. That they may be conferred upon us it is true; but when we undertake to cover our sins, or to gratify our pride, our vain ambition, or to exercise control or dominion or compulsion upon the souls of the children of men, in any degree of unrighteousness, behold, the heavens withdraw themselves; the Spirit of the Lord is grieved; and when it is withdrawn, amen to the priesthood or the authority of that man**. Behold, ere he is aware, he is left unto himself, to kick against the pricks, to persecute the saints, and to fight against God. We have learned by sad experience that it is the **nature and disposition of almost all men, as soon as they get a little authority, as they suppose, they will immediately begin to exercise unrighteous dominion**. Hence many are called, but few are chosen. **No power or influence can or ought to be maintained by virtue of the priesthood, only by persuasion, by long-suffering, by gentleness and meekness, and by love unfeigned. By kindness and pure knowledge**, which shall greatly enlarge the soul without hypocrisy, and without guile—Reproving betimes with sharpness, when moved upon by the Holy Ghost; and then showing forth afterwards an increase of love toward him whom thou has reproved, lest he esteem thee to be his enemy; That he may know that thy faithfulness is stronger* *than the cords of death. Let thy bowels also be full of charity towards all men, and to the household of faith, and let virtue garnish thy thoughts unceasingly; then shall thy confidence wax strong in the presence of God; and the **doctrine of the priesthood shall distill upon thy soul as the dews from heaven.** (Doctrine and Covenants, section 121:34–45)*

*Now the **great and grand secret** of the whole matter, and the summum and bonum of the whole subject that is lying before us, **consists in obtaining the powers of the Holy Priesthood.** For him **to whom these keys are given** there is **no difficulty in obtaining a knowledge of facts in relation to the salvation of the children of men, both as well for the dead as for the living.** (Doctrine and Covenants, section 128:11)*

In these latter days, the Aaronic priesthood was restored to Joseph Smith by John the Baptist, whereas the Melchizedek priesthood was restored to Joseph Smith by the hands of Peter, James, and John, who in turn received it at the hands of Jesus Christ, who received it from God the Father.

*For I have conferred upon you the **keys and power of the priesthood, wherein I restore all things,** and make known unto you all things in due time. And verily, verily, I say unto you, that whatsoever **you seal on earth shall be sealed in heaven;** and whatsoever you bind on earth, in my name and by my word saith the Lord, it shall be **eternally bound in the heavens**; and whatsoever sins you remit on earth shall be remitted eternally in the heavens; and whatsoever sins you retain on earth shall be retained in heaven. And again, verily I say, whomsoever you bless I will bless, and whomsoever you curse I will curse, saith the Lord; for I the Lord, am thy God. (Doctrine and Covenants, section 132:45–47)*

So there you have it, from eternity to eternity. The priesthood is passed physically by the laying on of hands by those who have already received it in like manner. The priesthood is like the father and is independent of the mother, the church. We have always existed in the beginning, starting as intelligences, and we will always exist through the love and mercy of our great God, but it all depends on us, as to the quality of our existence. *"And no man taketh this honour unto himself, but he that is called of God as was Aaron."* (Hebrew 5:4, KJV)

We need to live every minute of our lives as though it depended on eternity. I hope this chapter enables the reader to get a glimpse of the vastness of eternity. When we get the vision of God and what He is about, it will take our breaths away. I, for one, want to get just as close to Him as I can. I have these two priesthoods I have spoken about, and I can testify to you of the blessings that have come because of them. The knowledge and the hope of something better than just "death do us part" is worth striving for. I pray that my family can get this vision and never settle for anything less than the best eternity has to offer. Through the priesthood, your families can be sealed together for time and all eternity. I couldn't bear the thought that the family I love so dearly will be separated from me after death.

Here the author sees fit to add his genealogy of his priesthood authority, for the benefit of his loved ones, and to preserve it, even as the Bible records the genealogy of our forefathers. My Father, Raymond Rexford Sego, before he died wrote his line of authority on paper and handed it to me, so that I would have it.

I, Steven Sego, was ordained an Elder, unto the Melchizedek Priesthood by the hand of my Father, Raymond R. Sego, in May of 1977. He in turn was ordained a Seventy, and later to the office of High Priest, March 17, 1946, by the hand of S. Dilworth Young.

S. Dilworth Young was ordained January 9, 1920, by Seymour B. Young. He received it from Edmund Ellsworth February 18, 1857, who in turn received it from Joseph Young March 8, 1843. Joseph Young received it February 28, 1835, at the hand of the prophet, Joseph Smith. Joseph Smith was ordained by Peter, James, and John, and they were ordained by Jesus Christ, as recorded in the New Testament of the Bible.(John 15:16, KJV)

"For whatsoever things remain are by me; and whatsoever are not by me shall **be shaken and destroyed."** *"Therefore if a man marry a wife in the world[by contract, marriage license], and he marry her not by me nor by my word, and he <u>covenant with her so long as he is in the world[till death do they part] and she with him, their covenant and marriage are</u>* **not of force when they are dead,** *and when they are out of the world; **therefore they are not bound by any law when they are out of the world."** "Therefore, when they are out of the world **they neither marry nor are given in marriage;** <u>but are appointed angels in heaven,</u> which angels <u>are ministering servants,</u> to **minister for those***

*who are worthy of a far more, and an exceeding, and an eternal weight of glory." "For these angels did not abide by my law; therefore, they cannot be enlarged, but remain separately and singly, **without exaltation, in their saved condition, to all eternity;** and from henceforth are not gods, but are angels of God forever and ever." "And again, verily I say unto you, if a man marry a wife, and make a covenant with her for time and for all eternity, if that covenant is not **by me or by my word,which is my law, and is not sealed by the Holy Spirit of promise** , **through him whom I have anointed and appointed unto this power**[by one/High Priest holding the Melchizedek Priesthood], **then it is not valid neither of force when they are out of the world, because they are not joined by me, saith the Lord, neither by my word; when they are out of the world** it cannot be received there, because the angels and the gods are appointed there, by whom they cannot **pass; they cannot therefore, inherit m y glory; for my house is a house of order, saith the Lord God."** (Section 132:14-18, Doctrine and Covenants)*

*"And again, verily I say unto you, if a man marry a wife by my word, which is my law[law of the priesthood],**and by the new and everlasting covenant, and it is sealed unto them by the Holy Spirit of promise,** by him who is annointed, unto whom I have appointed this power and the keys of the priesthood; **and it shall be said unto them---ye shall come forthin the first resurrection;** and if it be after the first resurrection , in the next resurrection; and shall **inherit thrones , kingdoms, principalities, and powers, dominions, all heights and depths—then shall** it be written that he shall **commit no murder whereby to shed innocent blood,** and if ye abide in my covenant, and commit no murder whereby to shed innocent blood, it shall be done unto them in all things that whatsoever my hath put upon them, in **time and through all eternity; and shall be of full force when they are out of the world; and they shall pass by the angels and the gods, which are there, to their exaltation and glory in all things, as hath been sealed upon their heads, which glory shall be a fulness and a continuation of seeds forever and ever."** "Then shall theymbe gods, because they have no end; therefore shall they be from **everlasting to everlasting,** because they continue; **then shall they be above all, because all things are subject unto them. Then shall they be gods because they have all power, and the angels are subject unto them."** "Verily, verily, I say unto you, **except ye abide my law ye cannot attain to this glory."** "For*

strait is the gate, and narrow the way that leadeth unto the **exaltation and continuation of the lives, and few there be that find it, because ye receive me not in the world neither do ye know me.** *(Section 132:19-22, Doctrine and Covenants)*

"*Verily, verily, I say unto you, if a man marry a wife according to my word, and theya re sealed by the Holy Spirit of promise, according to my appointment, and he or she shall commit any sin or transgression of the new and everlasting covenant whatever, and all manner of blasphemies, and if they commit no* **murder** *wherein they shed innocent blood,* **yet they shall come forth in the first resurrection, and enter into their exaltation; but they shall be destroyed in the flesh, and shall be delivered unto the buffetings of Satan**

ACKNOWLEDGMENTS

I would like to recognize and acknowledge those who have inspired me in this work, but mainly, I recognize my God and Father in Heaven for bringing me out of discouraging and frustrating circumstances and situations and for giving me the knowledge and the fortitude to stand tall. I also recognize my beautiful and good wife for her relentless and unwavering support throughout the years, some of which have been hard and trying times. God has certainly blessed me when He sent her into my life. I also recognize and acknowledge my great children, whom I love dearly, especially my immediate children, Stevana, Jordan, Olivia, and Grace. It is for the specific purpose of building this bridge that I am writing this book, in hopes of giving the ones who read it a little more insight into what it will be like when facing eternity.

I also acknowledge other friends and family members. You know who you are as there are too many to name. All of you are the ones I wrote this book for, hopefully to inspire you all to finish the race standing up and strong in the faith of God to the end, that we will all be together in the kingdom of our heavenly Father and His Son, Jesus Christ.

I want to especially thank my daughter, Stevana W. Sego for her artwork in the form of a chart, used on the cover of this book, and also Timothy A. Emmett, for helping me to design a chart to graphically explain the Gospel of Jesus Christ, included on an inner page, as an illustration.

HELL
(& DESTRUC

- **Telestial—Kingdom**

- **Democracy** (Other Terms)

  - S0Ci8liSN

  - Fascsn
  - Nazism

In Ancient Terms

- Egynt
- World
- whole o\ ai1 the earth
- The Beast

- The great and abominate church
- Great and spacious building Lehi S4w
- Wilderness

- **State-Run Religion**

- **Probationary State**

Isa 4:0 — My people are destroyed from lack of knowledge

Satan – Lucifer

Acts 5:3
Lies = Language of The Devil

International Bankers

Mark 11:15
And Jesus began to cast out them... overthrew the tables of the money changers

MONEY CHANGERS
and
COUNTERFEITERS

Jewish Talmud · Cabala
SECRET ORDERS
Knights of Templar
Illuminati · Skull & Bones
Masonic Orders · Etc

Ten-Planks of the Communist-Manifesto

1. Abolition of property ownership.
2. Heavy income tax
3. Abolition of inheritances.
4. Confiscation of emigrants & rebel property.
5. Centralized credit banking.
6. Centralized community and transport

7. All state owned business & wasteland redemption
8. Industrial armies especially for agriculture
9. Abolition of town and country distinction
10. Public education combined with industry

Uniform Commercial Codes
(SBte · Codes)

John 8:32 ~ Ye shall know the truth and the truth shall make you free

2 Nephi 15:13-14 ~ My people are gone into captivity... Hell hath enlarged her mouth... (compare Isaiah 5)

2 Nephi 28:14 ~ All gone astray... but few

1 Nephi 8:23 ~ Mists of darkness

Ether 8:20-26 ~ Secret combinations

Doctrine & Covenants 84:45-53 ~ Truth is light, light is spirit, spirit is the power of God

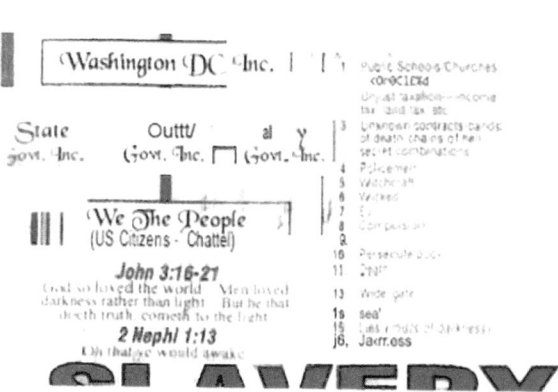

Washington DC Inc.

State govt. Inc.   Outtt/al Govt. Inc.   Govt. Inc.

We The People
(US Citizens · Chattel)

John 3:16-21
God so loved the world... Men loved darkness rather than light... But he that doeth truth, cometh to the light

2 Nephi 1:13
Oh that ye would awake

Public Schools/Churches cOrrOCl€Kd
Unjust taxation—income tax and tax etc
Unearned contracts, cards of death chains of hell, secret combinations
Policemen
Watchman
Wicked
Ev
Compulsion

Persecute poor
Craft
Wide gate
sea'
Last chains of darkness
Jackr.ess

SLAVERY

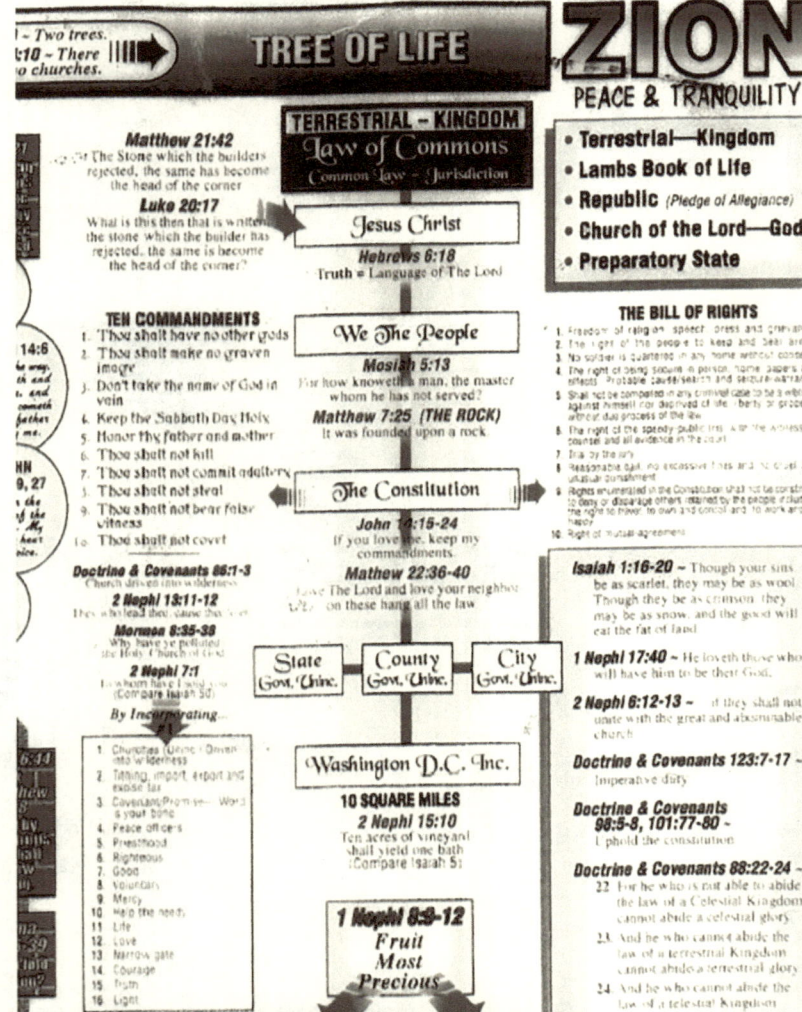

BIBLIOGRAPHY

Holy Bible (KJV)

Book of Mormon

Doctrine and Covenants

Pearl of Great Price.

Published October 1993 by:

The Corporation of the President of The Church
   of Jesus Christ of Latter Day Saints

Salt Lake City, Utah.

Smith, Joseph. *Joseph Smith's New Translation of the Bible.*
   Independence, MO: Herald Publishing House, 1970.

White, Ellen. *The Great Controversy.*

Reference: to Creation Science Evangelism, Creation
   Series, Kent Hovind, (Dr. Dino).

christianfilms.com -creation series, Amazon 2007 quote, page-6

Bates, Finis L. *The Escape and Suicide of John Wilkes Booth.*

Wikipedia. "Popes of the Catholic Church."

Anonymous. "Does Evil Exist?"

Wikipedia. "First Inaugural Address of Ronald Reagan."

Lee, John Doyle. *Deathbed Confessions*, 1877.

Chambers Encyclopedia. rev. ed. New York: Collier Publisher, 1890.

The Whistle Blower. 1st ed. Granite Falls, NC: Alice Publishing, 1998.

Sego, Steven. "Gospel of Jesus Christ." Rathdrum, Idaho, 2002. Chart.

The Informer [pseud.]. "The Beginning of the Lie, July 16, 2007. http://www.freedomdomain,com/sovereignty/inform 18.html.

Staley, Jim. "Nimrod, Great-Grandson of Noah." passionfortruth.com.

Paris, Edmond. *Secret History of the Jesuits.*

Bunch, Taylor. *Book of Revelation*, 1933.

Trudeau, Kevin. *More Natural Cures Revealed.* Elk Grove Village, IL: Alliance Publishing Group, Inc., 2006.

Tanner, Sandra. "Masonic Symbols and the LDS Temple."

Cain, Alexander. *Alive after the Fall.*

Turner, John G. https://www.nytimes.com/2012/10/21/books/review/brigham-young-pioneer-prophet-by-john-g-turner.html.

Dirkmaat, Gerrit, "Council of Fifty Notes," August 2017. www.fairmormon.org/conference/august-2017/lost-teachings-prophets.

Jackson, Steve. *Game of Conspiracy.*

"Masonry." www.churchofjesuschrist.org/study/history/topics/masonry?=eng.

Wikipedia. "Mormonism and Free Masonry." https://en.wikipedia.org/wiki/mormonism_and_freemasonry.

———. "Mormon Endowment."

———. "Penalty (Mormonism)."

"LDS (Mormons)." lds-mormon.com.

"Endowment Oaths and Ceremonies." *Salt Lake Tribune*, February 8, 1906. U.S. Senate document 486.

Eustis, Mimi L. Mardi Gras Secrets. 2005.

Young, Brigham. *Journal of Discourses.*

Federal Civil Judicial Procedure and Rules. 1997 edition. St. Paul, Minnesota: West Publishing Company, 1997.

Exmormon.org. "Conjecture on the Origins of Mormon Violence; Brigham Young and De Smet."

Thearmageddontimes.com.

http://theyig.ning.com/front-page-news/the-pastors-who-signed.

Mormonism101.com.

Baptistboard.com.

Worldslastchance.com.

Cleaver, Emanuel. "2012 meeting." *Daily Caller.*

Simcox, Tom, Israelmyglory.org, Who's Who in Daniel 11, July/August 2009

Noah's Ark Documentary, producer: Grizzly Adams Production, 2013, licensed by C3 Entertainment.

https:www.1.cbn.com/cbnnews/us/2016/september/rabbi-jonathan-ca HYPERLINK "https://www.1.cbn.com/cbnnews/us/2016/september/rabbi-jonathan-ca;by"; by Rabbi Jonathan Cahn, warns of America's Temple of Ba'al, September 28, 2016 on CBN News.

The Salt Lake Tribune; archive.sltrib.com January 26, 2017

DISCLAIMER

Before you read this book, you are encouraged to check with your friends, your politicians, your clergy, your relatives, your attorney, and anyone else you think will tell you the truth or who you think is smarter than you to give you an honest and unbiased opinion. You need to know that everything I say in this book is simply my opinion, and there are many people who may disagree with my conclusions and findings. If you do anything I recommend without the supervision of a licensed attorney, you do so at your own risk. The publisher, the author, the distributors, and bookstores present this information for educational purposes only.

I am not an attorney, nor do I claim to be, nor am I attempting to practice law without a license. This book is only my opinions, my thoughts, and my conclusions based on sound knowledge and experience. The information in this book is for educational purposes only, and you and only you are responsible if you so choose to do anything based on what you read in this book.

TWO CHURCHES ONLY

The Book describes life as intelligences while we were spirits and why we came to earth before we took on our earthly forms. It discusses the nature of God's work and glory as well as where we came from, why we're here, and where we're headed. It discusses God's grand plan to redeem humanity and how ingenious the plan is. It reveals two kingdoms or churches that have been in a constant state of conflict since the Garden of Eden, as well as how each of us fits into the larger scheme of things. The book reveals how each of us must make decisions about which master we will serve. The book additionally reveals the churches' loyalty to the king they are subservient to. It talks about government agencies and certain leaders and exposes their secrets. It also reveals great mysteries about God and why things are happening the way they are. This book explains the judgment and different phases in eternal progress; it explains who God is and talks about when he comes again and how. It also admonishes us to receive the gospel of Jesus Christ and become more like him. The theme, therefore, of this book begins at the time before creation and leads the reader through eternity.

ABOUT THE AUTHOR

Steven Sego

Sego was born in Alamosa, Colorado, on April 16, 1958, and is the thirteenth of fourteen brothers and sisters. Sego was born and raised in western Montana, primarily in and around Troy, Libby, and Noxon. Sego's desire to understand the nature of God grew as a result of his brother Daniel's work as a missionary for the Church of Jesus Christ of Latter-day Saints. He thought, prayed, and meditated to gain a better understanding of the afterlife after his younger brother, Michael, tragically died in an accident. His main areas of thought were where we came from, why we are here, and where we are going after we die. He has been blessed with four children and is happily married to his wife.